AMERICANS FROM HOLLAND

Books by Arnold Mulder

AMERICANS FROM HOLLAND

Novels

THE SAND DOCTOR
THE OUTBOUND ROAD
BRAM OF THE FIVE CORNERS
THE DOMINIE OF HARLEM

AMERICANS FROM HOLLAND

by Arnold Mulder

THE PEOPLES OF AMERICA SERIES
EDITED BY LOUIS ADAMIC

J. B. LIPPINCOTT COMPANY
PHILADELPHIA & NEW YORK

☆ THE PEOPLES OF AMERICA SERIES ☆

In the summer of 1943 the J. B. Lippincott Company invited me to become general editor of a group of books they had in mind, to be collectively titled THE PEOPLES OF AMERICA Series.

In content and scope, the Lippincott idea was essentially and in many particulars identical with one that had occurred to me in 1939, soon after I had begun my Plymouth Rock-Ellis Island project (as it came to be called). I had kept my idea to myself, intending to try to get some publisher interested in it after the war. But off and on I had wondered if I might not have difficulty in getting it started.

The idea was to tell the story of the United States of America in a new way: around the various elements in the population stemming from countries and regions in Europe, Africa and Asia, and from lands north and south of us in the Western Hemisphere; around the skills and ordinary labor—the constructiveness, the creativeness—of which they were capable on their arrival; around the economic, social, cultural and political ideas, impulses and ideals which they brought over with them and developed here. The emphasis would be on *people,* on their variety, on their pooling their talents and genius and brawn, and working together to create a new and unique civilization. The aim would be to help influence our national atmosphere in the direction of unity within diversity, as distinct from the old and still widely approved "Americanization" drives toward a homogeneity based on uniformity which had mainly negative results and could not now help prepare us, as a people and a power, for a constructive world function in the difficult times ahead. . . .

I felt that some of the best-known and most influential among the orthodox American historians might possibly look askance at my idea, and that that might cause publishers to hesitate to take it up. Now, of a sudden, I found that the Lippincott Company had thought of it by themselves as a venture under their imprint, which is nearly as old as

5

the United States; and that they had a title for the Series that was preferable to either of the two I had been tossing about in my mind.

In the course of my Plymouth Rock-Ellis Island project I got together considerable material on most of the groups. It was made available to the authors of the volumes in THE PEOPLES OF AMERICA Series:

Some "do's" and "don't's," some general and specific expectations, have come out of editorial conferences and discussions with authors:

Each volume is meant to be a comprehensive, scholarly story of the group it deals with. Research should not stick out. Sociology is permitted, even desired, but the books are not to be sociological treatises. No group is to be treated as a "problem" in relation to the rest of the population.

The story of each group begins with its Old World background (but that need not necessarily be Chapter I) and continues and ends with the group's chronicle from the arrival of the first colonists or immigrants down to the present day. The role played by each element in American life and the process by which it has been merging or blending into the American nation are to be stressed. Leaders and the more dramatic personalities should occupy a prominent place in the record, but the emphasis should be on people generally, on the masses of men and women who came here; on their labor and other functions; on the forces, ideas and problems that have sprung from the interplay of the varied humanity and the new continent.

If the author is himself an immigrant or of immigrant parentage, and is or has been personally involved in the story of the group of which he is writing, he need not hesitate to break into autobiography. Each volume should contain fresh material. No book in the Series is to be a mere reworking of other books. The thought-texture of each should be touched by creative imagination and purpose.

It is the aim of the Series not merely to assemble facts about the various groups of the American population but also to influence the groups and the population as a whole in the direction of a sound American culture drawing eagerly on all its roots and sources. It is hoped that no two volumes will be similar in pattern, emphases and conclusions.

The books are intended for the general reader and for college and high-school use. The hope is eventually to have the whole Series in every public and college library, in most high-school and private-school libraries, and on many private shelves or reading tables. It is expected that some of the books will be translated into old-country languages, thus helping to familiarize the Old World with the human composition of the New and to influence favorably our relations with other lands.

In 1944, when we started to plan the Series, the publishers and I expected to begin to publish the volumes late in '45, but that turned out to be impossible; many American writers were busy with war work of one kind or another until after V-J Day. This is the first volume to appear. Hereafter three or more will come every year.

In general, editorially speaking, the Series will explore and exploit what may be the greatest body of largely untouched Americana.

Louis Adamic

Milford, New Jersey,
Summer, 1947

CONTENTS

ILLUSTRATIONS

AMERICANS FROM HOLLAND

I

It Might Have Been

FOR A BRIEF moment in the story of mankind Holland gave evidence of a blind impulse to impart its culture to the whole of the North American continent. During less than half a century of official Dutch occupation of Manhattan Island and the Hudson River Valley, while Holland was enjoying its so-called Golden Age at home, the nation was half unconsciously extending its feelers into the unknown wilderness across the Atlantic; it was searching out a path along which Dutch trade and culture might travel during the centuries to come.

The other maritime nations of Europe were sending out similar feelers, and with similar half-consciousness of what it would mean for the far future—England to Virginia and Massachusetts, France and Sweden to other sections of North America, Spain and Portugal to South America. They were all, of course, after the immediate loot they saw lying loose for the taking—silver and gold, furs, precious woods, the profits of the slave trade. They were not thinking of the spread of their cultures across a continent that they hardly understood was a continent. There were loud protestations by some that the main purpose was the dissemination of the blessings of Christianity among savages so benighted that they actually believed a treaty was made to be observed, but the ruling motivation was profit. The same ships' captains who talked loudly about the spread of religion in America made ports of call of the harbors on the coasts of Africa and sent out expeditions to round up defenseless natives to serve as merchandise in the highly lucrative slave trade. As always, individuals were sincerely concerned about the souls of savages, but the national tentacles that reached out across the Atlantic were equipped with olfactory nerves for smelling out profit.

But that has always been, and is today, the way a civilization travels. The flag follows the trail made by the trader, and eventually that path turns into a road over which a culture can pass. The fact that the Dutch of the Netherlands'[1] Golden Age were not conscious of an impulse to impart their civilization to a new continent is not evidence of the absence of the impulse. The agents of empire are at least half-blind; such eyes as exist at the ends of national trade feelers are extremely near-sighted.

In retrospect it seems hardly an accident that Dutch tentacles should reach out to the best harbor on the American Atlantic seaboard—the harbor through which must enter the main stream of whatever culture would dominate the continent. In the seventeenth century Holland was certainly the principal maritime power in Europe; even England, its only serious rival on the sea, had to take second place during most of the era. Since the days of the "Sea Beggars" in the sixteenth century, when even social scum and riffraff and, yes, criminals played a decisive role in the drama of the rise of the Dutch republic under the leadership of William the Silent, the Hollanders had displayed a genius for life on the sea that had made them masters of strategic harbors all over the globe. Many years before one of their feelers reached out into New York Harbor, they had smelled out trade stations in the islands of the Pacific and on the coasts of Africa and South America.

By 1642 the dividends of the Dutch East India Company amounted to fifty per cent, and for many years previous they had never been less than twenty-five per cent. The shares of the company rose as high as five hundred per cent.[2] The adventurous Dutch sea captains employed by the staid psalm-singing directors of the East India Company understood on which side their employers' bread was buttered; they chose their harbors not for the beauty of the scenery; they killed off the natives who interfered with the processes of trade with a finesse that wins something like shuddering admiration even after three centuries. In brief, they were specialists in their profession. So long as they had

---

[1] In accordance with general practice, the terms "Holland" and "the Netherlands" are used interchangeably in this book; also "Holland" and "Dutch" when used either as noun or adjective.

[2] Petrus Johannes Blok, *History of the People of the Netherlands* (G. P. Putnam's Sons, 1907), Part IV, p. 77.

plenty of water under their ships' keels they knew what they were about, how to turn the wealth of the globe into guilders. They were at home in the world, and no country however remote was foreign soil to them. If there was one best harbor on the edge of a continent they were sure to find it.

It was by that breed of seafaring men that the West India Company was organized, modeled on the pattern of the East India Company. The new monopolistic concern received its charter from the Dutch government on June 3, 1621.[3] Interlocked with the board of directors of the East India Company, the commercial pilots of the new organization hoped for twenty-five and fifty per cent dividends from the trade with the coasts of America. Also like its elder brother in monopoly, the company was not purely commercial, but a kind of political arm of the government as well, by means of which injury could be inflicted on the enemy.[4]

Was it an accident that this concern soon had its grasp on the harbor of destiny? Those Dutch captains who swarmed over the Atlantic like ants over a picnic lunch were sure to find the choicest morsel sooner or later—rather sooner. True, they had been anticipated by Henry Hudson; and there had also been independent Dutch merchants who had been making a few honest guilders at the expense of, perhaps sometimes to the benefit of, the natives of Manhattan Island. But it was not until the shrewd directors of the West India Company appeared on the scene that the strategic commercial importance of the magnificent harbor was given anything like adequate assessment. A small colony of Walloons formed the nucleus of the settlement in 1624, and so New Netherland was born.

The Dutch race, with a culture that was the highest in Europe at the time, had won a bridgehead on the edge of a vast, unexplored world. Properly exploited, that bridgehead could have been used as a base from which Dutch civilization might have fanned out over the continent. For nearly half a century, in view of the strategic importance of the harbor the Hollanders held, there was at least an even chance that America would become Dutch, not English; perhaps the odds were somewhat better than even.

[3] *Ibid.*, p. 3.
[4] *Ibid.*

There was of course Jamestown to the south, and there was New England to the northeast, to say nothing of scattered settlements by other nations. Even if the Dutch had held on to and exploited New Netherland, the probabilities are that the Virginians would have crossed the Alleghenies in the eighteenth century and deployed onto the great meadow of Kentucky; and that the descendants of the Winthrops and Sewalls and Mathers would have followed the water routes to the plains of Ohio and points farther west when their stony New England soil had lost its primal fertility. English culture was almost certain to flow in two streams across the continent; at least so hindsight would make us believe. If the Dutch had held their bridgehead, the continent might have become the home of two civilizations. But it seems more likely that the Dutch would have assimilated the English, as in actual fact English culture has assimilated the Dutch. Not too great a strain is put on the imagination by suggesting that the possession of New York Harbor through the seventeenth and eighteenth centuries would have given Dutch culture a grip on the continent that nothing could have shaken loose.

What might have been, merely seems incredible to us because of what actually is; but its opposite would have appeared just as incredible if the cat of history had jumped in the other direction. It may not be too easy to imagine a Declaration of Independence worded in Dutch, written by a Hollander, and directed not against the government of George III but against that of the States-General of the Netherlands.

That it would have come to something of that kind was at least possible. For while the North American continent was not parcelled out between the English and the Dutch, those two on the whole occupied the most strategic positions for continental colonization. In both England and Holland the seeds of democracy had germinated sufficiently under the surface of the social and political soil so that they could be expected to sprout in the favorable frontier medium.

It would be disingenuous, however, to give the impression that they alone represented the push toward independence. St. Jean de Crève-coeur notes in his famous essay, "What Is an American?", that the American people of the eighteenth century were "a mixture of English, Scotch, Irish, French, Dutch, Germans, and Swedes." He describes the "race now called Americans" as a "promiscuous breed." It is conceivable that any other people than the English or the Dutch might have become the race of destiny to fill the American geographical vacuum, but in the eighteenth century the main rivalry on this continent appeared to be between England and Holland. And the American people of the colonial eighteenth century would have been American whether they stemmed from English stock or from Dutch—or, it might be added, from Scotch or Irish or French or German or Swedish.

As between English and Dutch the love of freedom was at least as strong in the hearts of Hollanders as of Englishmen. It is not too difficult to imagine descendants of Admirals Tromp and De Ruyter or of Stadtholder Jan De Witt producing a Dutch George Washington, or that fourscore and seven years after his day the descendants of those who opposed the slave trade in the seventeenth century should incubate a Dutch Abraham Lincoln.

Perhaps these Alice-in-Wonderland imaginings belong to fantasy rather than to sober history; but they are not without their uses in this record, if for no other reason than that of conditioning the mind to an appreciation of the epic nature of the march of a culture across a continent—of any culture, not Dutch or English alone. For something of the kind of thing that did happen in America was bound to happen there, regardless of the blood of the agents through whom the events came about. Given the pressure from across the Atlantic, and the geographical vacuums westward across the continent, the pattern of the history of America was determined not by blood or nationality but by a destiny that is very real even when the word "destiny" has been dissociated from its usual mystic connotations.

The details of the story would of course have undergone change, the actors in the continental drama would have been different. The war for independence might have come at another time, or perhaps eighteenth century Holland would have been too weak to wage such a war. But biology would have operated on this continent whether the parent stock was English or Dutch, or German or French or Swedish or Irish. Men and maidens would have fallen in love; children would have been born to occupy the land; climate, geography, the frontier would have developed in millions of simple men that self-reliance that needs freedom for its very existence as much as a lung demands oxygen for life. If Holland instead of England had given us our continental language we would not have had our Emersons or Thoreaus, our Washingtons or Lincolns, our Websters or Calhouns. But we would almost certainly have had others in their places. Even as it is, at least two of our greatest writers, Walt Whitman and Herman Melville, had Dutch blood in their veins. Genius is not the monopoly of any nationality, and the events that bring out latent powers in the souls of men are not erratic accidents but follow at least roughly the curve of history. That curve was fixed by forces far more compelling than that of nationality.

What manner of culture was it that for a moment in history reached out its tentacles to an empty land, seeking to perpetuate itself in generations yet to be born?

Comparisons of civilizations, as of individuals, are odious, but at least it is not necessary to make apologies for the culture of Holland in its Golden Age as compared with that of the English that displaced it in America. True, the Dutch had had no Elizabethan Age in literature. There had been no Shakespeare in the Netherlands. The dramatist-poet Joost van den Vondel came nearest to winning the right to be called great in a universal, not in a parochial, sense. But that intoxicating effervescence in literature that we call "Elizabethan" was not in even him. "He was not," says A. J. Barnouw, "as were the great navigators and scientists of seventeeth-century Holland, an explorer and discoverer. He was satisfied with being a follower. The creative genius of Holland does not tend toward the literary. Even the most gifted of Dutch writers had a self-conscious feeling of inferiority, which made them hesitate to strike out upon untrodden paths." [5]

Vondel was a dramatist in an age when the drama seemed the natural form of expression, at least in England. He was nineteen years old when Shakespeare died, and he outlived John Milton by five years. During those great years the Dutch language was not more provincial than the English. It seemed natural to men like Milton to know the language of Holland, and the great scholars of Europe were attracted to the universities of the Netherlands. Dutch scholars like Erasmus were on the whole more truly citizens of Europe than comparable scholars from Oxford or Cambridge. If Vondel, or any other Dutch writer, had been a minor Shakespeare, or even a Marlowe or Ben

Jonson, he would not have wanted for a European audience because of the bar of language. His theme in *Lucifer* was essentially the same as Milton's; if that drama had been even a minor *Paradise Lost,* it would have had a good chance to become a part of world literature, whereas it has remained a provincial work of art, for all its importance in Dutch national letters.

But if in literature Holland trailed behind her great commercial rival across the North Sea, in some of the other arts she far outshone the English. The Dutch school of realistic painters headed by Rembrandt was never approached by any school in England either in the seventeenth century or later. On canvas the Hollander was as superior to the Englishman as in literature the Englishman surpassed the Hollander. If painting is an evidence of civilization, then the Holland of the century during which it held Manhattan Island was one of the most highly civilized nations of Europe, not excluding even the France of Louis XIV.

And Holland was supreme in some other fields that may fairly be made the measure of culture. Hugo Grotius, who died two years before Peter Stuyvesant arrived in America as governor of New Netherland, was the greatest jurist of his day, one of the greatest of all time, and he was pre-eminent as historian and theologian as well. A mathematician and astronomer who may fairly be classed with Galileo was Simon Stevin, a many-sided genius who won distinction in several branches of seventeenth century science.[6] Christiaen Huygens, brother of the poet Constaintijn Huygens, was so highly regarded by Louis XIV of France that the Grand Monarch gave him a pension of six thousand francs and made him the first president of the French Academy of Science.[7] In the field of biology Jan Swammerdam was the first to discover that insects are not the result of spontaneous generation, a myth that continued to receive wide acceptance in many other countries for a century to come; he demonstrated that insect life comes from life. And the great but eccentric Anthony Van Leeuwenhoek, maker of microscope lenses, exposed to the view of mankind, for the first time in history, the fascinating world of microbes, and hence he may fairly be regarded as the father of modern bacteriology.

[6] *Ibid.,* p. 47.
[7] *Ibid.*

But perhaps the most highly civilized citizen of Holland during that country's Golden Age was Spinoza; he was in fact one of the most highly civilized men of the world of his day—or for that matter of any day. He belongs, by any fair test, among the original thinkers of history. Although seldom thought of as a Hollander, partly because he was a citizen of the universal land of the spirit, partly because as a Jew he was politically and culturally an alien, he was born in Holland and a resident of that country all his life. At any rate Holland was civilized enough not to persecute him because of his ideas; such mild persecution as he suffered came largely from his own Jewish teachers and associates. It would have been too much to expect that his heterodox ideas should have won acceptance from the Dutch public of his day; the mere fact that that public did not persecute him is in a way a measure of the degree of culture Holland had attained in the seventeenth century, at a time when the Dutch merchants and navigators formed a spearhead for the possible spread of that culture across a continent that was as yet hardly better known than the Gobi Desert in China.

In the field of education the Holland of the Golden Age was in the forefront of progress in Europe. While formal schooling is not necessarily an evidence of culture in the true sense, Holland's system of education was such that it penetrated through to the lives of the people and maintained for them a high level of literacy for that century. In an age when many English and French upperclass citizens were still only semi-literate, often worse than that, Dutch schools were laying the foundation for a truly popular system of education. As for higher learning, between 1584 and 1643 Holland founded no less than four great universities, which attracted the best minds of Europe, among them Descartes.

The products of those universities did not of course reach the frontier trading post of New Amsterdam on Manhattan Island, nor did perhaps even the products of the lower schools; those schools were for the most part for the prosperous, and the sons of the prosperous stayed at home. But if Dutch culture had taken root in America, as for a moment it promised to do, the educational system it would eventually have transplanted to this continent would have been quite as adequate for the needs of a future American republic as the systems that came to us from England, or those that were invented by us in answer to frontier needs.

Comparing the state of civilization in Holland with that of the English, a British writer says: "Holland was the higher developed of the two Maritime Powers." And comparing it with the culture of France, he adds: "France, the inspiration of the absolute monarchs of Europe, had a larger and more docile clientèle for the reception of her culture; but Holland, with a fraction of the population and area of France, was the real leading power of the age. . . . Holland built up an intellectual and artistic life before which the France of Louis XIV, for all its civilization, pales. . . . The mantle of sixteenth-century Italy fell naturally to seventeenth-century Holland, the outstanding and maturest middle class nation of the age." [8]

[8] P. C. Gordon Walker, in *A Modern History of Europe*, ed. J. Hampden Jackson (Harper & Brothers, 1935), p. 604.

II

The Comfortable Don't Emigrate

HOLLAND'S FAILURE TO win a continent was basically a failure in emigration. In the Golden Age the people of the Netherlands were too comfortable to leave home. They were adventurous enough, and they had sufficient energy. But motivation was lacking for the slow, pedestrian occupation of a new land demanded by colonization. They were all for dramatic expeditions, exploits on the high seas, forays into the far places of the globe where resources could be quickly exploited. That was essentially what the West India Company had in mind; it established New Netherland as a trading post, not as a bridgehead of empire. This policy resulted in the loss of the greatest prize that was ever within Holland's near-grasp during the whole of her colonial history.

Even if the Company, and the government that was interlocked with it, had given all their energies to peopling the new land with true colonists instead of agents in the fur trade, it is doubtful if their efforts would have found the necessary response in Holland. The very fact that the era is known as the Golden Age shows that the Dutch home public was poor material for the blandishments of emigration advertising. The contented and the prosperous do not emigrate; exiles are pushed out, they do not voluntarily leave a home community that satisfies their needs.

The Dutch standard of living was higher in the seventeenth century than that of most of the rest of Europe. Poverty was of course present, and it would be disingenuous to suppose that "Golden Age" was synonymous with "Utopia." Definitions of such words as "poverty"

24

and "security" change, and it is virtually impossible to estimate, after the lapse of three centuries, how much poverty there was in Holland in terms of today. It seems likely that far fewer than one third of the Dutch population were "ill fed, ill clothed, and ill housed," as the late President F. D. Roosevelt, a descendant of those same Hollanders, asserted was true of twentieth century America.

Wealth as a matter of fact was flowing into Holland from the far reaches of the globe. The daring Dutch navigators were tapping the riches of Africa, Asia, the islands of the Pacific, and, a little later, of the Americas. The good people at home could not know about some of the methods employed by the great semi-official companies to get their clutches on the money; or if they knew, they were quite as adept at rationalization as the people of any age have been, or of any country, to square profit with ethics.

They knew, for instance, about the highly profitable slave trade, as the English of that day knew about their own slave trade, for it is a mistake to suppose that Hollanders were the only slavers. Those few who protested against it were squelched quite effectually by the leaders of thought. Pamphlets were fairly common not only defending the trade but exalting it as an instrument of Providence. God was so ordering things for the salvation of black souls!

Some of the other sources of wealth were hardly less questionable; there would be no point in denying, after three centuries, that the gold of Holland's Golden Age came, in part at least, from sources not far removed from piracy, although technically the word would not apply. The fact is that wealth was flowing into Holland in a constant stream, and although in the main it found its way into the coffers and the bank accounts of the few, the fact itself spelled commercial prosperity, which in turn spelled at least relative security for the masses that normally would form the raw material for emigration.

Given the opportunity to work, the Hollander of the seventeenth century, as of the twentieth, was sure to be busy. Work, then as now, was for him almost a religion. The same energy that caused him to bounce back within a year after the end of the Nazi occupation and begin to rebuild his wrecked towns through his own efforts, while the nationals of some other countries were folding their hands in impotent despair, animated him during the era when he saw his native land at the head of Europe's economic procession.

In fact, Holland was absorbing a considerable amount of the excess labor of other countries. A beehive of activity, it could use the artisans of France and England and Portugal; themselves more skilled than any guest workers, the Hollanders had no reason to fear such competition. Many of their shipyards could turn out a vessel a day, to the envy of the great industrialists of Louis XIV's France. And in nearly all the industrial arts the Hollanders were several steps ahead of the working classes of Europe in general. Dutch weavers and cloth makers had been famous for centuries; Holland's goldsmiths competed successfully with those of Italy; Amsterdam was even then a center for the diamond cutting trade. In the less aristocratic crafts and trades as well, the nation led Europe. At the opening of the seventeenth century the skilful practice of the industrial arts had resulted in a close-knit economic system that offered jobs to all who were willing to work.

Is it reasonable to suppose that such a population of craftsmen, many of them essentially industrial artists, should emigrate to a wilderness where the best they could hope for was to become what later would be called lumberjacks, or farmers who would have to raise meager crops with sweat and toil? Nor was Holland's farm population a much better reservoir of emigration. As was true of the rest of Europe, the Dutch farmer was, psychologically at least, still a kind of bondman. Politically a citizen of a republic, he was spiritually still bound to his bit of earth, a part of it like his horse or his cow. To most of the farm village dwellers of seventeenth century Holland emigration would have been wholly inconceivable. The idea of self-reliance was relatively new, in rural Holland as elsewhere, if in fact it existed at all in the modern sense. Village folk might have joined in a migration out of sheer desperation, but a powerful impulse from the outside would have been required to galvanize them into an action so dramatic for them. The Man with the Hoe, "brother to the ox," does not of his own initiative suddenly metamorphose himself into one of Walt Whitman's Pioneers. Two centuries had to pass before he was ready for that.

The motivating force that pushed many English artisans and farmers out of the home nest, religious persecution, was lacking in Holland. There was no reason why Hollanders of whatever class should leave home to seek freedom of worship. They had it in Holland to perhaps a higher degree than the people of any other country enjoyed. The English Puritans understood that, when they sought temporary asylum in the Netherlands. The Jews of Europe had for years acted on a similar knowledge; and such countries as Portugal had lost to Holland some of their best human material and most skilled artisans and financiers, because the spirit of religious toleration that had animated William the Silent had leavened the mass of the Dutch population. Spinoza had at least been able to keep his head on his shoulders in Holland, a feat that would have been impossible in most other countries, perhaps even in England. Says a modern historian of the Dutch people:

The mercantile government of the United Netherlands understood that by bringing religious differences to the fore it would in time make native and foreigner averse to inhabiting and visiting these regions, and, considering the fact that in all Europe the number of the Reformed faith could scarcely be calculated at one twentieth of the population, it regarded its interest to lie in the adoption of freedom of worship for all, so far as possible, for one of its maxims. The Reformed Church remained privileged above all, and it alone enjoyed complete freedom in accordance with the Dort principles fixed in 1618 and 1619, which the government repeatedly declared its wish to maintain, but all attempts to carry these principles to their utmost consequences were steadily thwarted, and the actual rights of an exclusive state church were never obtained by it. The placards against adherents of other opinions continued to be upheld in name, and the government apparently listened now and then to those who desired measures against the heterodox and dissenters, but the latter could be sure of toleration, provided they did not assert themselves too publicly.[1]

Hence there were in Holland not only no considerable numbers of religious leaders who sought asylum for themselves in America; what is perhaps more important, they did not harangue and encourage and organize whole congregations to seek a new home, as similar men did in England, and also as similar men did in Holland two centuries later. On the contrary, the men who might have become the best leaders and most effective advertisers of colonization encouraged simple

[1] Blok, *People of the Netherlands,* Part IV, p. 276.

people to abide at home, people who might otherwise have emigrated under the spur of such economic pressures as existed; quite naturally a minister does not want to lose his congregation—and his job.

There was also failure in propaganda from the American side of the Atlantic. A few voices there were that urged Hollanders to throw in their lot with the settlers on the first Dutch frontier in America, but they were too weak to convince large numbers.

By contrast both Jamestown and New England were served by writers the works of several of whom have become an integral part of American literature. Actually those Englishmen were enterprising promoters of immigration, sometimes consciously so, sometimes not. So early as the first quarter of the century the live-wire Captain John Smith turned himself into what today would be called a "booster"; in doing so he became one of the most delightful liars of modern history, although very probably he was unconscious of any serious departure from sober fact—as "boosters" frequently are to this day. In his eagerness to "sell" Virginia to the people at home, and later New England— a name, by the way, that he coined—he achieved what with liberal allowance is today classified as "literature." But he was not trying to get into the anthologies of American literature three centuries later; he was attempting to "sell" his colony, and he understood the twentieth century connotation of the word even though he lacked the word itself in its later application. And the Puritans of Massachusetts were also excellent community salesmen, although their methods were different. The letters home of John Winthrop—some of which are authentically literature—and other documents of that kind were widely circulated and read in England, and were extremely effective sales talks. In part because of this—other forces were also operative—the population of the English settlements was constantly being increased by recruits from home.

As a result, when in 1664 New Amsterdam became New York, the Puritans wresting a living from the stony soil of New England had at least three times the population the Hollanders had attained on richer land and with the help of their matchless harbor. The English in Virginia had increased correspondingly. New Netherland's population, by contrast, was not in excess of twelve thousand after a little more than four decades of official Dutch occupation, perhaps not much more than ten thousand. Moreover, it is estimated that about a third were of British blood, for there had been a considerable infiltration of English subjects by that time, some from New England, some from Virginia, and some direct from England. After the turnover in New York from Dutch to British rule the same influences that had attracted immigration since early in the century continued to operate, and with accelerated tempo, so that by the end of the century Holland's maritime rival in Europe had established twelve vigorous colonies along the North American Atlantic coast. By that time Holland had none.

Lacking a heavy flow of immigration from home, New Netherland was bound to lose in the competition with her British neighbors. The fact that there was an appreciable infiltration of English nationals was ominous; the Dutch frontier government was in the position of a nation whose birth rate is so low that it must recruit its population from rival countries. It is never enough for a settlement on the edge of a vast continent merely to hold its own or to grow only a little; if it does not swarm it is presently so dwarfed by the vastness of its backdrop that it will lack the strength to cut out even a cowpath of empire. No settlement in America, during the seventeenth century, could count on mere natural increase of population to provide necessary growth. If, for instance, Jamestown and Plymouth had depended on birth rate alone, even after they had become well established, they would quickly have lost out in the race across America. Although the birth rate in New Netherland, at the close of the Dutch official occupation, was high enough for a settled community that has achieved a population equilibrium, it was not adequate for an outpost of culture that seeks to propel itself into a geographical vacuum.

Even without aspiring to occupy a continent the founders of New Netherland could have used ten times the ten thousand Hollanders that were lured to America, and then ten thousand times ten thousand more, merely to occupy the land the government had already staked out for itself. The actual size was somewhat indeterminate and the boundaries were somewhat vague. Manhattan Island and New York Harbor and a part of Long Island were included; also the Hudson River, with territory east of it to the Connecticut River, and westward as far as could be tapped for skins in the Indian fur trade. Most of

New Jersey, almost all of Delaware, and a part of Pennsylvania were also included.

But it was not land so much the Hollanders wanted as strategic spots for trading posts. There were only thirty families in the first "wave" of immigrants that sailed from Holland in 1624 and settled on Manhattan and Staten Islands and near what is now Albany. To the northern settlement they gave the dynastic name of Fort Orange; the village on Manhattan Island became Nieuw Amsterdam; the area as a whole inevitably became known as Nieuw Nederland.

There would be no point, after three centuries, setting down the minutiae of the adventures and misadventures, the little triumphs and equally little disasters that befell the early settlers who were persuaded by the agents of the West India Company to seek their fortunes in New Netherland. They enjoyed success and experienced failure, they were subject to hope and despair, as are settlers on any frontier; they made love and raised families; they traded with the Indians and did a little farming, though not so much as they should have done. In time some became discouraged and went back home. Most of them stayed, perhaps because there was nothing else they could do.

But New Netherland never was a Dutch frontier in the same sense in which Plymouth and Jamestown were outlets for the pressures of English surplus population. There was little pressure from the home front, and the Dutch government was apathetic about the settlement in America. Holland rather expected the original Walloons, and their successors, to make possible the coveted twenty-five per cent annual dividends on the West India Company's shares, and was hardly thinking in terms of the settlers' welfare, still less in terms of the westward course of their empire across the new continent. So slight was the support the settlers of succeeding years received from their own government that "hundreds of the better class of Dutch withdrew from New York, returning to Holland or settling in the West and East Indies, not a few going to Virginia and the Carolinas." [2] The settlers appealed to the home government from time to time, with negligible results. They were small change to a government that, during much of the period of the history of New Netherland, was playing what may almost be called global politics, at least in so far as anything could be

[2] William Elliott Griffis, *The Story of New Netherland*, p. 148.

called global in the seventeenth century. The government was more interested in such speculations as that of the capture of the famous "silver fleet" of Spain by Vice Admiral Piet Heyn, a speculation that had been carefully prepared for, with probabilities and risks estimated with the shrewdness of good Dutch businessmen.

The episode, which was successfully staged a few years after the boatload of Walloons settled on Manhattan Island, has gone down in Dutch history as an important event, though its real significance is negligible, while the colonization experiment at New Netherland was regarded as a pedestrian bit of small business, that moreover committed the unpardonable sin of not only failing to pay dividends but of requiring help from the parent government. In the long view—but a hindsight view, it must fairly be admitted—the bridgehead on Manhattan, with its potentialities for the capture of a continent and the winning of the wealth of a new world, was far more dramatic than the capture of the "silver fleet." But the latter event held immediate drama and it had color, and, most important of all, it turned in quick profits. Dutch poets did not write popular songs about Manhattan, as they did about the exploit of Piet Heyn, whose name had a punch and a brevity that lent itself to the lilt of folk poetry and music: "Piet Heyn! Piet Heyn!" sang the Hollanders for three centuries after he had gone the way of all flesh, "his name was small but his deeds were great, for he conquered the silver fleet." In Dutch the lines rhyme and the words almost sing themselves.

The exploit, it must be confessed, was impressive if not important in terms of national interests. With thirty-one ships, off the coast of Cuba, Piet Heyn, almost without a fight, captured the Spanish "silver fleet" of fifteen vessels that was known to be going home laden with rich spoils from the Spanish American holdings. The imagination of the Dutch government, as well as of the home people, was excited by the fabulous treasures of silver, gold, pearls, indigo, sugar, campeachy wood, and costly furs, which sold in the Netherlands for no less than fifteen million guilders.[3] It was exploits of that kind—basically commercial ventures—that interested the States-General and the Dutch public. It would be too much to expect them to penetrate the veil of the future, or to see that while they were preoccupied with such de-

---

[3] Blok, *op. cit.*, Part IV, p. 37.

tails they were letting a much richer prize slip through their fingers, a prize moreover that gave promise of making them a political world power.

Within two years after the capture of the "silver fleet" the West India Company ran into such financial straits that it had to borrow to keep afloat. It is fascinating to imagine how the course of history would have been changed if the Dutch government and the Dutch people had had the wisdom to invest the equivalent of the profits of Piet Heyn's exploit in their New Netherland colonizing venture. Instead, they put off their colonial wards largely with promises that could be conveniently forgotten when payment in harder coin became inconvenient. The Company, on its part, followed the unwise policy of converting profits into dividends, neglecting to provide a working reserve.[4]

A single attempt was made to achieve emigration on a permanent basis and in adequate numbers. At least on paper the patroon system had that purpose. A number of Dutch tycoons were presented with vast tracts of land in the Hudson River Valley on condition that they would actually colonize the holdings with settlers. The grants were impressive domains, that of Kiliaen Van Rensselaer in the Albany area comprising seven hundred thousand acres. But even the patroons, and many of their settlers, were usually more interested in beaver skins than in raising Indian corn and Dutch wheat and potatoes. As colonizers the patroonships were not brilliantly successful. All of them, with the single exception of Rensselaerswyck, had failed when the official Dutch occupation of New Netherand came to an end.

[4] *Ibid.*, p. 38.

III

Too Little, Too Late

THE SIMPLE HISTORICAL record of the fall of New Netherland hardly
rates a footnote in world history, and most of the English and even
Dutch historians dispose of it in a paragraph, if they mention it at all.
The settlement that Holland had founded in 1624, and had developed
and administered during the next four decades, was forced to surrender to the English in 1664—while England and Holland were at
peace—for no better reason than that the Duke of York, brother of
Charles II, wanted the territory for his personal revenue, and the fort
at New Amsterdam was too weak to resist.

The "capture" was little more than international highway robbery
that could be successful only because Holland had failed to keep its
guard up on the frontier. A century later Philip Freneau, the "poet of
the Revolution," sneered that the only claim England had had to the
territory was "that Cabot had looked on it first." The British pretext
was threadbare, but the English could make good their claim by reason
of military strength. If the Dutch government had been reasonably
prudent, or if its agents, the colonial governors, had been other than
small men, New Netherland could hardly have become the victim of
international robbery without striking a blow. The settlement was administered by a succession of directors-general, nearly all of whom
were failures; a possible exception was Peter Stuyvesant, who was serving at the time of the surrender. They failed, in part because they
were too small for their jobs, narrow-guage traders instead of builders
of empire, but more particularly because the support given them and

33

their people by the Company and their country's government was always "too little and too late."

Some of those glorified general managers of empire may be ignored. Three names have managed to survive—Wouter Van Twiller, Wilhelmus Kieft, and Peter Stuyvesant. In so far as the souls of men get translated into the events of history, the spiritual stature of these three men goes far to explain the basic reason for the fall of New Netherland.

Wouter Van Twiller, who after a fashion at least has entered history over the road of burlesque, was perhaps more fool than knave, or more mediocrity than either fool or knave. A Captain David Pietersen De Vries, who has left a record of his connection with the New Netherland settlement, expresses surprise "that the West India Company should send such fools into this country who knew nothing except to drink; that they could not come to be assistants in the East Indies; and the Company by such management must come to naught." He asserted that whereas in the East India service only governors were named who had been prepared for their positions by long service in subordinate positions, the West India Company "sent in the first instance as superior officers persons who had never had command in their lives."[1]

The charges are numerous that Van Twiller was given to drink; and although drinking was rather taken for granted on the first Dutch frontier in America, the governor's weakness was pronounced enough to draw a protest from his uncle in Holland, the mighty Kiliaen Van Rensselaer. Pride was another count made against him, at least by some who disliked the man; he was described as being "puffed up," which may well have been true of a man too small for his official shoes. Lacking prudence and the kind of hard-headed business sense that characterized the successful Hollander of his day, he appears to have neglected even a proper system of bookkeeping, and to have more or less disdained the pedestrian routine of turning in systematic reports to his company.

So many charges were made against him in the gossip of the Dutch

[1] Mrs. Schuyler Van Rensselaer, *History of the City of New York in the Seventeenth Century* (The Macmillan Company, 1909), I, 137.

settlement that only his uncle's influence kept him in his official seat the last few years. His enemies and rivals openly suggested successors, but he weathered the storms of opposition because the directors of the Company listened to Van Rensselaer, and the States-General was for the time being at least too apathetic to trouble itself much about the details of administration of New Netherland. The mere director-general of a few hundred Dutch semi-exiles three thousand miles away was a fairly small administrative detail to politicians who were confronted with the threat of a great naval war.

From the Company's point of view Governor Van Twiller's main fault was his failure to produce dividends; on the contrary, the New Netherland speculation continued to be a liability, a drain on their coffers. If this had been balanced by contentment and happiness of the folk of the settlement, history might absolve the governor even if his employers did not. But things were not going well for the Hollanders in the New World. Some physical improvements were made in the little village and fort of New Amsterdam, and there was some activity in extending the settlements along the Hudson and toward the south, but this was done as much in spite of the governor as because of him. With all their faults the people of New Netherland were usually wiser and more enterprising than their rulers; they had something of an instinct for empire, and all they needed was a guiding hand to give it direction. Such guidance could hardly be expected from a mediocrity who was on the whole too neutral to be a knave. Although one of his enemies called him a "child of the devil, a consummate villain," the term had application to his negative looseness of life rather than to active wickedness.

The fact should be noted in his favor that although he was pompous and often a fool, he was at least not hypocritical. He did not profess a piety that he did not feel, which may have been one of the reasons why he was unpopular. Not a good politician even in this, he antagonized those forces in his community that were reaching out toward a conventional and ordered ecclesiastical way of life. It is not difficult to think of him as a fool, but not as a hypocritical fool. And he should also be credited with wholesomeness in his relations with the Indians. There were no Indian uprisings during his administration such as disgraced the regime of his immediate successor and even of Peter Stuyvesant. This may in part have been the result of mere apathy, of a reluctance to stir up sleeping dogs. On the whole the Indians were realizing a profit out of the Hollanders and were fairly content to keep the peace. But that was still true later when trouble came in spite of it. At least Governor Van Twiller did not wantonly attack the red men but appears to have treated them fairly.

But such negative virtues as he displayed hardly marked Van Twiller as an agent of empire. He did not look beyond the somewhat shadowy boundaries of the Company's domain, and hardly that far; the little village of New Amsterdam was usually about as much as he could handle. He was hardly even a little frog in a vast pool. Empires are not built by such as he; nor by people capable of selecting such as he to sit in the seats of power; nor by a government that delegates monopolistic privileges to such people and that is more deeply interested in immediate profits than in long-term advantages.

For it was of course finally Van Twiller's failure to turn in a profit that caused his recall, not the charges that he sometimes got drunk, or that he was in a general sense a fool, or that he was wanting in statesmanship and could not see far beyond the tip of his nose. The seventeenth-century Hollanders were about the best businessmen in their world, far better for instance than were the English or the French; but theirs was a type of business that was built on an economic theory of quick turnover; they could not see the wisdom of an investment that would pay dividends only to their great-grandchildren. Not that Wouter Van Twiller was the man to provide them with that type of dividends, but because he failed to turn in quick profits he lost his job to one who, it was hoped, would make the investment pay.

Whereas Wouter Van Twiller was a weak governor, his successor Wilhelmus Kieft was a seventeenth century Little Caesar without the genius that alone can carry a Caesar's name down the ages. He devised the peculiar system, not of the one-man dictatorship familiar to the twentieth century but of government by a two-man council. The council consisted of himself and one more, hand-picked by him. Then he took the further precaution of giving the other member one vote while for himself he reserved two. In other words, he invented the veto power three hundred years before the UN thought of it. Later the people wrested from him at least a semblance of a government by a more numerous and more representative board but it was rather appearance than reality. In the main he governed by edict—"which his people thought too severe as well as too autocratic." [2] Schooled in democracy at home, the Hollanders did not take kindly to arbitrary government.

In one respect Kieft was an improvement on Van Twiller; he did not drink, a virtue rare in his day. Hence whatever sins he committed were not the fruit of befuddlement, but were deliberate. He was not weak or neutral, but a man of abounding energy. The only trouble was that he employed his energy in ways that made his name a byword and a reproach among his own people and especially among the Indians, who had in the main been friendly up until this time.

Not only did he keep his own wits about him, he knew on occasion how to make use of the weaknesses of others, especially of their fondness for drink. On one occasion certain influential citizens of New Amsterdam forced him to replace with a church the barn in which divine services had been held. To raise the money the governor hit on the plan of passing a subscription list, but he waited until a wedding feast with its inevitable drinking had mellowed the hearts of the people. When he deemed them ready for his designs he passed the list, and provoked competition by setting a liberal example. "Each then, with a light head, subscribed away at a handsome rate," a participant recorded. When they sobered up and prudence returned, it was too late.

If all his acts and devices had been as innocent as that, Kieft might have gone down in history as a man of some credit. A contemporary pamphlet said of him: "Kieft thus being made Director had now a path wherein, with good appearance and without being subject to much being said, he could have acquired honor and distinction." [3] But when he planned and provoked a bloody massacre of relatively peaceful Indians, he won a right to the term applied to his predecessor, "consummate villain."

For a long time he had been turning over in his mind the idea of getting even with Indian tribes of New Netherland for their refusal to pay what they considered an unjust tax. The red men, quite reason-

[2] *Ibid.*, p. 152.
[3] Quoted from *Breeden Raedt* by Mrs. Schuyler Van Rensselaer, *op. cit.*, I, 172.

ably from their point of view, denied the governor's right to impose the levy. The massacre that resulted was carefully planned and deliberately carried out in cold blood and with complete surprise to the savages. Kieft's henchmen murdered eighty Indians in a single night, many of them in their sleep. Captain De Vries reports that "infants were torn from their mothers' breasts, and hacked to pieces in the presence of the parents, and the pieces thrown into the fire and in the water, and other sucklings were bound to small boards, and then cut, stuck, and pierced, and miserably massacred in a manner to move a heart of stone."

Kieft's relations with the Indians would be a blot on his name even if he had shown statesmanlike traits in other respects. Killing off and plundering savages for the killers' own benefit was a fairly well recognized technique of many of the Europeans of the seventeenth century, English and French and Swedes as well as Hollanders; on the whole the record of the Dutch is good. But from the point of view of the Company and the government he represented, Kieft is to be convicted of stupidity as much as of wanton cruelty. His "war" on the Indians accomplished nothing of benefit to the colonists and paid no dividends to the West India Company. It was wanton and unprovoked. And on a later occasion he deliberately accused the Raritan Indians of Staten Island of having made depredations actually committed by white men. In the mob scene that grew out of the accusation several Indians were killed, some cruelly maltreated. The tribe of course retaliated, and because Captain De Vries happened to be living on Staten Island his farm bore the brunt of the savages' wrath, although he had always opposed Kieft's Indian policies.

Such was the man to whom the Dutch government had entrusted its dream of an empire in America. Empire builders have often been ruthless and cruel and still successful. But they have never been both stupid and successful. In terms of history stupidity is a greater crime than ruthlessness. Wilhelmus Kieft had both traits. Holland paid for it with the loss of its chance to build an empire in America.

Kieft himself lost his life by shipwreck on his return voyage to Holland. One writer reports that "his death was generally regarded as an act of retributive justice." The folk of New Amsterdam who so regarded it failed to explain, even to themselves, the wastefulness, to say nothing of the injustice, of a Providence that drowned eighty innocent shipmates to get rid of a single villain!

Peter Stuyvesant, whom the Indians called "Wooden Leg," was chosen director-general of the province as a kind of forlorn hope. He arrived in New Amsterdam in 1647, and his administration necessarily came to its reluctant end in 1664 with the surrender to the English. Not only was he far the ablest and most reliable of the governors, he served longer than anyone else. He was not strong enough to correct the tragic blunders of his predecessors; by the time he appeared upon the scene, weakness and stupidity and villainy had given so strong a direction to Holland's American experiment that nothing short of personal greatness and political genius could have turned back the current. And greatness can hardly be attributed to Stuyvesant, although some of the man's biographers have worked hard at the attempt. They have been able to give him the semblance of greatness only by contrast with the small stature of his predecessors. Among Lilliputians even a midget Gulliver is a giant.

The man's real size can perhaps be gathered from the recorded fact that he kept a delegation standing in his presence for more than an hour with heads uncovered; and he sent away another delegation that had come to confer with him for the defense of New Amsterdam with the implied reproof: "We derive our authority from God and the Company, not from a few ignorant subjects, and we alone can call the inhabitants together." Such an attitude robs the final scene of his career in America of some of the dignity of tragedy its setting suggests when this same Peter Stuyvesant had to surrender to English Colonel Nicolls in spite of "God and the Company," forced by those same "ignorant subjects" to sign the surrender.

Some excuse for Stuyvesant perhaps lies in the fact that social stratification in the seventeenth century was more pronounced than it is in the twentieth. Although Holland was a republic, there was a wide chasm between rulers and subjects, as of course there was in England. Moreover, Stuyvesant was the son of a clergyman in Friesland, and the clergy in Holland during the sixteenth and seventeenth centuries formed an aristocracy of a sort. It is only fair to judge the man by the standards of his own age and background.

More serious is the fact that he misunderstood the nature of the new setting in which his official lot was cast. He appears to have had little conception of the inevitable modifications in human character and social institutions that a frontier environment would bring about. His "ignorant subjects" were away ahead of him in this respect. They finally forced out of him concessions that a true statesman would have initiated, a statesman who served the demands of empire rather than of short-sighted business. But Stuyvesant honestly felt that the frontier needed an autocrat; just as he honestly believed with a twentieth century American leader that the "people were too damned dumb" to decide on issues of statecraft and of peace and war; theirs but to do and die—in the seventeenth century as in the twentieth. It is fair to report that Stuyvesant was a tyrant by conviction; he subscribed to the theory of the "strong man" on the frontier.

He may have been right. Given true force of character he might have turned his very liabilities into assets for the empire; men of steel who have moved the world have not by any means always been good husbands and fathers and pleasant companions. But Stuyvesant was opinionated and stubborn, short-sighted and convinced of his own wisdom, rather than truly wise. It is hardly necessary to add that he had not the slightest idea of a possible Dutch continental destiny; he remained to the end the employe of a commercial concern; there was in him nothing of the spirit of a Cecil Rhodes or of some of the eighteenth century English and Dutch buccaneers in the Far East.

Stuyvesant stands convicted, moreover, of a trait that has been alien to Dutch character during the whole of Holland's history—intolerance. He was working against the grain of his tribe when he attempted religious persecution on his own account in New Netherland. Officially he was serving the state church of Holland—the Reformed Church—and it may be that he was sincerely devoted to it in a personal sense. In any event, he tried his hand at forcing all his "subjects" to conform to the only legal religion in the province, and in so doing he organized a little parochial Inquisition of his own, and administered it with a savagery such as usually springs from religious intolerance.

A public proclamation made it a crime to hold a religious meeting not sanctioned by the Reformed Church. Penalty for violation was a fine of one hundred pounds, and anyone attending an unauthorized religious meeting was subject to a fine of twenty-five pounds.[4] When fines failed, the governor resorted to harsher measures. A Quaker, Robert Hodgson, was thrown into a dungeon, then fined six hundred guilders and sentenced to labor for two years at a wheelbarrow with a Negro. Chained to the barrow, he refused to work. The Negro was forced to beat him into unconsciousness with a tarred rope. Stuyvesant's order called for a daily whipping. Hodgson was even hung to the ceiling by his hands and lashed until his flesh had been lacerated. But the governor found his match in the gentle Quaker, who refused to yield.[5]

In the end the West India Company, more enlightened than its employe, saw that religious fanaticism did not mix with dividends. Rather peremptorily, it ordered the governor to cease from his persecutions, and he complied. There is a strong suggestion in the extant record that with Stuyvesant presecution was less a case of religious zeal than pride of authority. As head of the state he had a right to dictate belief, and anyone who ventured to follow another God than Stuyvesant's was committing a species of political treason, or at least lese majesty. The theocratic governors of Puritan New England had a similar point of view, and Stuyvesant may have caught the disease from them. The governor of New Netherland was not out of step with his age, but he was miles behind the public opinion of his country and even of the "subjects" he despised.

But he was at least personally honest, and his private life was reasonably blameless. Far from being the "father" of New Netherland, as some of his biographers have described him, under slightly more favorable conditions he might have taken his place with at least the minor heroes of history. Conscientiousness in the performance of his duty as he saw it was a ruling trait of his nature, and in some respects he has as much right to be held up as a sentimental example for youth as have other "heroes" whose feet of clay have been discreetly hidden by the myth makers of history in the patent leather boots of chauvinistic romanticism.

In the final summing up he looms bigger than his Company or his government. Had he been given halfway decent support during the

---

[4] John S. C. Abbott, *Peter Stuyvesant, the Last Dutch Governor of New Amsterdam,* p. 192.
[5] *Ibid.,* pp. 198-200.

final act of tragedy, and had Company and government had a little of the prudence they demanded of their director-general, he would not have had to submit to the shame of surrendering New Netherland without a blow being struck in its defense. In fact, he stands out at the last in a light that comes near to making him seem heroic. Perusing the record of three centuries ago we are driven to the conviction that for once a leader declaring he intended to defend his fort to the last drop of blood, literally meant his own blood, not that of the men under his command. But the Dutch government had allowed the British to pull political wool over their eyes that were focused on quick returns as usual, and when Colonel Nicolls and his fleet appeared before New Amsterdam it was too late. The people were of course right in forcing Stuyvesant to sign the act of surrender; the alternative would have been useless slaughter, with not even a gambler's chance of holding out until the procrastinating home government could send aid.

Such were the leaders of Dutch empire in America during the seventeenth century. In basic fact, empires like nations are built out of the souls of men. And only in great souls may be found the raw materials out of which to build them.

IV

The Patroon: Vestige of Feudalism

How to attract real farmers to their holdings in America was from the beginning a pressing problem for the West India Company—a problem that was never solved. The directors-general of the concern cast envious eyes at New England that in a dozen years attracted a population of some twenty-six thousand, most of them true colonists, not mere traders locating in the New World for what they could get out of it in the fur trade. Known for its stony soil, New England yet attracted far more farmers than did the fertile acres of New Netherland.

In an attempt to lure Dutch farmers and other real workers away from their relatively comfortable Holland, the West India Company in 1629 instituted what later became known as the patroon system. In intention it was sensible, and also honest enough from the point of view of the Company and the Dutch government. Providing enough producers to balance the number of traders obviously represented the only hope of success in colonization. The latter were by no means idle drones, but neither did they develop the country. They were there not to put something into the land but to get out of it whatever they could.

The patroon system was intended to correct the imbalance. The Company was shrewd enough to appeal to Dutch self-interest to get its vacant land settled with working colonists. It issued a charter of "Privileges and Exemptions" to members of the Company who would recruit settlers and develop the land. Any man of wealth who, within a period of four years, should settle fifty adult persons in homes along the Hudson or its tributaries was to receive a liberal grant of land and the title "Patroon," with various rights and privileges appertaining thereunto.

From the point of view of the patroons it was a wonderful opportunity to become aristocrats in a new land. The typical patroon thought of himself as a kind of Dutch earl. By outfitting at his own expense a company of fifty adult settlers who would engage actually to occupy and cultivate the land, a man of wealth had it in his power to confer a title of sorts on himself and at the same time do his bank account a good turn, or so he hoped. He received a grant of sixteen English miles along the seacoast or on one side of a navigable river, or eight miles along both sides of a river. If he imported more settlers he became lord of more lands. How impressive those Dutch "earldoms" might become is illustrated by the statistics of the Van Rensselaer patroonship. Granted to Kiliaen Van Rensselaer, an Amsterdam trader in pearls and precious stones, the estate, which one included what is now the city of Albany, contained 700,000 acres, or 1,150 square miles. It covered most of the present Albany, Rensselaer, and Schenectady counties, as well as almost all of Columbia County, and part of Greene.

The patroons were sometimes absentee landlords. They were little Dutch lords in whom and their heirs the title to the lands in America was "vested forever," and they were entitled to an "oath of fealty from all tenants," and a flag which all passing vessels were required to salute. This attempt to transplant in the American wilderness a bit of the feudalism of Europe may seem grotesquely comic today. The patroons took it with solemn seriousness. One of Kiliaen Van Rensselaer's deputies began a letter to his boss as follows: "Laus Deo! At the Manhattans this 16th June, 1643. Most honorable, wise, powerful, and right discreet Lord, my Lord Patroon." And yet even those Dutch traders in pearls and precious stones were not wholly lacking in a sense of humor, as the ancient records prove.

There was something of a land rush among the members of the West India Company when the 1629 charter of "Privileges and Exemptions" was published, but only three actually took practical steps for settlement the first year. Those three located in what is now Delaware, in lower New York state on Staten Island and the present sites of Hoboken and Jersey City, and on the upper Hudson in the Albany region.

The Delaware patroonship was acquired by Samuel Godyn and

Samuel Blommaert, both directors of the Company. The settlement in the area of New Amsterdam was made in 1630 by o᷎ Michiel Pauw, also a West India Company director. The patroon᷎ ᷎rt Orange, which came to be known as Rensselaerswy᷎ ᷎ly one that proved truly successful in a permane᷎ ᷎d by the great Kiliaen Van Rensselaer, who was so᷎ ᷎han a mere director of the Company; rather the power ᷎ ᷎ throne, the maker and unmaker of governors-general of New᷎ etherland.

The Delaware venture began with a section sixteen miles square. Five other directors joined the original two to increase the capital; and colonists, tools, and cattle were shipped from Holland. One of the two vessels was captured by pirates, but the other landed its thirty-two settlers and their equipment. The settlement came to be known as Zwaanendaal—Valley of Swans. In spite of its idyllic name, the settlement was soon attacked by Indians, and the partners fell out among themselves. The land titles were presently resold to the Company, and that was the somewhat ignominious end of the first patroonship.

The story of the settlement in the region of Fort Amsterdam was not much different. It was a small colony, founded in 1630, and bore the somewhat pretentious name of Pavonia, the Latinized form of the name of the founder, Michiel Pauw. It lasted seven years but was never on a paying basis, and it had to contend with many frontier difficulties. Capital proved inadequate. The title of this patroonship too reverted to the Company.

Most typical and most successful of the patroonships was that of Rensselaerswyck on the upper Hudson, in the Albany sector. Originally Kiliaen Van Rensselaer had five partners in the venture, but the others soon dropped out and the Van Rensselaer family acquired control "in perpetuity." That the words were more than a phrase appeared two hundred years later when, in the forties and fifties of the nineteenth century, the descendants of the settlers staged their dramatic Anti-Rent War against the descendants of the patroon.

The first group of emigrants reached Fort Orange in June, 1630. Since Rensselaerswyck was the most typical and the most successful of the patroonships, the story of its settlement and development provides the most reliable as well as the most picturesque data for the patroon system as a whole.

The system was an anachronism when it began. The frontier was the most inappropriate place to reintroduce a system that had been repudiated in the mother country, for Holland had outgrown the serfdom the patroon system represented as long as three centuries earlier. The businessmen who managed the West India Company do not seem to have understood that the very air of the frontier was sure to doom the experiment, that the pressures of frontier life were all in the direction of personal independence and self-reliance.

The patroon was almost completely the owner of his tenants, body and soul. He owned the land the tenant worked, not for the time being but "in perpetuity." The Van Rensselaer family still owned their seventeenth century acres in the nineteenth century, and the nineteenth century tenants were still "serfs" all but in name. The master of the estate had exclusive hunting and fishing rights within his holdings. He was chief magistrate on his estate, and although there were some restrictions on his powers in a technical sense, practically he had almost despotic power over his tenants and their families.

The tenant farmers at Rensselaerswyck were given exemption from taxation for a period of ten years, but this seeming privilege had to be paid for dearly in loss of personal freedom and mobility. The tenant could not leave the estate during that period or sell his services elsewhere. In addition to paying rent in stock or produce, the tenant was required to yield up to the patroon a part of his crop and of the increase in his cattle. Also, the patroon had the first bid on anything the tenant raised on his farm that he did not need for his own family. Which meant that the tenant could not sell anything until the patroon had refused to buy it.

There were other galling provisions, such as the tenant's being forced to pay tribute to his patroon for having his grain ground—he was not allowed to have it done in a competitive market. Most humiliating of all was the provision that the patroon was the tenant's legal heir if he died without leaving a will, no matter how many dependents he might leave.

The patroon had most of the privileges, the tenants most of the duties and obligations:

How hard were the terms on which the tenants held their leases is apparent from a report written by the guardians and tutors of Jan Van

Rensselaer, a later patroon of Rensselaerswyck. The patroon reserved for himself the tenth of all the grains, fruits, and other products raised on the *bouwerie*. The tenant was bound, in addition to his rent of five hundred guilders or two hundred dollars, to keep up the roads, repair the buildings, cut ten pieces of fir wood, and bring the same to the shore; he must also every year give the patroon three days' service with his horses and wagons; each year he was to cut, split, and bring to the waterside two fathoms of firewood; and he was further to deliver yearly to the Director as quitrent two bushels of wheat, twenty-five pounds of butter, and two pairs of fowls.[1]

It is an amazing fact that some of those provisions were still in force two centuries later, at the time of the Anti-Rent War, and still had legal standing in the courts. Meanwhile there had been a Declaration of Independence, and the Revolutionary War had been fought and won, in part by the descendants of these same tenants. The techniques and sanctions had been changed, to bring the system into conformity with political democracy, but to all intents and purposes the "serfs" were still "serfs." The feudalism imposed upon the Dutch farmers of the Hudson River Valley by the patroons of the seventeenth century died hard. That system links the seventeenth century with the nineteenth, after most of the other links, such as language and political institutions, had been broken.

The interests of the patroons and those of the Company in due time came into conflict, as was almost inevitable. Kiliaen Van Rensselaer and his associates were suspected of aiming to supplant the Company. The fur trade became a serious bone of contention. The patroons argued that they were at heavy expense in colonizing their holdings and could not hope to make the venture pay out of the returns of agriculture alone. There was big money in the fur trade, and it seemed reasonable, at least to Kiliaen Van Rensselaer, who as an absentee patroon was keenly interested in the dividends from his American investment, that some of that business should come his way as a reward for his patriotic endeavors. There is difference of opinion as to how disinterested Van Rensselaer was. Did he establish his patroonship to get his fingers on the profits in furs, or was he sincere in demanding a share in that business because he wished to make the colonizing

[1] From *Dutch and English on the Hudson,* by Maude Wilder Goodwin, Vol. 7, *The Chronicles of America* Series. Copyright Yale University Press.

venture a success for himself and his country? He himself wrote, in 1638: "I am firmly resolved not knowingly and intentionally to injure the West India Company in their rights in the least, as my principal object is directed toward farming and things connected therewith." [2]

With all its troubles and difficulties, the patroonship at Rensselaerswyck was at least permanent, which is more than can be said of the others. All of them that existed at least in name in 1664, when the Dutch occupation came to an end, were transformed by the English into manorial grants, and other manors were added to the list. Politically and technically the end of the Dutch regime meant "thirty" for the patroons and their system; actually the system that had been fastened on the valley continued to play a determining part in the history of the region.

[2] Bertus Harry Wabeke, *Dutch Immigration to North America 1624-1860*, p. 31.

V

The Folk of New Netherland

THE WIT WHO said that even if money does not make you happy, it at least lets you be miserable in comfort might have won understanding from the folk of New Netherland. They respected money, and they were but little disposed to exchange material advantages for the more intangible treasures that moth does not corrupt. There were comparatively few "God-intoxicated" men among them. Their way of life was on the whole materialistic; they had a deep and abiding respect for common sense and business acumen, both Dutch tribal traits. Even though the wealth they dealt in was mostly in the form of beaver skins, and the people they traded with were savages, they had a talent for business and they understood devotion to it. To their own hurt they were less agricultural than commercial.

If an aptitude for trade is a fault, that fault may fairly be attributed to the folk of New Netherland. Some other charges have less validity. Many of the reports of what those people were like have come to us from the English, who of course were rivals of the Dutch on the American frontier. The emphasis has often been placed on their love of drink, and that was without question one of their vices; and on their "fornication and adultery," and again it must honestly be confessed that there was a good deal of that. But they were not so lost to the decencies and amenities of an ordered social life as some of their rivals would have us believe. One of their early ministers, a Domine Michaelius, described them to a friend in Holland as "somewhat rough and loose" but, generally speaking, "good people." They had nothing of the social viciousness and abandoned lawlessness that history and fiction have always associated with the winning of our own West.

They were twitted by their English judges—and tradition has uncritically adopted the aspersion—with boorishness and a low standard of living. Many of them committed the crime of dwelling in hovels, with sunken clay floors. But again, in the West, later on, pioneers invented sod houses, and clay floors have been familiar to frontiersmen since time immemorial. The folk of New Netherland were as ready as any pioneers to reproduce the comforts of the home land in their raw communities as soon as conditions would allow. In *The History of the City of New York* Mrs. Schuyler Van Rensselaer reports:

On the outlying bouweries the farmers built substantially and lived in comfort. Jonas Bronck had a stone house roofed with tiles which, as is shown by the 'plat' of his land in the State archives, stood near the site of the present Morrisania station of the Harlem River railroad. An inventory taken in 1643, after his death, mentions good furniture and clothes, some curiosities including a 'Japanese cutlass,' table silver and pewter, eleven pictures 'big and little,' twenty books in Danish, Dutch and German, eighteen 'old printed pamphlets,' and 'seventeen manuscript books which are old.'

That was nearly twenty years after the colony was established. Time is required to bring the amenities of life to any frontier. Quite a different picture, also a true one, could be painted of the life of the Dutch folk during the early years. Thus Augustus Van Buren writes of the settlers, in the *Proceedings of the New York Historical Society:* [1]

Most of them could neither read nor write. They were a wild, uncouth, rough, and most of the time a drunken crowd. They lived in small log huts, thatched with straw. They wore rough clothes, and in winter dressed in skins. They subsisted on a little corn, game, and fish. They were afraid of neither man, God, nor the devil.

But fact and truth are not necessarily synonymous. The chances are that every item in that picture is authentic, but when the damning details are grouped together to form an indictment their essential truth evaporates. The early comers to New Netherland were doubtless illiterate; so were very many of the first waves of immigrants on any American frontiers throughout our history. They were inclined to be

[1] Quoted by Dixon Wecter, *The Saga of American Society* (Charles Scribner's Sons, 1937), p. 53.

"uncouth" and "rough." When have frontiersmen been otherwise? That they should build small log huts thatched with straw was inevitable; logs constituted their only building material, and peasant huts in the Netherlands, in fact throughout the Europe of that day, used straw for thatching. Their clothes would certainly be rough, and in winter skins would be the most available material; the Dutch folk were merely showing their common sense by adapting themselves to their new environment. As for their diet—a "little corn" and a more plentiful supply of game and fish—what else could have been expected? Corn was hard to raise in soil that had to be cleared first of trees and stumps and roots; game and fish were more readily available.

There remain the charges that they were "most of the time a drunken crowd" and that "they were afraid of neither man, God, nor the devil." A good deal of drinking there was, all records agree; this is not merely a charge brought by envious rivals of the Dutch folk, it is substantiated by their own documents. But it need not surprise a public too much that takes as a matter of course the Bret Harte "Roaring Camps" and the San Francisco saloons of the gold rush of 1849. The alleged lack of fear of "man, God, or the devil" presents a completely distorted picture. For those same folk soon forced a reluctant governor to make provision for the proper education of their children; they laid the foundations, through their own initiative and somewhat in despite of their political leaders, of what presently grew into a great church organization, the Reformed Church in America. As for their fear of the devil, whatever that phrase means, one of their early ministers paints quite a different picture; Domine Michaelius says of them that they were "respectful to their minister."

As the years passed and more immigrants arrived in New Netherland, until at its peak the province had a population of perhaps twelve thousand, the grimness and roughness of life were gradually replaced by more gracious modes of existence. Frontier camps became villages, log shelters were replaced by homes that boasted of some comforts and beauty, and the "wild, uncouth, and rough crowd" imperceptibly turned into a society of reasonably responsible citizens who felt their identity with an orderly community.

As early as 1643 the Dutch people of New Amsterdam had raised a fund to build a schoolhouse. It is important to note, if the true character of the folk is to be justly appraised, that the people did this of their own initiative and that they voluntarily laid upon themselves this financial burden. The West India Company had promised to establish a school system in the province similar to the one the people had been used to at home, but that promise had been more or less a dead letter. Holland's public school system at the time was not unlike America's today, at least in principle. The people of New Netherland may have been "wild and uncouth"; they were intelligent enough to understand the value of a truly democratic education for their children. By comparison it is revealing to recall that in Plymouth there was no public school for fifty-two years after the founding of the colony.[2]

As for institutional religion, long before the colony could afford a regular minister, it maintained two lay readers known as "comforters of the sick," who read to the people on Sundays from the Scriptures. And long before the church was finally built, in Governor Kieft's time, a large room over a "horse-mill" was used to accommodate the congregation. The people even equipped their temporary church with a bell captured in a West India Company military expedition. Such were the humble beginnings of the Reformed Church. Presently ministers came from Holland and the church grew with the community. But again, it is worth remembering that their church institution was not imposed upon the folk from above; the West India Company was a business concern, inclined to be apathetic about institutions that did not promise to return cash dividends; the people demanded the church.

Perhaps the clearest evidence that the Dutch folk of New Netherland were potentially better empire builders than their commercial and political rulers is found in their instinct for democratic government. It was of course not called that; the word "democracy" was still a term of reproach throughout America so late as the early nineteenth century. But the Dutch folk of New Netherland, like their brothers and cousins in Holland, were sure that they wanted to hoe their own row —commercially, politically, and in every other way. They wanted "to breathe after their own fashion," to attribute Emerson's phrase to them. They refused to be docile under dictatorship. Governor Stuyvesant might indulge in the pompous claim that he derived his authority from "God and the Company"; he might call the people "ignorant

[2] Mrs. Schuyler Van Rensselaer, *op. cit.* I, 205.

subjects." Those same "ignorant" men asserted their charter of democratic rights with a spirit not unlike that shown by Jefferson more than a century later in the Declaration of Independence. In their famous *Remonstrance and Petition to the Director-General and Council of New Netherland* they used the words that had the unmistakable ring of a system that was to be born on this continent long after the writers had been gathered unto their fathers:

We humbly conceive that our rights and privileges are the same, harmonizing in every respect with those of the Netherlands, being a member dependent on that State and in no wise a people conquered or subjugated, but settled here on a mutual covenant and contract entered into with the Lords Masters and with the consent of the natives, the first proprietors of these lands, from whom we purchased the soil with our own funds.[3]

In other words, the people of New Netherland were citizens of Holland, as the British colonists later claimed to be citizens of England. They refused to be regarded as dependents or wards. Since Holland was a republic and Holland's citizens were free men, they were determined to be free.

In domestic affairs they progressively wrested rights of self-government from the directors-general of the West India Company. All the governors, without exception, tried to establish dictatorships, Stuyvesant most insistently of all. The people resisted them and gradually compelled them to yield up a share in the government. Though the phrase, "taxation without representation," was not coined until the days of the American Revolution, the people of New Netherland understood its meaning. It was not with them, as it later became in America, a mere political theory; they instinctively felt that it was not good economic and political sense to lay burdens upon people without their consent.

And if tolerance and freedom from superstition are marks of civilization, then the "wild and uncouth" folk of New Netherland were rather highly civilized, in a relative sense at least, whatever their deficiencies may have been in etiquette or even in morals. As compared with the Puritans of New England, whose writers were persistently depreciating them, they were "advanced," almost "civilized," giving the words their modern connotations. The Puritans chased out

[3] *Ibid.,* I, 346.

Roger Williams, whom Ludwig Lewisohn, perhaps too dogmatically, has described as "the only Christian of his day in America." The Hollanders not only admitted all victims of religious intolerance and fanaticism, they invited them to take refuge in New Netherland, promising them freedom of conscience and the right to worship God in their own way.

Although this tolerance was in some measure the fruit of Dutch business acumen, it was also, in part, an outgrowth of something in Dutch nature that had its roots deep below the surface of economic sagacity. It had been hardly an accident, rather the result of a racial trait, that in a day when Luther, a German, and Calvin, a Frenchman, had been building their ecclesiastical systems on a denial of toleration, Erasmus, a Hollander, had been the great European foe of intolerance. The spirit of Erasmus was still alive in Holland in the seventeenth century, and the contrast between its manifestation in New Netherland and the lack of such a spirit in New England is so great that it is startling.

Governor Stuyvesant alone tried to dictate to men's consciences. He never had the support of the folk of New Netherland, and when the directors of the West India Company got around to it they compelled him to desist. And his attempt was the sole instance of religious intolerance in the history of the Dutch experiment in colonization in America. Some of the other directors-general may have been "consummate villains"; their villainy did not take the form of a self-righteous insistence on conformity to their own brand of worship.

Nor do we find in the annals of New Netherland any of the grim cruelty often recorded in the story of the dealings of the Puritans with the sinners of their community. For the Dutch folk were not only tolerant of others' beliefs, they were inclined to deal somewhat gently even with those of their own persuasion who fell into sin. Had there been a Hawthorne among the descendants of those Hollanders he could hardly have found material for a *Scarlet Letter* in the annals of the province. There was comparatively little sadism in the hearts of the folk of the province; the reason—there was comparatively little fanaticism in their natures.

But the folk of New Netherland can hardly be spoken of as a unit. They came from widely separated sections of the Netherlands and out of many different backgrounds. There were peasants among them, but fewer than would have been desirable; farming conditions were not unfavorable in Holland. In like manner, the Dutch citizens who had a trade guild standing were not inclined to emigrate. It would be a mistake to think of the population of New Netherland as made up of self-reliant immigrants who possessed special skills. In course of the years they developed industrial acumen and personal self-reliance, in response to the urgencies of the frontier, but many joined the adventure in the New World who were not of that stamp.

Governor Stuyvesant complained to his Company that New Netherland was being "peopled by the scrapings of all sorts of nationalities," but that may have been an exaggeration. It was natural for the governor-general to complain; if he had poor material to work with he could not be held so greatly responsible for lack of success. But though there were many "scrapings" among them—Norwegians and Danes and Germans and Finns sent over to satisfy the terms of immigration contracts, Stuyvesant's word calls for qualification; some of those people were engaged because their skills were needed in the frontier economy.

The New Netherland colony was not the fruit of a spontaneous movement. Most of the people there were *sent* for one reason or another. The West India Company needed workers and it engaged the best it could get. Similarly the patroons needed men, and some of them went to the length of paying a bounty to anyone who supplied them with an indentured servant who could be counted as a "colonist." If a man had a knack as a lumberman or carpenter or mason, and could be lured by glowing pictures of opportunities on the frontier to chance the adventure, he was eagerly accepted as a colonist.

The folk of New Netherland emigrated for a variety of reasons. Many of them left home because they were unsuccessful there. Some responded to the mirage of easy money in a new country. But among the emigrants there was a respectable sprinkling of ambitious young men who had carefully gaged the possibilities and probabilities on the frontier. Many of those did well and found a place for themselves.

Whatever their background or reasons for emigration, the large majority drifted into trade—which meant the fur trade. Too few became farmers. But farmers are precisely the type of workers any frontier needs. While the general quality of the New Netherland population was not inferior to that of the English of New England, the latter were more inclined to put their trust in the good earth. "Scarcely three good farmers were to be found among the 507 settlers with which the city of Amsterdam hoped to establish her colony." [4]

Perhaps it was their common sense attitude on the subject of witchcraft that marks the New Netherland folk as being in advance of their time. There were no witchcraft trials of any kind in New Netherland history. The only New Netherlander ever put on trial on such a charge was accused by New England Puritans, at Hartford, where she was a resident.

The belief in witches was rather general in Europe during the seventeenth century. It is therefore not remarkable that New England Puritans took such things seriously even toward the close of the century. Not yet that it was not exclusively the ignorant who yielded to such superstitions. Cotton Mather, who wrote what is surely one of the most dreadful books of all time, *The Wonders of the Invisible World,* in which he described in considerable detail the trials of the witches, was one of the most highly educated men of his day. The wonder is that the simple common sense of Dutch colonials, who were almost next-door neighbors to people capable even in the succeeding generation of such fantastic superstitions, should have been potent enough to stand out against the drift of fanaticism on the American frontier.

That that fanaticism was genuinely dangerous to innocent people is shown by the statistics of the punishments meted out by the Puritan men of God to the victims of their superstition. So late as a generation after the fall of New Netherland, in June of 1692, the first New England victim was sent to the gallows; in July, five more; in August there were six; and in September, fourteen. An eighty-year old man was pressed to death under heavy stones. Some two hundred persons were accused or suspected. A special court was instituted to try the witchcraft cases, which dragged on for many months. The testimony as set down by Cotton Mather in all seriousness is so fantastic that to the mind of today it reads almost like burlesque.

The people of New Netherland may have been "wild, uncouth, and rough"; in their tolerance and instinctive resistance to the spirit of

[4] Bertus Harry Wabeke, *Dutch Immigration,* p. 19.

superstition of the age they were nearly a century ahead of those whose destiny it was to supplant them as the colonizers of America in a continental sense.

The folk of New Netherland in terms of the wave of what was their future were far more enlightened than their leaders who tried to govern them with supercilious contempt. An objective examination of the record, honestly allowing for all their faults and weaknesses, shows that they were worthy of becoming the bearers of their country's culture across our continent. The ineptness and short-sightedness of politicians and traders robbed them of that destiny, but their defeat was only partial, as the subsequent story of the life of their nationality in America shows.

There is a footnote to the story of the Dutch colonial episode on the American continent. In less than a decade after the surrender to the English the Dutch recaptured New York, during the war that broke out between England and Holland in 1672. The folk of New Netherland industriously set about restoring their own institutions, even to the extent of wiping out many of the English place names and substituting for them the Dutch words by which they had been known for half a century. It was a last instinctive attempt to impose their culture on America.

But once more their government in Holland failed them. Three months after the recapture of New Amsterdam a compromise peace between Holland and England nullified the fruits of military victory in the New World. One of the articles of the treaty read:

Whatsoever countries, islands, ports, towns, castles or forts have been taken on both sides, since the time that the late unhappy war broke out, either in Europe or elsewhere, shall be restored to the former lord or proprietor in the same condition they shall be in when peace itself shall be proclaimed.

Holland had other fish to fry—European fish—and threw in her few thousand American colonists to gain her ends on her own side of the Atlantic.

VI

Washington Irving's Hollanders

IT WAS THOSE people, potential empire builders, or at least men and women of good sense, tolerance, and industriousness, whom Washington Irving purported to describe in *Knickerbocker's History of New York*. They came out of his mill of burlesque as buffoons, almost like figures in a modern comic strip. Now and again some Hollanders, a few of them highly influential, have objected to the portrayal as a libel on their nationality. Even Walt Whitman, who was of Dutch stock on his mother's side, called the book "shallow burlesque, full of clown's wit."

Irving himself was driven to disclaiming any intention of disrespect to the breed from which some of his closest friends were descended— James K. Paulding, for instance, who had collaborated with him in writing the *Salmagundi* papers and who had been a boyhood chum. The creator of Diedrich Knickerbocker, moreover, remained on terms of intimacy with not a few of the socially highly placed Dutch families in the Hudson River Valley. And with notable exceptions, Hollanders and descendants of Hollanders have enjoyed the *Knickerbocker History* as much as have other readers; they have accepted it for what it is—burlesque, and good foolery. Van Wyck Brooks, whose Dutch blood comes from New Netherland ancestry, asks: "Who could quarrel seriously with such a ripe expression of a mind that was so well-furnished and so good-natured?"

Such differences of opinion make *Knickerbocker's History* a part of the story of Americans from Holland. The book's publication date—it appeared in 1809—would chronologically place a discussion of the

58

subject at a later moment in this record, but its subject matter focuses attention on it at this point while the historical character of the Dutch folk is fresh in mind.

Knickerbocker's History has a right to be judged in terms of what Irving meant it to be—burlesque, not realistic history; and burlesque has its own laws, and hence its own immunities. Moreover, the fact has been generally ignored by those who resent Irving's lampoons that he wields as wicked a pen describing New Englanders as he does portraying the ancestors of present-day Hollanders. New England does not get so much space, by reason of the nature of the subject, but when its people appear on the stage they are burlesqued with the same glorious abandon employed in lampooning the seventeenth century Dutch worthies. The pictures of witchcraft among the Puritans, or the caricatures of the New Englanders' ridiculously long and pompous speeches, could be resented by Americans of English stock with as much reason as citizens of Dutch extraction could resent the lampoons of Wouter Van Twiller, Wilhelmus Kieft, and Peter Stuyvesant. If Irving, a humorist and satirist invested with satire's license, can be fairly accused of libeling the Hollanders he can just as fairly be charged with wronging his own great-ancestors.

And that same thing goes for the people of Swedish birth. In the course of the imaginary narrative Governor Peter Stuyvesant enters upon a campaign against Fort Christina held by the Swedes. It would be quite as fair for descendants of Swedish nationals to object as it is for Hollanders to take exception to a story that belongs to actual history in about the same degree that *Alice in Wonderland* belongs to real life. Can anyone easily forget the caricature of Swedish Governor Jan Risingh, the commander of the fort, shaving himself with a "villainously dull razor," causing him to "make a series of horrible grimaces, that heightened exceedingly the grizzly terrors of his visage" while he was receiving Governor Stuyvesant's emissaries? The portrait is extravagantly glorious spoofing and can no more be taken seriously than it would be possible to take seriously the exploits of Ally Oop in the Kingdom of Moo.

Paradoxical though it may sound, the *History of New York* is not about the Hollanders at all; it is purely and simply a satire on the Americans of Washington Irving's own day. Not only are Irving's

Hollanders of the seventeenth century occupation of New Netherland mythical, almost too obviously mythical, they are so clearly used as a stick with which to belabor nineteenth century Americans, that if there is to be objection to Irving's burseque it can come most legitimately from the descendants of those Americans.

To see Irving's burlesque in proper perspective it is necessary to become acquainted with a series of papers that preceded the writing of the *History*. In 1807 the then very young Irving joined forces with two other very young men, his brother William and James K. Paulding, to publish what they thought of as an American *Spectator*. The serial papers went under the burlesque title of *Salmagundi: or, the Whim-Whams and Opinions of Launcelot Langstaff, Esq.* Some of the numbers are still readable, especially those in which the young authors burlesqued the manners and customs, the habits and foibles, of their fellow townsmen in the little city of New York and of the American people in general.

Certain American traits are singled out for repeated attack. The American government should be called a *logocracy*—government by talk. It was all talk, talk, talk. The American people were bent on talking themselves and everybody else to death. Ours was a government of mediocrities, for mediocrities, by mediocrities. America, the authors charged, was being governed at the moment by a windy clown (Thomas Jefferson). Irving describes him as "a man of superlative ventosity, and comparable to nothing but a huge bladder of wind." He burlesqued other public men of the moment, and political caucuses, and state dinners, and all sorts of manifestations of the life of the time, much as Addison and Steele had satirized similar social and political manifestations in England, and in the same spirit of good-natured spoofing.

Neither in England nor in America was it burlesque directed against any nationality. The charge occasionally made against Irving is that in the *History* he was exploiting an unfair and narrow racial prejudice. But *Salmagundi* does not so much as mention Hollander or Swede or German or any other national. And the *History of New York* is merely an amplification of the basic burlesque developed in briefer scope in the earlier work. The Hollanders and their seventeenth century colonizing exploits at New Amsterdam are merely used as a means for dramatizing a young American writer's attacks on Americans.

The suggestion of the *History* came from a solemnly pompous piece of community publicity under the title, *The Picture of New York,* by a Dr. Samuel Latham Mitchell, who was a professor of chemistry and zoology at Columbia College. This appeared in 1807, at the very time when the young *Salmagundi* authors were having their light-hearted fun at the expense of the American people. The Mitchell opus was the sort of thing that has become painfully familiar in our own age of "publicity." But it was less well recognized at the time for what it actually was, and hence it was more potent in debauching the good taste of the public than we find similar contemporary volumes. It was pompous and trite, as such documents usually are, and it gave the impression that New York had a monopoly on civilization, on good taste, on business morals, that it came as near being a Utopia as could be expected in a land where God's in his heaven and all's right with the world. The little city of some sixty thousand was beginning to feel its oats, and it was not at all averse to swallowing the largest dose of self-commendation that any publicity dispenser could administer.

Here clearly was a subject for *Salmagundi* burlesque. That, it seems likely, was all that was intended at first. Irving drew his brother Peter into the project, but fortunately the latter soon dropped out and left the job to a real master of burlesque. The subject grew on the young author, and before he knew it he was thinking in terms of a book that would match in size the volume it meant to lampoon. Although the processes of authorship are mysterious, and can seldom be traced accurately, in retrospect, even by the author himself, it is not too hazardous to suggest that the Irving *History* did not at first contemplate a detailed narrative of Dutch occupation in the seventeenth century. It seems more likely that the story of that episode was meant merely as a springboard for the burlesque, but that it proved such good fun that the author finally decided to confine himself to one period alone. All Irving himself says is that the choice of the period was dictated by an artistic demand for narrative unity.

At the very start he saw an opportunity to kill two birds with one stone. Mitchell's book was not only pompous, a worse fault was that it was long-winded—as such books almost invariably are. But long-windedness had been a characteristic of native American writers for a century or more. The Cotton Mathers and their kind were inclined to begin so far in the past of any subject they treated that, by the time the real narrative or exposition opened, the readers had already been drugged with words into a state of intellectual insensibility. The opening movement of the *History* therefore was designed to satirize both the specific Mitchell book and the works of all the more characteristic writers in the field of American letters.

For Diedrich Knickerbocker was not content to open his history with the landing of the Hollanders on American soil; not even with the beginning of the Dutch nation in Europe; nor with the first emergence of Dutch nationals in the days of Julius Caesar; he was satisfied with nothing less than opening the story with the beginning of the world. And so before a Hollander is so much as mentioned we have been treated to a series of chapters in which burlesque authorities are solemnly treated in terms of burlesque, with burlesque footnotes and burlesque balancing of "facts" against "facts."

But at long last the mythical historian gets the colonists of the West India Company landed on Manhattan Island. There is just enough real history to make the migration recognizable, but the details are such a glorious mixture of fact, fable, and pure invention—chiefly the latter—that it seems grotesque it could ever have been taken seriously by so much as a single reader. The very dates cited are often a little vague. Not because Irving did not know the facts; there is much more historical scholarship in the book than appears on the surface. But most of that scholarship consists in what the author does not say. Historical data were deliberately blurred because that was in the very nature of the art form in which Irving wrote—burlesque.

In due course of his satirically leisurely narrative Diedrich Knickerbocker gets Governor Wouter Van Twiller on the stage. Seen against the background of burlesque, he turns out to be not a Hollander but a lampoon of the same American government officials that the authors of *Salmagundi* had been satirizing in that work. Then, even as now, presidents and congressmen were often accused of being do-nothing rulers. The ecstasies that had inspired such earlier men as Tom Paine, and that had carried the Revolution to its triumphant close, had given way long since to the prose of the latter days of Washington and particularly to the doldrums of the Adams administration. As a loyal member of the Federalist party Irving probably did not feel free to tie the Wouter Van Twiller mask on any particular living politician, but the general political atmosphere of the early days of our own republic is strongly suggested in that figure and the mythical Hollanders who surrounded him.

There were no such inhibitions when the author came to the administration of the next governor, Wilhelmus Kieft. For here was an opportunity to satirize President Jefferson, who was just then in the closing period of his second administration. The young author disliked Jefferson and all his works, not merely the way a good Federalist would be likely to hate a "democrat," the dislike was also temperamental and personal. Like many of the best men of that age, including Washington and Hamilton, Irving both distrusted "democracy" and was temperamentally repelled by the "people." To him, as to many other very able and patriotic men, Jefferson was the incarnation of everything that was cheap and vulgar in the mass mind. Irving and those of like mind could not believe that Jefferson was not playing to the galleries and appealing to mob sentimentalism.

The young author was of course wrong about Jefferson; before he died, exactly fifty years after the publication of the *History of New York,* he recognized the fact that Jefferson had been riding the wave of the future and that he had been one of the truly great builders of America. The fairness of the burlesque of Jefferson is not in question here, merely the fact that it was not a burlesque of a long-forgotten Dutch governor of New Netherland, but of an American president who was daily, almost hourly, in the public eye.

The Jefferson personality was fatally adapted to burlesque. Jefferson was not merely a public man, he was daily putting his oar into everything that was going on. A kind of early nineteenth century Theodore Roosevelt, he had his say about everything, from the dress of young girls to the philosophies of savants; he had a thousand interests; his ideas were inclined to be unconventional; and he was not averse to administering wholesome shocks to the American people. All this to the delight and admiration of his followers, but equally to the disgust of his political and personal opponents. Nearly every day this "busybody" in the White House made them a little sick to the stomach.

What more natural than that the young Irving, almost intoxicated with the art form he had made his own in *Salmagundi,* should leap into the battle with youthful glee? Almost any other particular Hollander than Wilhelmus Kieft would have done quite as well, or for that matter almost any other half-mythical person out of the twilight history of any other country. President Jefferson was Irving's game, and in the portrayal he let his victim have it with both barrels. Hollanders who object to the *Knickerbocker History* have forgotten the real victim and think only of the blunderbuss Irving used to dispatch him.

Actually the portrait of Wilhelmus Kieft is less successful as a creative achievement than that of his successor, one-legged Peter Stuyvesant. Was the young writer inhibited too much by reason of the fact that every reader would mentally substitute the name "Jefferson" whenever the name "Wilhelmus Kieft" appeared in the text? A president is after all a president, even though he is head of the other party. A definite, specific, living person cannot be lampooned with the unrestraint that may be employed in the case of a generalized mass personality, such as was the case with the story of the administration of Peter Stuyvesant.

Whatever the reason, readers have remembered Peter Stuyvesant and have more or less forgotten Governor Kieft. Rightly so, because Knickerbocker's Stuyvesant has much more real red blood in his fictional veins. Irving let himself go in creating Stuyvesant. He was portraying Public Official, not a specific Thomas Jefferson or anybody else. The material out of which he made the figure had in it the stuff of eternal life. For readers who have forgotten the politics of the time, Kieft may require an identifying footnote; the Stuyvesant portrait cannot become obsolete or outmoded and it will never require specific identification.

Nor will the atmosphere in which the governor lives and breathes and has his being. For it is the atmosphere that Irving had been slowly generating in *Salmagundi.* This is the America of his own day he is deluging with ribald laughter. First of all politics. All his life Irving was fascinated by politics, not as a participant but as an observer. Man as a political animal was of perennial interest to him, and in his opinion much of the American national's most delicious super-foolish-

HET VERLEENEN VAN DEN NAAM AMSTERDAM, 25 APRIL 1625, AAN HET LATER
HERDOOPTE NEW-YORK.

Soo haest den ringh sloot ten naeste by ghemaeckt sal
zyn sal den Commis Verhulst ende den Raet terstont
by de hant doen nemen de fortificatie volgende het con-
cept N° C. twelck ghenaemt sal werden Amsterdam, daer
aen doende graven soo veel volcx als eenichsints uyt de
bouw-lieden, bootsgesellen ende coloniers konnen gemist
werden   VAN RAPPARD DOCUMENT E, FOL. 11.

Top: DUTCH MAN-OF-WAR IN HOLLAND'S GOLDEN AGE
Bottom: OFFICIAL PATENT NAMING NEW AMSTERDAM

Netherlands Information Bureau

CONTEMPORARY PORTRAIT OF KILIAEN VAN RENSSELAER

Not the Amsterdam merchant who founded Rensselaerswyck but a descendant who ruled the vast estate after New Netherland had become British. The costume suggests the regal splendor in which the Lords of the Manor lived.

Netherlands Information Bureau

ness found expression in his political activities. The travesties on the politics of the Jefferson era, as shadowed forth in the world of Peter Stuyvesant, are lively in themselves and they are excellent social satire. Are they fair, from the point of view of the politician or statesman? That's quite another question. When has satire or burlesque been scrupulously fair? There would be a contradiction in terms involved in such an idea.

Then there were such other booberies as conventions and official dinners and all the other techniques developed for the smooth operation of municipal and national life. The very readers who took such things with portentous seriousness laughed until their ribs ached, just as in our day we who were the victims of Sinclair Lewis's lampoons paid our good money for *Main Street* and *Babbitt*. And also in the same way we have been laughing for two hundred years at the antics of the Lilliputians and the Brobdingnagians, electing to forget for the moment that we are laughing at our own petty souls.

And women's clothes and men's clothes were of course inevitable game; they always are for any satirist anywhere at any time. Irving was not lampooning *Dutch* costume as such. Nor was he lampooning Dutch ancestor worship; he was aiming his shafts at what he considered the pretentiousness of such organizations as the New York Historical Society of his day. And at the humorless awe with which many of the Dutch aristocrats of the Jefferson era spoke about their forebears of the seventeenth century. Ancestor worship was exactly the same in the nineteenth century as it was in the seventeenth, the same in the seventeenth as it is in the twentieth. In describing it in terms' of half-mythical Dutch history Irving was portraying it for his own time and for all time.

Chauvinism was another American trait that the story of the reign of Peter Stuyvesant throws into bold relief. In Irving's day that spirit was just beginning to get a stranglehold on the American mind. The American people were convinced they could "lick" the whole world, and they were rather sorry the job would be such an easy one. Our great-great-grandfathers had forgotten Washington's wise injunction, in his Farewell Address, not to get tangled up in European quarrels because they were as yet too weak to mind anybody else's business. Too weak! That was a laugh. One American with a squirrel rifle was more than a match for half a dozen Englishmen or Frenchmen armed with cannon and mortars.

Of course they took most of this out in talk. But that made it all the better target for burlesque. How Peter Stuyvesant postures and prances, and how he talks and blusters and threatens! And how everybody else talks! How they pass resolutions and draw up documents in defiance of the powers of the world and the devil! A *logocracy*—a talking people who are convinced they can scare the world into fits by mere bluster. That was Irving's conception of his countrymen, and that is the picture that comes out of the history of the administration of Peter Stuyvesant. The fact that the real Stuyvesant was not in any sense like that, that the Hollanders over whom he ruled were not like that, is of course completely irrelevant. There would be no point in confusing burlesque with history.

There are many other themes for burlesque, too many to be enumerated here. The sterile scholarship, for instance, of the intellectuals of Irving's own day and of the Puritans of the eighteenth century. The whole tone of the *History* is a broad, an almost slapdash, burlesque of that type of learning. Some Hollanders have interpreted it as an attack on their own national savants, forgetting that the breed is always the same, yesterday, today, and forever. Then there is the type of religion that is merely conventional; and patriotism that thinks in terms of dollars and cents; and party politics that tries to hide behind the mask of alleged statesmanship. And there are many incidental, even local, targets. In some respects the *History of New York* is journalism, a journalism that must have been exceedingly effective in the early nineteenth century; today many of the allusions that Irving made casually as a matter of course are somewhat shadowy—the names of once popular clubs, movements whose goofy nature we can no longer fully appreciate, all sorts of topical interests instantly intelligible to the readers of that day.

To the very close of the book Irving kept his own day in the foreground of his burlesque, using his Hollanders only as a means to an end. Thus, with his eye very probably on Napoleon—the year was 1809, when the Corsican was at the peak of his madness—he thus described the death of Peter Stuyvesant: "Thus died Peter Stuyvesant, a valiant soldier—a loyal subject—an upright governor, and an honest

Dutchman—who wanted only a few empires to desolate to have immortalized him as a hero."

Always it was his own time Irving was satirizing. It is one of American literature's little ironies that his legend has for nearly a century and a half credited him with burlesquing the Hollanders of the seventeenth century.

VII

Vestiges of the Occupation

THE SUCCESS OF Irving's book is a strong indication that there were still, at the time of its publication, numerous vestiges of the Dutch occupation. A basic necessity for successful satire is reader familiarity with the things satirized. The youthful author of *Knickerbocker's History* knew that he could depend on the response of his local public. That response, in terms of sales, would indicate, even if there were no other proof, that Dutch culture had not been wholly replaced by that of the English, 145 years after the occupation came to an end.

But there is ample proof from other sources; even overwhelming proof. In 1809 New York and Albany, as well as the whole of the Hudson River Valley and parts of New Jersey, Delaware, and Pennsylvania, were still strongly tinctured, some places even dominated, by Dutch mores. Those ten or twelve thousand Hollanders who had occupied the region officially for only four decades, had succeeded in so stamping upon its life and institutions the impress of their own national culture that it had not been erased after a century and a half. Not only had it not been erased, it was still so strong that it gave the tone to the region at the beginning of the nineteenth century. New York did not have a Dutch section, as New Orleans to this day has a French quarter; but its life as a whole was flavored, perhaps spiced, by the spirit of the descendants of the men and women who founded New Amsterdam. Albany, at the beginning of the nineteenth century was still more distinctively Dutch in its tone; and many other communities of the area once included in New Netherland retained so many vestiges of the occupation that as communities they were far more Dutch than English.

Perhaps the most readily identifiable vestige of a culture is language. There is something so intimately personal about a country's speech, even about its idiom, that men instinctively cling to their own as long as they can. They feel that the tongue of their fathers is almost a part of their own flesh. At least the Hollanders in the Hudson Valley showed by the tenacity with which they clung to Dutch speech that they considered it not merely a utilitarian means of communication, that to them there was something almost sacrosanct in the speech of their ancestors. H. L. Mencken, in *The American Language: Supplement One*, notes the stubborn tenacity with which the Hudson Valley clung to the speechways of New Netherland:

> The English tried to wipe out Dutch in New York after the conquest of the colony in 1664, but it carried on an underground existence for many years, and so late as the second half of the Eighteenth Century an English observer was reporting that it was "still so much used in some counties that the sheriffs find it difficult to obtain persons sufficiently acquainted with the English tongue to serve as jurors in the courts of law." Dutch, indeed, was the first language in some of the remoter parts of the Hudson valley until our own time, and also in parts of New Jersey.[1]

Albany, so late as the first decade of the twentieth century, still contained a church that held its services in the Dutch language and imported its pastors from Holland.[2] When a new constitution for the state of New York was under discussion in 1846, a suggestion was seriously made that no one should be allowed to vote who could not read both English and Dutch; there were at least some who regarded Dutch as one of the state's indigenous languages.

But by that time the language had largely lost its battle for survival, as of course any language loses in competition with the prevailing speech of a vast continent. Most tongues lose out much more quickly. The marvel is that Dutch held its own even in isolated districts. A half century earlier, toward the close of the eighteenth century when Washington Irving roamed as a boy through the environs of Tarrytown, Dutch was far from being a mere survival. He loved to go fishing with boys who bore Dutch names, and to visit the friendly kitchens of the mothers of those chums. During such prowlings he unconsciously absorbed much of the lore that later reappeared, transmogrified, in such tales as "Rip Van Winkle" and "The Legend of Sleepy Hollow."

And Noah Webster, he of the dictionary fame, reports that he used to listen to Dutch sermons in Albany so late as 1786. The astonishing part of that statement is not that eccentric and cranky old Noah should report the fact itself—he set down all sorts of curious lore—but that he should regard it as almost a matter of course that he, non-Hollander though he was, should be familiar with the language; he understood that Dutch was an important component element in the formation of the American speech that even then was beginning to displace English proper in the United States. As a matter of fact, no English sermons were permitted in the pulpits of the Reformed Church throughout the area formerly occupied by New Netherland, until 1764—exactly a century after the surrender to the English—and it was not until the end of the eighteenth century that English finally largely displaced Dutch as the language of the sermons preached in the pulpits of the church.[3]

Mencken develops the amusing theory that the word which is perhaps most characteristically American of all words—"Yankee"—is a vestige of the Dutch occupation. It is supposed to have been a combination of two Dutch words, *Jan* and *kaas,* the latter in time corrupted to *kees. Kaas* is Dutch for "cheese," and the name originally was one of opprobrium meaning "John Cheese." First applied by the English sailors to Dutch buccaneers, the New Netherland Dutch later seized upon it to sneer at English settlers. Thus it came to be fixed on New Englanders, and they presently accepted it as descriptive of their sagacity. By the time of the Revolution the English applied it indiscriminately to Americans in general.[4] It is a curious thought that "Yankee Doodle" itself is, indirectly at least, a kind of vestige of the Dutch occupation of New Netherland!

If language is an important vehicle of a culture, then the language vestiges of the occupation still clearly identifiable in the region a century and a half, even two centuries, after the official transfer of the

[3] *Ibid.,* II, 143.
[4] H. L. Mencken, *op. cit.,* pp. 192-93.

province to England bear witness to the vitality of the Hollanders' unconscious impulse to fill the American vacuum. The tongue of a feeble civilization could not have maintained itself for half that length of time.

All immigrant languages in time become, to some degree, a part of the American philological blood stream. Alien words suffer a sea change and in the course of the years are not even recognized as alien. The tongue of the New Netherland folk played this rôle also. Mencken, among others, has traced the origin of the Americanism "boss" to the Dutch word *baas,* the two words so identical in idiomatic meaning that they could be used interchangeably. Another writer makes the curious observation that the American slang term "boodle" is identical in sound with, and is obviously derived from, *boedel,* a respectable Dutch word meaning "household stuff." [5] The same writer derives our "cooky" from *koekje,* a little cake.

A few samples these of vestiges in language of the Dutch occupation; it is doubtful if anyone could list them all, because some of them seem so indigenous to our speechways that their origin is not even suspected. But enough have been identified to suggest that all of us in America are daily using a speech that has in it many linguistic echoes of the language imported by the Hollanders who occupied New Netherland.[6]

Walt Whitman deprecated the American habit of giving European place names to our cities and rivers and mountains. He was all for using Indian nomenclature, both because such words are indigenous and almost invariably euphonious; he rolled them over his tongue with gusto and made a face over the unimaginative commonplaceness of the names transferred from the map of Europe to our own.

But that was in the nineteenth century, when the nation was filling up. While the Hollanders, in the seventeenth century, lived precariously on the edge of the continent—and the same was true of the English and the Swedes and the French—they took joy in transplanting the dear names from home; it gave them, a little, the sensation of home itself. *"Nieuw Nederland"* was as inevitable as "New England," and *"Nieuw Amsterdam"* as "Plymouth." In any event, the Hollanders

---

[5] Mrs. Schuyler Van Rensselaer, *op. cit.,* II, 150.
[6] For a more exhaustive account see Mencken's *The American Language: Supplement I,* pp. 186-97.

spattered their own place names all over the map of the section they
occupied, and today those names are the most ineradicable vestiges of
the occupation. Some of them have suffered change, so that they are
not identified by the average American as Dutch in origin. "Brook-
lyn" is the best example. It was originally called *Breuckelen,* a name
that is all Dutch; later it went through half a dozen transformations,
until the present spelling became permanent. "Yonkers" is another
example. Originally the area was known as *de Jonkheer's Landt,* that
is, "the young sir's land." Although the spelling has changed, the
pronunciation of the city's present name is not markedly different from
the way the Hollanders said it.

The place name survivals of the Dutch occupation are so numerous
that it would be tedious to catalogue them all. A few samples will
suffice. "Catskill" was originally *Kaaterskil*—*kil* in Dutch means
"channel." "Peekskill" was named for the channel of a citizen named
"Peek." "Watervliet" is literally "fleet water," and "Bergen" is the
Dutch plural for "hills." "Spuytenduyvil" means, literally, "spouting
devil"; its spelling has remained unchanged but the word is often
erroneously translated as "spitting devil." "Haverstraw" has been only
slightly changed in spelling and pronunciation; the Hollanders called
it *Haverstro;* its meaning in Dutch was about the same as in English.
"Sandy Hook" was Dutch in origin, as are all place names ending in
"Hook"; the Dutch word, spelled *Hoek,* means "corner." Such place
names as "Barnegat" also are Dutch in origin; *gat,* in that language,
signifies "mouth of a harbor," and not a few Hollanders settling at
such a mouth added their family name to the suffix to form a new
word destined to outlast centuries. "The Bronx" was named for Jonas
Bronck, a Dane, to whom Governor Kieft granted a land patent in
1639. Bronck laid out the first farm and erected a building above the
Harlem River. This district was named after him; also Bronxville,
Bronx Park, and Bronx River.

There is of course an "Amsterdam" in New York state, as of course
there is a "London" in Canada, and some other Netherlands place
names have been transferred to the map of America without change.
But many others naturally grew into names from mere words of
identification. For the most part they were hardly places that needed
a name when the words were first associated with them by which they

were destined to be called. It was somebody's *kil* or someone else's corner or harbor mouth that was identified. Later, in many cases, villages and cities grew up on those spots and names were born. For better or for worse, in spite of Walt Whitman's distaste, the Hollanders stamped themselves indelibly on the American map on the eastern seaboard, as other Hollanders—they of the second migration—were to do two hundred years later on the map of Michigan, Iowa, Wisconsin, Minnesota, the Dakotas, and some other states.[7]

But the vestiges of the occupation represented in place names are not a reflection of the vitality of the culture from which they came; they were inevitable, and the names of a weak nation are about as likely to survive as those of a strong people. Institutions are a better index of vitality. One of those that the Hollanders imparted to their region was the state church of the mother country. It had its inception in the province in the early years of the occupation. Something like a definite congregation was organized when there were only three hundred souls in the settlement, many of them Walloons, to whom the Lord's Supper had to be administered in French, the only language they understood. The denomination known today as the Reformed Church in America is the oldest communion of the Presbyterian branch of Protestantism in the Western Hemisphere; its official records go back to 1639, although its actual life began much earlier. In early times the English referred to it as the Reformed Dutch Church in New York, and when it outgrew that state it was identified as the Reformed Protestant Dutch Church in America. That name was too cumbersome for popular use, so the institution was simply called the Reformed Dutch Church. But in the natural course of human events the *Dutch* of the name became obsolete; services were held in English, and almost as many of the communicants were non-Dutch as of Dutch ancestry. In 1867 the word "Dutch" was dropped from the name, and it is now officially, as it had long been popularly, the Reformed Church in America.[8]

Significant of Dutch social vitality is the fact that the church did not allow itself to be absorbed by the legal communion of the country that conquered New Netherland. The ten thousand or so Hollanders who

[7] See Mrs. Schuyler Van Rensselaer, *op. cit.*, II, 149-50.
[8] *Ibid.*, I, 84, 85.

formed the population of the province were compelled of necessity to adopt the political institutions of their conquerors; they clung to their own religion in spite of what most of them must have considered the devil of foreign occupation. They saw to it, in the articles of surrender, that they obtained the right to worship in their own way. The greatest menace to the permanence of the Dutch church did not come from official coercion, but from unconscious absorption. The English church would of course have been eager to take over and turn the Hollanders of New Netherland into Anglicans. Since this was the seventeenth century, when such transfers were more or less taken as a matter of course, the wonder is that the pressure was not greater than it proved to be. Doubtless the ecclesiastical officials of the conquerors understood that it was hopeless to try coercion on people who had been bred in the novel idea of religious toleration, but whose toleration did not mean indifference to their own faith. To that they clung with a tenacity that three centuries have not been able to weaken.

For many generations after the surrender the Reformed Church remained the dominant communion in New York and the Hudson Valley, in spite of the fact that the Anglican Church enjoyed official favor. The life of the Dutch folk of New Netherland perpetuated itself in this institution when it was blocked in its political advance.

It has been in such ways, through its institutions, that Holland has marched across the American continent in a very real sense. As the Dutch race advanced along the American settlement routes, not spectacularly or dramatically as a Covered Wagon anabasis, but soberly in the spirit of Dutch common sense, their national church has advanced with them; or rather the American ecclesiastical institution that has naturally developed out of their national church. For it remained in dependence on the Classis of Amsterdam only until 1772; then it became an American institution in its church government. Today the Reformed Church in America is not a Dutch institution in language or ritual. But its tone and spirit still have many vestiges of the church originally transplanted by the New Netherland folk from Holland to the American wilderness.

And there is nothing about the denomination today that suggests the moribund. The statistics for 1945 listed 452 congregations in the Eastern Synods of Albany, New Brunswick, and New York, and 290 in the Western Synods of Chicago and Iowa. The number of families in the Eastern Synods was 137,121, and in the Western group 33,415. Communicants in the Eastern branch totaled 103,804, in the Western branch 70,171. Those listed as adherents numbered 17,700 in the East, 5,264 in the West.[9]

For the sake of completeness it should be noted that another branch of the Dutch communion in America, the Christian Reformed Church, composed in large part of Hollanders and descendants of Hollanders, had, in 1945, 30,052 families, 74,778 communicant members, 132,990 total members, 312 congregations, and 268 ministers.[10]

But that is anticipating somewhat, to indicate that this vestige of the Dutch occupation of a part of the American continent three hundred years ago has shown a remarkable vitality and has been truly in keeping with the Hollanders' impulse to perpetuate their culture in America. The church wars that in the nineteenth century resulted in what is popularly known as a Secession—always spelled with an upper case S—were still far in the future when the Dutch advance across the continent had reached this point in the story. Those wars, and the new ecclesiastical institution of the Hollanders in America that grew out of them, will have to be described later in their proper setting and chronology.

Other vestiges of the occupation keep cropping out in the most unexpected places. When shortly before the Revolution St. Jean de Crèvecoeur, a Frenchman, asked his then startling and now famous question, "What is an American?", he recognized honestly with Gallic respect for things as they are, that Dutch culture formed an important element in the makeup of the *American* character of the race that had developed on this continent: "They [the Americans] are a mixture of English, Scotch, Irish, French, Dutch, Germans, and Swedes."

The order in this list, with the Dutch yielding precedence only to the French of the peoples listed for the European continent proper, was undoubtedly a reflection of de Crèvecoeur's judgment as to the importance, at that time, of the Dutch ingredient in the heady population brew he was attempting to describe. That he put his own native

[9] The Rev. Jacob Vander Meulen, *Hollanders: The Development of Their Objectives in Europe and America,* p. 58.
[10] *Yearbook of the Christian Reformed Church, 1946,* p. 26.

land ahead of Holland is but natural. A little later in the famous essay he unconsciously thinks of the Hollanders immediately after the English—which at that time was probably the true sequence: "I could point out to you a family whose grandfather was an Englishman, whose wife was Dutch, whose son married a French woman, and whose present four sons have now four wives of different nations."

And in his sketchy pageant of the religions on the American continent in his day de Crèvecoeur once more lists the Hollanders as an important element in the American scene; in fact, he gives rather more space to his description of the Hollanders' religion than to those devoted to other nationalities. And incidentally it may be noted that the realistic Frenchman does not ascribe to the Hollanders of his community the excessive piety that has sometimes been attributed to them; evidently he saw them as the records had revealed them during the occupation, wholesomely secular, at least without an admixture of the fanaticism that characterized the early Puritan New England:

Next again lives a Low Dutchman [thus runs de Crèvecoeur's account], who implicitly believes the rules laid down by the synod of Dort. He conceives no other idea of a clergyman than that of a hired man; if he does his work well he will pay him the stipulated sum; if not he will dismiss him, and do without his sermons, and let his church be shut up for years. But not withstanding this coarse idea, you will find his house and farm to be the neatest in all the country; and you will judge by his waggon and fat horses that he thinks more of the affairs of this world than of those of the next. He is sober and laborious, therefore he is all he ought to be as to the affairs of this life; as for those of the next, he must trust to the great Creator.

That was in the eighteenth century. Throughout the nineteenth, although the language of New Netherland had almost completely disappeared, the Dutch tradition persisted in the region. Writing, or at least publishing, in 1909, exactly a century after the appearance of *Knickerbocker's History*, Mrs. Schuyler Van Rensselaer, in her *History of the City of New York*, deposes:

New Yorkers are still very proud of Dutch descent even when it is masked under names of other origins. In family pride some of them are as tightly and complacently encased as any Virginian. In the more generous sentiment called pride of race they exceed all other Americans, and this feeling has strengthened instead of diminishing since the Revolution.

Some other writers are less positive on this point. All sorts of historical generalizations can be shown to have basis in fact, depending usually on what an author wishes to prove or establish. In any event, the New Netherland folk did not simply disappear from history. They left footprints clear and deep on the well-known sands of time. The men and women of the occupation had had character and vitality enough to win a kind of resurrection in the early nineteenth century, even if it was via burlesque. That rehabilitation was astonishing in itself and surprising in its aftermath. Irving remarks with some pride, in 1848, that "Knickerbocker" has become a "household word," and he lists with evident appreciation the many uses to which it has been put —Knickerbocker societies, Knickerbocker insurance companies, Knickerbocker steamboats and omnibuses and bread and ice. Then he adds with gentle malice: "And when I find New Yorkers of Dutch descent priding themselves on being 'genuine Knickerbockers,'—I please myself with the persuasion that I have struck the right chord."

In language, place names, ecclesiastical institutions, the vestiges of the Dutch occupation are fairly definite. There are also many survivals of the period that are less tangible and precise; instead of being footprints they are a lingering fragrance, like the memory of the presence of a vital personality.

Religious toleration is probably the most engaging of such Dutch vestiges. It has become the marrow of American bone; few remember, if they ever knew, how it developed in our world. To be fair, it would eventually have come anyway in answer to the time spirit, but it early became a part of us because it had been a part of the Hollanders who, officially for four decades and actually for three centuries, occupied a strategic section of our country. And with religious tolerance went freedom of speech and press, that has always been especially dear to Dutch hearts. The cardinal American principle of separation of church and state cannot legitimately be attributed to the Dutch alone; it evolved from several impulses in the hearts of men of several nations. But Hollanders of three centuries ago took the common sense of it at least tacitly for granted, in an age when the government of New England was definitely a theocracy and when hardly any nation anywhere in the world saw anything the matter with the church ruling the state or the state making the church a cog in the political machine.

"What is an American?" Whether de Crèvecoeur's answer is exhaustive or not, at least some of the ingredients that went to the making of this new national type during the past three centuries were contributed by the Dutch folk of New Netherland and their descendants who made this new world home.

VIII

Hybrid Hollanders

MONEY HAD BEGUN to breed early in New Netherland; the Dutch folk were often canny businessmen. So early as 1674, before the second and final surrender to the English, when a tax was levied on wealth for fortification improvement, it was found that 133 persons were each worth more than one thousand guilders "wumpum value." Sixty-five Dutch citizens were as a group worth 520,900 guilders in "Holland currency." [1] The richest man in the province at that time was Frederick Philipse, who was worth eighty thousand guilders.

Some of the future large fortunes had already made a beginning. That New York in due course became the American money center was in part due to its location and the strategic character of its harbor; the wealth of the world could hardly flow through such a commercial bottleneck without making the city rich that grew up around the harbor.

Most of the folk of New Netherland were simple people and of low economic and social standing. There were just enough of the other kind to give color of at least factual proof to the traditions of ancestral grandeur industriously propagated by some of the descendants of the Hollanders. Thus a Bishop William I. Kip, a descendant of a New Netherland family that played an important rôle in the province, exulted as follows:

The country was parcelled out among great proprietors. We can trace them from the city of New Amsterdam to the northern part of the State. In what is now the thickly populated city were the lands of the

[1] Mrs. Schuyler Van Rensselaer, *History of City of New York*, II, 116.

79

Stuyvesants, originally the *Bouwerie* of the old governor. Next above were the grant of the Kip family, called Kip's Bay, made in 1638. In the center of the island was the possessions of the De Lanceys. Opposite, on Long Island, was the grant of the Laurence family. We cross over Harlaem river and reach Morrisiania, given to the Morris family. Beyond this, on the East river, was De Lancey's farm, another grant to that powerful family; while on the Hudson to the west, was the lower Van Courtland manor, and the Phillipse manor. Above, at Peekskill, was the upper manor of Van Courtlands. Then came the manor of Kipsburg, purchased by the Kip family from the Indians in 1636, and made a royal grant by governor Dongan two years afterwards. Still higher up was the Van Rensselaer manor, twenty-four miles by forty-eight; and above that the possessions of the Schuylers.[2]

And so on endlessly, the paeans of family pride by all sorts of people. Yet this same Kip family was descended from a tailor in the Netherlands—a worthy man no doubt, honest and industrious and virtuous, but sans blue blood in his veins. Stuyvesant, the "old governor," we know was the son of a Friesian clergyman. The De Lanceys, mentioned next, "took their first rise from their commerce with pirates." [3] The Laurence family was descended from an Englishman, and the Morrises sprang from a Welshman; neither of them appears to have been an aristocrat. The Van Cortlandts made their money in the sugar refining business (as did, by the way, the Roosevelts, not mentioned in Kip's record). The Philipse family sprang originally from a Dutch carpenter. The founder of the American Van Rensselaer clan, Kiliaen Van Rensselaer, made his fortune trading in pearls and precious stones —which may or may not have coincided with blue blood; Kiliaen himself never set foot in America but he was a power in the affairs of New Netherland.

Kip mentions only a few of the "aristocratic" Dutch and Dutch-English families of quality whose scions in the eighteenth and nineteenth centuries, and still in the twentieth, prided themselves on ancestry. Many others prove to have had bourgeois origins, when the records are examined. As was true of the Roosevelts, for instance, sugar refining and other commercial ventures—often real estate operations—account for the fortunes of the Cuylers, the Rhinelanders, the Bogards, the Livingstons. (The fact that a name is English does not

---

[2] John S. C. Abbott, *Peter Stuyvesant*, p. 347.
[3] Dixon Wecter, *The Saga of American Society*, p. 58.

always mean that descendants do not pride themselves on their Dutch ancestry; after the surrender, Dutch and English possessions increasingly went through marriage ceremonies, and often the maternal ancestors of people whose family name is English were Dutch.) The brewery business accounted for the money of Colonel Henry Rutgers, of Rutgers College fame. And there were many other similar reasons for family pride; the founders of some families were dealers in imported crockery, they sold merchandise from Europe and India, they were general traders and shippers, they imported drygoods, they operated warehouses, they ran stores; some of them, like Isaac Roosevelt, advertised "loaf, lump, and strained sugar and sugar-house treacle." [4]

Nothing discreditable in this, of course. They were good Dutch, and Dutch-English, businessmen, and they lived by their gospel of common sense and commercial acumen. If there was any fault, it was not theirs but their descendants' who tried to put on airs on the basis of "family" where no "family" existed. And it should be remembered that those names of a dubious blue-blood distinction were the exceptions. Most of the men and women of the ten or twelve thousand inhabitants of New Netherland at the end of the occupation were humble people.

The one or two patroonships that succeeded wholly or in part later became merged with the Hudson Valley "manors" celebrated by the Kips and others of their kind. They were English as much as Dutch, and in so far as they constituted an aristocracy, it was an aristocracy foundationed on trade, not on blood. There were nine such manors in the Hudson Valley, established in the seventeenth and eighteenth centuries. Their owners sometimes bore English names—Livingston Manor and Morris Manor; sometimes Dutch names—Manor of Cortlandt and Rensselaerswyck. And in time many other families of wealth had a tendency to refer to their ancestral homes as "manors," echoing the English phraseology.

Inevitably, after the surrender in 1664, a hybrid civilization developed in the area covered by New Netherland. Throughout the eighteenth century the normal biological processes operated; English maidens fell in love with Dutch boys, or the sons of English families with the

[4] *Ibid.*, pp. 59-60.

daughters of Hollanders. That would have happened even if there had
been hostility between the two groups, as the experience of armies of
occupation in the two World Wars has proved. But during the eighteenth century Dutch and English occupied the Hudson Valley on terms
of friendship; they were in the process of ceasing to be either Dutch or
English and were evolving into the Americans de Crèvecoeur defined in
answering his famous question. They were bound to become a hybrid
population, and since hybridization is in the main a wholesome process,
making for biological vitality, it is not surprising that families arose in
the area that played leading rôles in American history.

But that process was truer of the metropolitan areas than of the rural
section. Dutch blood was defended much more stubbornly in the comparative isolation of the country than in the greater promiscuity of city
life. In some sections of what had been New Netherland there was for
a century or more after the surrender what almost amounted to in-
breeding, intermarriage keeping the families so unchanged that they
remained almost intact, with little or no intermixture of English blood.
It was of course in those sections that the Dutch language, and Dutch
institutions and customs, held their own throughout the eighteenth
century and even on into the nineteenth. Many of those people continued to use Dutch exclusively in the family intercourse throughout
the next hundred years, and they heard no other language even in
church. Only in isolation were such things possible, and then only
in the eighteenth century; in the nineteenth even the New Netherland
frontier had become too much one world to remain biologically and
culturally isolationist.

The quality families succumbed to the hybridization almost immediately. In addition to the inevitable compulsions of proximity, there
was the hardly less powerful motivation of economic advantage. Marriages of convenience between English and Dutch were doubtless
usually masked under the appearances of love matches; but normally
it was in all probability easier for a Dutch maiden to fall in love with
an English boy who had good prospects or whose father's estate ad-
·joined that of the girl's father than with a penniless Dutch boy. In any
event there was throughout the eighteenth century a brave joining of
fortunes in the Hudson Valley, and in the city of New York, that
resulted in some of the great concentrations of money and social posi-

tion of the nineteenth and twentieth centuries. Biology and economics joined in developing a hybrid culture in the area of America that presently became the seat of the American money power.

The history of the Roosevelt family illustrates the process of hybridization that has on the whole made for concentrations of wealth and for other types of distinction. The family originated in the Province of Zeeland, some branches of it on the island of Oud-Vossemeer. It was from that area, which a traveler just before the second World War described as "a sleepy, mildewy place that looked exactly no doubt as it must have centuries ago,"[5] that a Claes Martenszoon van't Rosevelt set out, in 1650, to make his fortune in New Netherland. His economic standing can be gathered from the fact that he emigrated at all, as well as from the fact that he crossed the Atlantic as a "settler,"—which, Theodore Roosevelt remarked, was "the euphemistic name for an immigrant who came over in the steerage of a sailing ship of the seventeenth century." This immigrant was the paternal ancestor of Franklin D. Roosevelt; the maternal ancestor was a Swedish officer, Martin Hoffman, who emigrated to America seven years later. Almost exactly a century after those founders of American families arrived on these shores, the two family streams united; then the great-grandson of Claes van't Rosevelt married the great-granddaughter of Martin Hoffman, and those two were the great-grandparents of F. D. Roosevelt.

But before the Dutch and Swedish blood streams joined, there had been other hybridization in the paternal branch of the family. The immediate descendants of the original immigrant intermarried with Puritan English stock—a British family of wheelwrights—and also with stock of Scotch-Irish and Quaker origin. The resulting blood brew was a rather complicated mixture, and one that might have served de Crèvecoeur as an excellent example in answer to his question, "What is an American?", had he known about it; but "at no pre-Revolutionary period was the family conspicuous or did any member of it attain distinction."[6] How often the bloodlines crossed in the three hundred year history of the family could doubtless be determined in the family record. The latest crossing occurred when James Roosevelt, father of

[5] Hendrik De Leeuw, *Crossroads of the Zuider Zee* (J. B. Lippincott Co., 1938), p. 153.
[6] Mrs. Schuyler Van Rensselaer, *op. cit.*, II, 79.

the late President, married Rebecca Howland, and as a second wife Sara Delano, mother of F.D.R. Franklin Roosevelt himself did not follow his father's example but married another Roosevelt from a distant branch of the clan, who in turn was the issue of intermarriages of Dutch and British stock.

The power of a name in perpetuating a sense of nationality is illustrated by the history of the Roosevelt family. The American people, generally speaking, think of all the Roosevelts, Eleanor Roosevelt included, as "Dutch." And most Hollanders who were of the late President's political persuasion claimed him with pride as one of them, whereas those of the Dutch folk who differed with him in politics almost too pointedly kept still about his nationality. In simple fact he was hardly more Dutch than British or even Swedish. If his paternal forebear, instead of the maternal ancestor, had been a Swede, and a Swedish name had been handed down to him, the admixture of Dutch blood would long since have been forgotten. There are many instances of Dutch blood being lost in British names, in the history of the Hollanders in New York and the Hudson Valley. The Roosevelt name has kept the American people conscious of the Dutch origin of at least one side of the family; but it has failed to teach many Americans how to pronounce the Dutch name.

A similar process of mingling of bloods went on in most of the other so-called "Knickerbocker families"—the Van Burens, the Cortelyous, the Vanderbilts, the Depews, the Cuylers, the Van Cortlandts, the Schuylers, the Beekmans, the Van Zandts, the Van Rensselaers, the Brevoorts, the Kips, and so on through the New York Social Register. An equally imposing list of British names could be culled from the same volume that would represent as large a proportion of Dutch blood. When an Alexander Hamilton married a Schuyler, the Dutch blood of their descendants was forgotten.

The Livingston family, of Livingston Manor fame, was an example of maternal Dutch blood resulting in distinction that is not recognized as Dutch distinction. Robert Livingston, a Scotchman born n 1654, established Livingston Manor in America in 1686. In 1679 he had married the rich widow of Nicholas Van Rensselaer, who was the daughter of the then not so well known Dutch Schuyler family. He had accumulated a considerable amount of worldly goods through his own operations of various kinds, and through his politic marriage with the widow of a member of the powerful family whose patroonship was at Rensselaerswyck he became one of the wealthiest men in America. At his death in 1728 the vast estate descended to Philip Livingston, the son, who once more mingled his blood with that of a Hollander, Sarah Van Brugh.

Their son, Robert Livingston, named for the founder of the family, was the third Lord of Livingston Manor. A descendant, Robert R. Livingston, was one of the committee of five appointed to draft the Declaration of Independence, and although he and the other members of the group eased the job on to the willing shoulders of youthful Thomas Jefferson, he had at least an advisory part in the task. Through a female descendant whose parents were proud enough of her Dutch blood to name her Sarah Van Brugh, the descendants of Chief Justice John Jay carried on the Dutch bloodline; for she became Jay's wife. There sprang from the Livingston line more than one justice of the Supreme Court and other men of distinction in American political and economic life, among them a secretary of the Treasury. All in all there was as much Dutch blood in the veins of the Livingstons as in those of the Roosevelts, but few think of crediting the distinctions won by members of this family to the Dutch maternal ancestors.

How great at least the economic vitality of Dutch blood still was in the nineteenth century is illustrated by the Vanderbilt clan. It became the richest American family of that century, and the founder of the fortune, Cornelius Vanderbilt, was the direct descendant of one of the humblest of the New Netherland folk. The family was wretchedly poor, trying to make a precarious living by farming on Staten Island. Its members continued among the poorest of the poor for four generations, and when Cornelius was born in 1794, one of nine children, his father was a farmer who made some extra money as a ferryman. Young Cornelius took to the water and at the early age of sixteen owned his own vessel for carrying passengers and freight. In a few years he acquired several sailing boats; but he was canny enough to understand the meaning of Fulton's *Clermont* experiment on the Hudson. So he pulled out of sail while getting out was still profitable, and what was more important for him, gambled on steam, and thus laid the foundation for his immense fortune.

A man of meager schooling, he nevertheless understood money-making, and by the time he was popularly known as Commodore Vanderbilt, and was laughed at behind his back for his ostentations and his no less marked parsimonies, by people who fawned on him to his face and secretly worshiped his success, he counted his money first in scores of millions and then in hundreds of millions. This son of a Dutch farmer-ferryman became America's first multi-millionaire and succeeded in putting the real content in that now commonplace word. In some ways a nickel-pincher, in unconscious response no doubt to his early poverty, he built himself a yacht that cost $1,500 a day to operate, and took his family and retainers on a European cruise that scandalized the English by its unashamed ostentation. After the close of the Civil War he became the guiding spirit of the New York Central Railroad, increasing his wealth so rapidly that it took the country's and the world's breath away. He was popularly credited—and the facts seem to show that this was not the usual myth—with increasing his wealth from ten million to a hundred million in twelve years.

The Vanderbilt fortune is still a power in America; for nearly a century and a half the economic know-how of this crude and unlettered son of a Dutch Staten Island farmer-ferryman, who himself had descended from a New Netherland immigrant of a century earlier, has in its own way been building America through the construction of railroads and steamship lines and a multitude of other businesses and "services." The story is quite different from that of the Roosevelts, the Livingstons, and others, whose Dutch blood appeared in statesmen, Supreme Court justices and secretaries of the Treasury. But it was potent in its own way.

Although politically the Dutch occupation came to an end in 1664, actually it has never come to an end. The Hollanders occupied the land by right of their ability to conquer and develop it. And that not merely in an agricultural sense; in fact, chiefly in other ways. They had it in them, those Netherland folk, to build empires. When the record is examined of what their descendants have done, it is no longer fantastic to imagine that if the political control of their bridgehead in

America had not been wrested from them because of the short-sightedness of their own government, they would have had as good a chance to fill the vacuum on this continent as the English won for themselves. The propulsive power of their culture would seem to have been great enough to win a continent. When as a group they were robbed of political power, and what was still more important, of language, the chief vehicle of civilization, they yet displayed their vitality as individuals and held for themselves and for their children for several generations the bridgehead they had won. More than that, they succeeded in propelling their culture across the continent and making it a part of the pattern of Americanism.

The story of that continental march, although it is not dramatic and spectacular, is as fascinating as the history of the winning and losing of New Netherland.

For about a century after the surrender in 1664 there was comparatively little immigration from Holland. A group of Dutch Quakers founded Germantown in 1683-90, but the number was not large and by 1709 all traces of the Dutch origin of the town had disappeared. Another group, known as the Labadists, settled in Maryland in 1683, but the community soon disintegrated. Not more than three hundred persons were involved in the two migrations. There was little other activity in immigration from Holland until Revolutionary times, although individuals of course continued to come over.

The Hollanders living in what had been New Netherland remained where they were, most of them—tenants of the manorial lords, independent farmers, businessmen in such thriving towns as the little city of New York. During the decades while the Revolution was in the making they played about the same part in the life of the emerging nation as that taken by other nationals. That is, some of them were what came to be known as Royalists, others favored the break with England. The records prove that this was true of the manorial class, English, hybrid, Dutch. Naturally there are fewer statistics about the attitudes of the Dutch masses. They were doubtless as confused, at least during the early stages of the pre-Revolutionary agitation, as average people anywhere would be, reacting emotionally to the times that tried men's souls and responding to local sentiment. When the crisis finally came many of them found their way into the Continental armies.

Immigration from Holland, on a very small scale, hardly more than by individuals, came into public notice again after a formal treaty of trade and friendship was concluded between the Dutch Republic and the United States, in 1782. The immigrants were mostly Dutch businessmen and diplomats. They were on the lookout for business opportunities. One, for instance, named Van Hasselt, experimented with raising silkworms at Charleston. Others engaged in ventures almost as picturesque, but the number of immigrants involved remained insignificant. Along with businessmen, who were usually men of means, came some humbler people—tradesmen, professional men, artisans—but their number, too, remained small. Also there were a few Dutch speculators, and some political refugees.

Among the latter the most picturesque figure was one Francis Adrian van der Kamp, a Mennonite minister of Leyden. He had taken part in what amounted to an attempted revolution in Holland in 1787, and he had to seek refuge in America. Van der Kamp was a man of great learning. Governor Clinton, who visited him in his village home in New York state, called him "the most learned man in America," and John Adams described him as "a star of the first magnitude." Harvard conferred on him a doctor's degree, and Governor Clinton assigned him the job of translating the records of the West India Company. He died in 1829, still an exile.[7]

But he was more picturesque than important. Nor was Dutch immigration as a whole important during this period. There was about it little to grip the imagination; it was almost completely lacking in the dramatic elements that characterized the mass migrations some decades later led by such men as Van Raalte and Scholte.

There were many political, economic, and commercial ties between Holland and the United States during and immediately following the Revolution. But all that belongs to the political and diplomatic history of the two countries; it is not a part of the story of Americans from Holland.

[7] Bertus Harry Wabeke, *Dutch Emigration*, pp. 71-83.

IX

Hollanders in American Literature

IT WAS NOT in hundred-million-dollar fortunes alone, or in politics or in the church, that the seminal vitality of the Dutch folk of New Netherland and their descendants revealed itself. Dutch plasma in the blood stream of American literature is usually ignored, the unconscious assumption being that it does not exist. It is only fair to admit that literature has not been the principal means of self-expression for the Hollanders in America; their genius lies rather in the field of finance, and even the men of wealth in the days of the patroons were more inclined to buy works of art than to make them, to collect libraries than to write them. That they were avid collectors is proved by the catalogues of their possessions that sometimes broke into public notice when their wills were probated. Nor were the *objets d'art* and the libraries they acquired mere articles cherished for their money value, although those oldtime Hollanders had a lively sense of art and literature as an investment. Judging by what some of them unconsciously revealed in their legacies, they were not unlike Soames Forsyte in their attitude; Dutch common sense and economic astuteness dictated the purchase of such things as would appreciate, not depreciate, in value, but the Hollanders also loved their rare old volumes, their china, their pictures.

Jonas Bronck's collection of books in Danish, Dutch, and German, and "old printed pamphlets" and "manuscript books, together with eleven pictures and articles in silver and pewter," was not unique. And since the Bronck will was probated so early as 1643, less than twenty years after the province was founded, his was naturally a much smaller and less pretentious collection than those of a later period. During the eighteenth century there was manorial magnificence about the furnishings of many of the Dutch homes in the Hudson Valley, and the book collections of the lords of the manor who favored the title "patroon" were often impressive.

And John Adams, in 1774, on the occasion of a horseback trip from Boston to New York, had the opportunity to contrast the simplicity and puritanic austerity of the Boston home with the elegance of domestic life in Dutch New York. He describes with special emphasis the architectural splendor of the manors he visited and notes the fact that a new church in the city was being built at the cost of a hundred thousand dollars.

But it must be freely granted that the austere simplicity of New England resulted in the production of more literature than did the magnificence of manorial life in New York and the Hudson Valley. When John Adams made that entry in his diary Franklin had written a part of one of the half-dozen greatest autobiographies of all time; Jonathan Edwards had enriched American letters with *Personal Narrative,* which is true literature by any fair standard; de Crèvecoeur had published *Letters from an American Farmer;* and Tom Paine was soon to begin the four books that have kept his name green in our national letters. Later still would come the flowering of New England.

The Dutch or their descendants played no such part in the creation of American literature, or a part that comes anywhere near to approaching the British record. But what else could be expected? English after all had become the continental language; if history had assigned that rôle to the Dutch tongue, would not the positions in literature of the two countries have been reversed?

But if Dutch culture did not contribute many writers to American literature even at secondhand as French culture contributed de Crèvecoeur, it provided American letters with what may not too unfairly be claimed as the first body of imaginative subject matter. The honor of being the subject of a national literature is hardly less great than that of creating it.

Washington Irving at least felt that for purposes of imaginative literature America so late as the opening of the nineteenth century was almost hopelessly deficient in that wealth of tradition out of which great writing comes. Our literary soil was extremely shallow; Hawthorne, some years later, made exactly the same complaint. Dutch mythology somewhat mitigated the drabness of the picture, as Irving saw it, and he had the wit to take advantage of it.

The main object of my work [writes Irving] in fact, had a bearing wide from the sober aim of history; but one which, I trust, will meet with some indulgence from poetic minds. It was to embody the traditions of the city in an amusing form; to illustrate its local humors, customs, and peculiarities; to clothe home scenes and places and familiar names with those imaginative and whimsical associations so seldom met with in our new country, but which live like charms and spells about the cities of the old world, binding the heart of the native inhabitant to his home.

In this I have reason to believe I have in some measure succeeded. Before the appearance of my work the popular traditions of our city were unrecorded; the peculiar and racy customs and usages derived from our Dutch progenitors were unnoticed or regarded with indifference, or adverted to with a sneer. Now they form a convivial currency, and are brought forward on all occasions; they link our whole community together in good-humor and good fellowship; they are the rallying points of home feeling, the seasoning of our civic festivities, the staple of local tales and local pleasantries, and are so harped upon by our writers of popular fiction, that I find myself almost crowded off the legendary ground which I was first to explore, by the host who have followed in my footsteps.[1]

In other words, Irving had given the American imaginative writer a subject, a generation before Hawthorne discovered Puritan New England as a theme, and some years before Cooper saw the possibilities of the Indian as subject matter of American literature. A writer of genius the Hudson Valley Hollanders had not yet produced, two hundred years after they had arrived, but they had at least done the next best thing, they had furnished our literature with a theme.

Ten years later, with the publication of *The Sketch Book*, Irving drew the primitive Dutch settlers into American literature once more, this time in an art form that has turned out to be distinctively American. For though the short story has been written in all lands, so that America has no monopoly on it, it is thought of as being more indigenous to our literature than to that of other countries; and "Rip

---

[1] "The Author's Apology," prefixed to the 1848 edition of *Knickerbocker's History of New York*.

Van Winkle" may be regarded as almost the beginning of the American short story.

That tale's perennial popularity has drawn Holland into another art form in America that is seldom associated with the culture of the Dutch people. Joe Jefferson's *Rip Van Winkle* snared the interest of ten thousand for every thousand caught by the charm of Irving's original character. In the field of the drama American literature of the nineteenth and early twentieth centuries was largely a Sahara Desert, and Jefferson's *Rip* was certainly not supremely great drama; but it was at least as good as most things in that field until the revival of American drama in the second decade of our century with the coming of such writers as Eugene O'Neill. Such mythology as our relatively young country affords played its part as the subject matter of what had almost the status of folk drama in our literature; and that mythology was distilled from the primitive history of the life of the Hollanders on this continent.[2]

It is obvious, even to the casual student of our national literature, that Hollanders have come into American letters more often as subjects than as authors. Irving was of unmixed Anglican ancestry, and so was John Lothrop Motley, whose *The Rise of the Dutch Republic,* because of its tone of almost lyrical partisanship, might give the unwary the impression that his admiration was racial. As one of the group of artist historians that flourished in the middle of the nineteenth century, Motley belongs to our literature rather than to our writers of history. The world has cherished him for nearly a century (the *Rise* was published in 1856) because his best-known book is a distinguished work of the imagination; we read it in spite of its shortcomings as history, for the same reason that we read *Paradise Lost* in spite of the fact that its science and theology have long been obsolete. Hollanders thus became the subject of the best-known and most popular evocation of history in our nineteenth century literature.

Motley identified Holland's story with the universal struggle for freedom in which America, England, and Holland were co-actors. He

---

[2] A twentieth century writer about the Dutch, William Elliott Griffis, denies that *Rip* came out of the primitive history of the Hollanders on this continent: "Washington Irving . . . took the world wide myth, which has nothing in it peculiarly Dutch, out of its setting in Germany, located it in the Catskills and made a funny picture of New Netherland men and ways." But that is any imaginative writer's privilege. Irving was writing a story, not history.

said of the rôle of the Low Countries in that drama: "The maintenance of the right by the little provinces of Holland and Zeeland in the sixteenth, by Holland and England united in the seventeenth, and by the United States of America in the eighteenth centuries, forms but a single chapter in the great volume of human fate; for the so-called revolutions of Holland, England, and America, are like links in one chain."

That would seem to make Motley's book a part of the story of Americans from Holland. When he began his labors the history of the Hollanders on this continent was not unlike a movie that a theatre-goer has picked up in the middle; in supplying the opening scenes Motley made the plot complete for the hundreds of thousands of general American readers who turned *The Rise of the Dutch Republic* into a best seller. It gave them a lively conception of Holland's story as a prelude to Dutch settlement in America. And although Motley's classic, like most books, has been more talked about than read since its initial spurt of popularity, its general substance has seeped down to the public consciousness, as all great books have a way of doing.

The Rise of the Dutch Republic captured the readers of its day because it was a good story. The structure was firm and the fabric tightly woven. Motley at no point dissipated his plot-building powers. The book was felt to have a "beginning, middle, and end" in the Aristotelian sense. It began like a novel with the literary tapestry piece of the abdication of Charles V, a magnificent scene that gave its readers the illusion of a curtain rising on a great drama. Then followed, in a crescendo of violence and passion, a rising action of sadism, of violent death for thousands, highlighted by dramatic scenes like the execution of Egmont and Horn. And finally there was the grand climax of the assassination of William of Orange with which the book closes. For the Americans of Motley's day sixteenth century Holland had leaped into life.

Not the least of the aesthetic appeal of Motley lay for his nineteenth century public in his management of scene. His readers learned to know him essentially as a tapestry painter. Again and again he staged scenes for them that stimulated the imagination through the sheer virtuosity of his skill in pictorial art. Some of those pieces, like the relief of Leyden, quickly took on a life of their own, independent of the work as a whole. They became the favorites of the American anthologists, and the magnificence of their rhetoric made them ideal for this purpose. Occasionally they were sneered at as "purple patches," but they have not lost their power to move the imagination, even after nearly a century. By themselves they were perhaps not justified. If the woof had not been firm of which they were the warp they would soon have disappeared from the anthologies, along with the mere preciosities of the same time that once cluttered the school books. But when, for instance, the execution of Egmont and Horn was felt by the nineteenth century American reader to be an integral part of the solid fabric of the drama Motley had written, the fact that the scene was deliberately staged and brilliantly lighted did not detract from its effectiveness. As a magnificent picture painted for its own sake it could stand alone; as a part of the drama of a nation's agony it did double duty through its pictorial magnificence and dramatic effect.

But a creative writer, factual or imaginative, must finally be judged by his management of his characters. Did Motley's men and women come alive, the readers of his day asked. It is hardly too much to assert that for the American public Motley turned William of Orange from a merely magnificent historical shadow into a man of flesh. In so doing he provided Americans of Dutch blood with an unconscious reason for legitimate tribal pride which served to make them better Americans while it reminded them of their Dutch blood. It was heartening for them, even two centuries after the event, to feel a William in their racial past, as it will be heartening for native Americans, for centuries to come, to know that their race once produced a Lincoln.

William was of course Motley's main figure. Motley admitted himself that his *Rise of the Dutch Republic* was at the same time Orange's biography. William was designed as much to be the main character of the history as Hamlet is the chief figure in Shakespeare's play, or Soames Forsyte in *The Forsyte Saga*. The book closed when the life blood of the devoted patriot ebbed away as the result of the act of his assassin, and Motley came near to grandiloquence in his closing phrase: "and when he died the little children cried in the streets." But he quickly assured his readers in a footnote that this was not mere rhetoric but that it was the "literal expression of the official report." When William fell, the curtain, of necessity, had to come down.

Motley was not a post-Stracheyan biographer of William; he was unashamedly devoted to the cult of hero worship, as were his nineteenth century American readers. To him William of Orange was definitely a superman. He was what Washington had been to the Americans of the generation of Parson Weems, what Lincoln became to the closing decades of the nineteenth century. Motley considered it to be his business to defend William against any and all aspersions. Occasionally he protested too much, and now and then he gave the impression of skating quickly over thin ice. But such was the method of the nineteenth century biographers. The important thing for Americans from Holland, and for Americans in general, was that William came alive—a little too fully dressed sometimes in moral virtue, a little too conspicuously heroic, but alive none the less.

Motley drew his portrait almost as much by indirection as through deliberate portrayal. History had of course presented him with a villain in Philip II; Motley converted him into a villain of melodrama, to serve as a foil to the hero. Almost too meticulously and deliberately, by as much as William was raised above the level of mere ordinary mortals Philip was lowered beneath that line. Where Motley's William was brave his Philip was a coward, where the Prince was shrewd the King was dull and stupid; the patriot stadholder was almost mathematically as kindly and compassionate as Philip was cruel and vindictive.

But it was Philip's mental incapacity that Motley held up to scorn rather than his vindictiveness. Orange had his paid spy among Philip's private secretaries, a spy who kept his master informed from day to day of the King's most secret decisions; the King was putty in the hands of the master statesman of the Netherlands. Philip, as painted by Motley, was slow-witted, severely limited in intelligence, an anachronism even in the sixteenth century. Worst of all—at least Motley gave that impression—he was ridiculously wordy. His biographer returned to that indictment again and again, and he cited numerous examples of tautology in Philip's letters and dispatches.

Was that meant as a contrast to William's *silence*? If so, the trick rather failed, for nothing can have struck Motley's original readers with more surprise than the loquacity of William the *Silent*. He spawned speeches, political, economic, and theological: and they were never by any chance Gettysburg Addresses. William rose to power, and maintained himself there under almost hopeless difficulties, through a Niagara of words. Those speeches—and even then some of them have not been preserved—fill volumes; and the letters fill more volumes, for he was as ready with the pen as with the tongue. But in Philip loquacity and prolixity was a crime to be held up to scorn; apparently in William, one of the most mistaken legends of history, that he was a silent man, was for Motley sufficient apologia for wordiness.

Scenes and characters like these captivated the American readers of the mid-nineteenth century as a Sandburg's Lincoln has stimulated those of the twentieth. The publication of *The Rise of the Dutch Republic* was not merely an event in book history; it provided the Dutch frontier in America with a background and setting that served to preserve in the Americans of Dutch blood a sense of racial identity. Moreover, this story of Holland's heroic age by a New England scion of British Puritans became an integral part of Holland's rôle in American literature, and hence of the Dutch rôle in the drama of American life.

Mock history, the short story, the drama, and authentic history—in all these, in the broad field of American literature, Holland played a no unimportant part, although the objective limner of the Dutch race will hardly be disposed to overemphasize the importance of the rôle. The moment we review the history of our country's literature we are driven to the conclusion that, as was almost inevitable, the literature of England for the most part nourished our poets and novelists and essayists. The wonder is not that this is so, rather that so small a land as Holland, with a culture so different from that of the land of Shakespeare and Milton, should yet have played so considerable a part in our national letters—at least as subject matter.

But not quite as subject matter only. In at least two instances the Dutch racial strain comes into the story as author, and that in persons no less distinguished than Herman Melville and Walt Whitman. Holland speaks through the blood of comparatively few of our novelists and poets, but the ones through whom it does speak are at least of first rank. For there is of course no longer any doubt that Melville and Whitman belong not only among America's greatest but among the world's truly great.

HOLLANDERS IN THE REVOLUTIONARY WAR
Contemporary engraving of the address by the first Dutch Ambassador, Johan Van Berckel, to the Congress in Princeton.

Netherlands Information Bureau

IOWA FRONTIER

Top left: The Reverend H. P. Scholte, founder of Pella, Iowa, as a youthful leader.

Top right: Treasure chest for community's gold.

Bottom: House the Iowa leader built for his art-loving wife.

Pella, Iowa, Museum

It would be ridiculously chauvinistic, from the Dutch racial angle, to account for the greatness of *Moby Dick* and *Leaves of Grass* by their creators' Dutch ancestry. For one thing, in each case it came from only one side of the family; for another, it was fairly far in the past. More important than either, *Moby Dick* and *Leaves of Grass* are so obviously the expression of the self-relying and individualistic "Sayers" that Emerson identifies with the true poet that their possible racial genesis loses point.

But the fact remains that Herman Melville was connected by direct line, through his mother Maria Gansevoort, with those same Hollanders Irving burlesqued in *Knickerbocker's History;* and the Dutch blood in Walt Whitman is equally well authenticated. Whitman, in fact, was not quite free from Dutch racial chauvinism. Not only did he resent *Knickerbocker's History*, he emphasized the fact of his Dutch blood as if almost afraid it would be forgotten because of his Quaker name— ". . . you liberty-lover of the Netherlands! (you stock whence I myself have descended)." And if it is reasonable to note that the genius of Hawthorne and Emerson and Thoreau and Lowell and most of the others who gave distinction to American literature had its roots in English culture and owed its vitality to English blood, why is it unreasonable to claim for Dutch blood some of the virtue of one of our greatest novelists and one of the world's greatest poets?

There is obviously an "otherness" about both Melville and Whitman that makes a search for explanation legitimate. *Moby Dick* has so much strange fire in it that it is hard to believe that all of it was kindled on a familiar English hearth; and *Leaves of Grass* is such a surprise in the company of the decorous Longfellows and Lowells of the period that the mind instinctively casts about for reasons. Along with other explanations, why not assume that blood is thicker than ink?

That point is capable of broader application; namely, that the Americanization of American literature owes much to non-English influences. Holland's culture, among others, has helped to give to our national letters a flavor that could not be produced by the blood of any single country, no matter how many Shakespeares and Miltons it claims. Admit freely that there have not been numerous works of art in our literature that have Hollanders or Holland's story for their subject matter; that there have been comparatively few Hollanders who have contributed directly to our collection of poetry and prose. Both of these facts are in the very nature of things; the same point could be made about nearly all other non-English cultures. But Holland, more so even than some other countries, has played an important rôle in enriching the blood stream of our culture. Our literature of the twentieth century has depth and richness almost in proportion to the variety of its racial sources. The flowering of New England was primarily an English flowering. We of this century have not surpassed it (however, we still have many years to go); but we are winning Nobel prizes, not because we are echoing our Hawthornes and Lowells, or even our Emersons and Thoreaus, but because immigrants from many lands, or perhaps their sons or grandsons, are unconsciously enriching our novels and plays and poems with the life-giving juices of their racial cultures.

Of Holland's rôle in American literature of the twentieth century it is much too early to make an estimate. The books that have Holland as subject matter, or that have been written by Hollanders or descendants of Hollanders, are not fewer in this century than they were in the last. Such names as those of Edward Bok and Hendrik Willem Van Loon will instantly come to mind. Moreover, not a few of the descendants of the nineteenth century immigration have been writing novels and poems and plays and essays. Others are doing their part as editors or publishers in bringing contemporary American literature to birth.

But who is wise enough to determine which contemporary books time will insist on enrolling in the canon of our national literature? As is true also of history, the cat of literature has a way of jumping with erratic illogic. Trying to guess where that feline is going to land belongs to sorcery, not to sober criticism. But the rôle Hollanders have played in the history of our national letters gives promise of tomorrows that will match our yesterdays.

X

Dutch Puritans

AT THE TIME when Motley was doing his research in The Hague and at the great Dutch universities for *The Rise of the Dutch Republic,* Holland was still echoing with the reverberations of a mass migration that might have been expected to appeal to the historian's creative imagination. It is doubtful, however, that, in the early fifties, he gained a clear conception of what had been going on in the Netherlands during the preceding decade; his eyes were focused on the epic events of the sixteenth century and he probably missed the near view of history in the nineteenth.

It would be unfair, moreover, to expect him to understand that the same qualities of heart and mind that had made millions of Hollanders heroic in the period he was describing had animated the few thousand simple peasants and villagers and artisans and preachers who had been giving trouble to the authorities. Motley can hardly have understood that those disturbances had been the prelude to, and the reason for, one of the most remarkable migrations of the century.

Nor, in all probability, did the historian-descendant of Massachusetts Puritans note the parallel between the Dutch village Hampdens of the nineteenth century and the English exiles of the sixteenth. The New Englanders had found asylum in Holland for several years and had been treated with sympathy and understanding. Their own British government had been so stupid that it had forced out some of the country's best human material. The Hollanders of the nineteenth century had no temporary asylum where they could get their second wind before taking the irrevocable plunge, but their own government, like

99

Britain, had run true to the form of officialdom that has lost touch with the source of its power; the descendants of the clan of William the Silent, through sheer stupidity and lack of social imagination, forced out of Holland some of the most desirable human material the race had evolved. For although, like the English Puritans, they were for the most part humble and relatively unlettered, their culture was not merely skin-deep but went through to the heart of them; in spite of their simplicity they carried in their blood stream and in their mind-stuff the potentialities of a race of people biologically strong, intellectually vigorous. A blundering and confused government could hardly be expected to understand this; it could see only the uncouthness of the human material it was dealing with. Holland's rulers lacked the wit to look very far beyond the tips of their own aristocratic noses.

The pattern of events so clear in retrospect was of course obscure and confused to those rulers, as well as to the general Dutch population. Or rather, there was as yet no pattern at all. The Weaver was busily spinning his web, using men and women as his threads—and government decrees, and Dutch supreme court decisions, and fanatical devotions of ordinary people to a few simple theological dogmas, and even the ravages of cholera and the visitation of "potato blight," and an economic depression, and a system of taxation that bore most heavily on those least able to pay, and other minor events and movements and social accidents that all combined to form the tapestry of a minor sequence in nineteenth century history.

Mass migrations are often mysterious in their inner motivation. A half century after Waterloo Tolstoi saw in the Napoleonic wars the occasion for a needed shifting of populations of Europe; or rather he saw the necessity for such shifting as the real cause of those wars. A hundred years after the Dutch migration of the middle of the nineteenth century it is becoming possible to see that the upheaval was not a mere result of something else or of other events, that it was self-determining and hence in a true sense inevitable. That sounds transcendental, but history is in retrospect often like that.

It would, however, be naive to see this migration only from the point of view of those who carried it to a successful issue, or from that of their descendants. How did it look to the Dutch government, not a century after the event but at the moment it was taking shape? Can something be said for the authorities who during the forties of the nineteenth century forced thousands to pull up stakes and find asylum in far-off America?

From their viewpoint, the government officials were forced by the fiscal and political exigencies of their position to apply what they considered the law of their country to a few thousand religious agitators. Authority, in its very nature, is always hostile to those who upset applecarts. Those agitators were dissenters, political as well as religious, and so they naturally came into collision with government. To authority they were fanatical Calvinists; history, especially as written by their descendants, has chosen to regard them as champions of liberty.

It may prove illuminating, at least it can do no harm, to look at the situation for a moment from the government's point of view—mistaken in terms of history, not wholly unreasonable as of the moment when that history was being made. The dissenters constituted only a sprinkling of the Dutch population, but they insisted on interpreting Dutch law for themselves. A state church was an integral part of the Dutch government. The state was guaranteeing the salaries of the clergy; and always, in all ages and countries, the power that pays the piper calls the tunes. Those fanatics—the word is used purely from the government's point of view—insisted on organizing churches of their own. In seceding from the state church they were in effect seceding from a branch of their government. From the angle of authority there was only a thin line between that and a kind of mass treason, or perhaps insurrection. It is always government's business to protect itself, and when a minority, and a very small minority at that, threatens to disturb the social equilibrium responsible government considers it a duty to take the necessary steps to correct the imbalance.

To the dissenters the question was religious and theological, to the government it was largely political and economic. To the dissenters the steps taken by the government spelled persecution; to the government, necessary correction. To the former the issues were of eternal significance, to the latter they were the theological hairsplittings of a group of fanatical eccentrics. The government, even from its own point of view, was not big enough to subscribe to the doctrine that in matters of conscience people must have the right to be wrong if they can be said to be free at all; that there is no liberty in a country that imposes coercion on men's thinking, religious or otherwise; that a government that is not strong enough to carry even fools in solution is too weak to have the moral right to exist.

The Dutch government believed that it was dealing with fools and fanatics—obviously a mistaken notion in the light of history; even if this had been true the steps it took were still those of official weakness and stupidity, not of strength and wisdom. The uncouth peasants and artisans were far wiser, fanatical though some of them may have been, than the aristocratic ruling caste that took upon itself the duty of correcting them and protecting them from their own follies. The folk had the instinct to be free, and that instinct was in the direct line of descent from their heroic forebears of the sixteenth century; the Dutch rulers of the nineteenth were decadents, for all their surface culture and sophistication.

But once more from the point of view of authority, it should be fairly admitted that there was fanaticism in the attitude of the dissenting groups. It was not surprising that the Dutch government authorities took the dissenters' peculiarities with less than complete seriousness. As those people inflexibly applied their rules of conduct with almost ludicrous earnestness, they met with an increasing hostility from the government.

That many thousands of average Dutch citizens felt the same way is also understandable; for astonishing though the migration was in numbers and geographical extent, the people who took part in it were after all so small a minority that their departure hardly caused a ripple in the life of the Dutch nation. Nothing could be more mistaken than the assumption that somehow in the middle of the nineteenth century the bulk of the population of Holland suddenly transferred itself to the shores of America. Yet that is sometimes almost the impression left by partisan writers who conceive it to be their business to glorify the importance of their ancestors. They do not say any such thing in so many words; they leave things unsaid that belong in the record. Many elements in the populace of Holland were hostile to the "agitators." We read of a crowd of boys following certain members of the group "with shouts and indecent taunts"; [1] and when authority sided with the young hoodlums rather than with the dissenters the latter "were forced to leave while the howling mob through which they had to pass threw stones at them." [2]

To assume that those boys and that "howling mob" acted completely out of unalloyed viciousness seems hardly realistic; after all, they too were a part of the Dutch folk of the day. People who are too inflexibly certain that they are one hundred per cent right are not always the easiest type to live with; they are likely to be too free with their criticisms of ways of life other than their own, and criticism expressed without much sense of tact is likely to beget hostility. A certain portion of the Netherland public appears to have felt toward the dissenters the way the Maypole dancers of "Merrie Mount" felt toward Governor Bradford and his followers in Massachusetts, and for similar reasons. The future pioneers on the Dutch frontier in America were heroic enough when their whole story is told so that it is unnecessary to deny their more unlovely side. And portraying them in the round makes them psychologically more credible.

The dissenters themselves were of course not conscious of fanaticism. No dissenter ever is, it is always the other person or the other side that displays this unhappy trait; to himself it is always strength of convictions. Perhaps the hostility displayed toward the dissenters was the fruit of tactlessness coupled with a too public display of a piety that was certainly sincere and that constituted one of the main elements of their strength and their stamina in the face of hardship and danger. On the frontier those qualities were an asset; in the home community, the end product of the usual compromises and adjustments, they must often have struck a sour note.

Later when the emigrants had arrived on the frontier and were confronted with the job of cutting down their first tree for the erection of their first log hut, they began the task by offering a "fervent prayer." In the wilderness, faced by a grim and unknown future, such a ritual at such a time does not seem too incongruous. Such scanty records as there are of their life in Holland before the migration was undertaken give the impression that their "unconverted" neighbors—they were

---

[1] Aleida J. Pieters, *A Dutch Settlement in Michigan*, p. 26.
[2] *Ibid.*, p. 27.

"unconverted" so long as they did not formally join them—did not always attribute equal congruity to their persistent and unremitting preoccupation with public prayer.

Nor could many of them sympathize with the dissenters' passionate condemnation of what was considered innocent amusement. To the dissenting group there were no innocent amusements; life was real, life was earnest, though that phrase had not yet been coined at the time. They had a sense of traveling through a vale of tears. And since they had, to a rather exaggerated degree, the racial trait of being logical, how could they make merry with things that were not fashioned in the pattern of eternity? To them the theatre was sinful, and they were vocal in their expression of the conviction. Card playing and dancing were equally on the proscribed list of amusements, as were many other activities that their very descendants the next generation accepted as legitimate. It is not too difficult to understand why such people were not popular, why the very persecutions they suffered at the hands of government were in part at least a reflection of the general public attitude toward them.

They carried their sense of religious propriety to rather extreme lengths in some instances. One of their formal reasons for separating themselves from the state church and organizing a communion of their own was that gospel hymns were used in the established church. They were convinced, on the basis of scriptural authority, that only the Psalms of the Old Testament canon were worthy of being sung in church worship. The synod of the state church had compiled a collection of sacred hymns to be used in conjunction with the Psalms. Theoretically the dissenters were within their human rights in refusing to have hymns forced upon them that they did not want; the authorities were of course stupid in making the attempt. But an objective examination of the facts leads to the suspicion that the dissenters' opposition was not wholly motivated by scruples of conscience, and that an ounce of tact and mental flexibility could have solved the difficulty. Instead, the men of the congregation would put on their hats when a hymn was announced by the state church minister, to indicate that they were spiritually absent while the singing was going on, or, still more drastically, they would leave the church, returning only when the last notes had died away.[3] One of the dissenting religious leaders described the collection of hymns as "one hundred ninety-two siren songs" designed to draw the members of the state church "from their saviour and to carry them into the false doctrine of lies." [4]

Such evidence as is extant points to a very strong supposition that the Dutch Separatists were inclined to be over-righteous, in their own eyes and in those of their neighbors—sincerely so, on their part, without any doubt. It would be less than intelligent to cast even the slightest doubt on their utter sincerity; their willingness to suffer and sacrifice for the ideas they considered vital is sufficient answer to all doubts on that score. Mere official piety wilts when it is subjected to strong opposition; Holland's Puritans were quite as constant in their unrelenting devotion to their own religious point of view as their English prototypes in Massachusetts had been two centuries earlier.

In all fairness it should be added that the Dutch Puritans, again like their English prototypes, were as hard on themselves as on others. Later, on the Michigan frontier, an elder rose in meeting and resigned his holy office because he had failed to prevent his son from going to a dance the night before. He considered himself unfit to be a ruler of the people when he could not rule his own household. Such utter sincerity wins reluctant admiration even a century after it was displayed, but it must have been difficult for those people of the Netherlands who considered such "sins" as going to a dance merely venial, or even among the graces of life, to bear with a spirit of that kind. And the Separatists were few in a dense population.

It seems all the more necessary to dwell on this point because the history of the Dutch Puritans has sometimes been written by those who unconsciously looked through the eyes of those Puritans. The temptation has often been too strong to cast the Separatists for the heroes of the play, and all the others—Dutch government, the general Dutch population—for the villains. The result is likely to be melodrama, with the inherent defects of that form. For life is almost never like that. Heroes often have feet of clay, and more often still they are ungracious and hard to live with; villains sometimes are rather delightful scoundrels, and in not a few instances they have qualities

---

[3] The Rev. Jacob Vander Meulen, *Hollanders*, p. 22.
[4] Aleida J. Pieters, *op. cit.*, p. 18.

of heart and mind that deserve sincere admiration. It is the business of the true dramatist to present the strange mixture of the good and the bad as life dishes it up. The easy thing to do is simply to condemn all those whose pressures drove a company of "heroes" into the foreign wilderness and consign them to the censure of history.

But the Dutch people as a whole did not suddenly lose all their tribal virtues. The picture suffers distortion if melodrama is allowed to take the place of true drama, if a dichotomy of "heroes" and "villains" is offered as a substitute for objectively realistic history. In the end, for Hollanders who paint such a picture it involves the humiliation of admitting that in the nineteenth century the Dutch race had lost its sense of tolerance and justice and fair play. But in the twentieth the third and fourth generation descendants of those "villains" of the nineteenth proved, during the Nazi occupation, that they possessed the tribal virtues of their race. Their grandfathers cannot have been all bad. It is unsafe to forget that the mass migration to America in the 1840's and 1850's was only an episode in the national life of Holland, and that very many good people, both Protestant and Catholic, were not even conscious of it at the time.

One of the more curious elements of the village drama is the fact that it lacked for the most part the saving grace of humor. Given that ingredient, the *dénouement* might have been quite different. But unfortunately, intense moral earnestness—"fanaticism" to those who disagree with it—is almost invariably without humor. It may be that its very power lies in this fact, that the survival value of this negative trait makes its elimination instinctive. At least it is next to impossible to imagine the accomplishments of a Savonarola if the great Italian had now and again had a gleam of merriment in his eyes. And the New England Pilgrim Fathers would hardly have won in the battle with their "rockbound coast" if they had been so much as capable of smiling at themselves when their Cotton Mathers preached two-hour sermons at a young woman who was about to die on the scaffold.

Laughter is potent in the relaxation of social tensions. People who are incapable of laughing at themselves usually become the subject of the laughter of others. There was no *Hudibras* in the story of the Dutch Puritans, but perhaps only because there was no Samuel Butler among their enemies to write it. There has been many a village

Macaulay both in their day and in later times to portray them as a species of demigods. Admittedly both pictures are distorted; but when a *Hudibras* parallels a Macaulay, the result at least approaches reality. In the story of the Dutch Puritans this has not happened, partly perhaps because from the point of view of universal history the migration has remained an episode, an incident that presently was lost in the welter of American history.

The almost complete lack of humor in the movement hardly justifies the conclusion that want of humor is, or was, a Dutch racial trait. Quite the contrary; humor has always been an important ingredient in Holland's literature, and Dutch national fiction and poetry prove that humor has always been present in rich abundance in the life of the people. The Hollander of the sixteenth, seventeenth, and eighteenth centuries was not normally dour, any more than was the Englishman who laughed at Shakespeare's comedies. Yet it was from among those Englishmen that the inflexible and for the most part humorless Puritans issued, and it was from among a similarly laughing Dutch population that Holland's Puritans went forth to a land where, for them, life was indeed real and life was earnest.

Nor does that quite tell the whole story. For human nature is so incomprehensibly strange that it is possible for people to possess a sense of humor and to be without it at one and the same time. This was true of the New England Puritans; Samuel Sewall's diary is sufficient proof of the point. And the Dutch Separatists were about as ready as their neighbors to laugh in the normal course of living, to indulge in satire, to deal in innuendo and the *double-entendre,* to roll their family jests over their tongues. Taken by themselves the official records give an utterly distorted conception of them. It was only at what they regarded as sacred things that the Hollanders were incapable of laughter. Humor to them was secular, seriousness was sacred. The wholesome idea of laughter in heaven would have scandalized them; that it did not was for the simple reason that they were utterly incapable of entertaining the idea. But humor in church they could at least imagine, even if they did not practice it. Generations later laughter at a church service was still frowned upon. Back there in the Netherlands, while the tensions were straining toward the breaking point, laughter was for weekdays not for Sundays. It was in part at least because the general Dutch public insisted on the propriety of Sunday laughter that trouble resulted.

Such were the Dutch Puritans who have flashed into the incandescence of history, in a small way at least, because they engaged in one of the most curious, and perhaps one of the more important, movements of modern times. They differed materially from many of the European nationals who came to America in millions during the nineteenth century in the fact that their coming was genuinely a migration, while many of the others came as families or individuals. Because this was a mass movement it has been necessary to describe the people as a mass. It has seemed desirable to correct the distortions that have imperceptibly been painted into the picture, and to place the portrait against the background of its own day.

XI

Souls or Bodies?

Was it the hunger of the souls of the Dutch folk or the necessities of their bodies that chiefly motivated their mass migration to America? The question has found no definitive answer during a century of discussion. An objective presentation of the facts may serve as a basis for judgment. It seems likely that both souls and bodies must be taken into account.

When Napoleon swept over Holland, much in the same way Hitler did in our time, the glorious Golden Age came to a final inglorious close. After the Corsican's fall the new Dutch government inherited his Code, which among other restrictions prohibited gatherings of more than twenty persons "whose object is to meet daily or on special days appointed for the observance of religious, literary, political, or other purposes." Such bodies were not to "organize themselves without the consent of the government or otherwise than under the conditions which it may please the public authorities to impose upon the society." The prohibition applied not only to the members of such an association but to any person granting the use of his "house or of his apartment in whole or in part for the meeting of the members." Appropriate fines were provided for in case of violations.

Napoleon merely had self-protection in mind, the prevention of the formation of groups of conspirators. When the government of the Netherlands as an independent state was reconstituted, with William I as king, its constitution guaranteed religious freedom, but the King was canny enough to gather into his own hands the strings that made all the country's ecclesiastical puppets jump. The salaries of the ministers of the state church were paid out of the public exchequer; church property was transferred to the state. The faculties of three universities for the education of the clergy were made state officers and hence directly subservient to the state. William had the state church in his vest pocket, and he regarded it as his property.

Hence the bitterness of the animus against those who refused to submit to the dictates of the authorities. It was not merely a religious or theological revolt, it was dangerously political in its nature. The provisions in the Code of Napoleon, not in any sense intended for this purpose, were employed to control the "insurrection," two decades after the fall of the Corsican. In due course the legal question reached the supreme court; that body did not so much read the election returns as observe the countenance of the royal master. In any event, the judges ruled that the constitutional provision for freedom of worship and the prosecution of dissenters under the offensive clause of the Code were not incompatible. The King and the members of his government turned themselves into petty persecutors while meticulously observing the forms of law. Technically the Separatists did not have a leg to stand on; actually they were insisting on liberty of conscience.

In the reorganization of the government a new name had been given to the state church—*Hervormde Kerk*—which in effect means "Reorganized Church." Before Napoleon the name of the Dutch church had been *Gereformeerde Kerk*—"Reformed Church"—the implication of the term being that it had gone through a process of spiritual cleansing. For the general reader it is perhaps wise to keep clear of the complexities of Dutch ecclesiastical government and church nomenclature and to focus his attention on the broad lines of a very human struggle that went on under the theological forms. Tyranny in whatever dress can be understood by all, and whatever the Dutch state church was called, or whatever name the dissenters went by, their bitter struggle is all too understandable.

During the twenties a kind of Oxford Movement, begun in Switzerland, had spread to Holland. Certain members of the generally subservient state clergy became convinced that dry rot had set in in their organization and that a spiritual reformation was overdue. In the first half of the decade of the thirties the movement resulted in formal secession from the state church by a number of congregations under the leadership of half a dozen fiery Dutch Savonarolas who carried their flocks into a new communion that threatened the prestige, the revenue, and the political power of the state ecclesiastical body. The two leaders who were destined to become best known in the American part of the Hollanders' story were the Reverend Hendrik Pieter Scholte and the Reverend Albertus Christiaan Van Raalte. The former became the founder of the Dutch settlement on the prairies of Iowa, the latter conducted many of his people to the forests of Michigan and attracted thousands of others to the same place by the force of his personality.

But before the actual mass migration got under way in the summer of 1846 a decade intervened of agitation, of recrimination, of disgracefully petty persecution, of determined opposition to arbitrary power. There were arrests and imprisonments. The Separatists insisted on disobeying the edicts of a tyrannical government. They were "village Hampdens" who with "dauntless breasts" stood up to the powers of law and alleged order. By people of Dutch blood who cherish the honor of a country that has for centuries been a leader in the never-ending battle for tolerance and liberty of conscience, the ten years from 1836 to 1846 are thought of as the "tragic era" in Holland's story.

And not the least of the tragedy lies in the fact that the persecutions by the government were in the main petty. There is often something grimly splendid in the ruthlessness of tyrants who stop at nothing to attain their ends. When two centuries earlier the Duke of Alva cut off the heads of Egmont and Horn, and beheaded and burned and drowned scores of thousands—sometimes allowing a victim to be buried alive as a special mark of clemency—the story took on a shuddering drama whose horror redeemed it from the shabbiness that motivated many of the later persecutions. Nothing could redeem the petty campaign of fines organized by the government of William I. The government did not have the courage to engage in persecutions that would challenge the opposition of men of good will in its own population, whatever their faith or creed, or draw the attention of the lovers of justice in other lands. It was a persecution by small men of a group of people made up for the most part of the socially undistinguished.

That is, the rank and file were of that type; the leaders were university men, certainly as well educated as the Bradfords and the Winthrops who had ruled the Puritans of New England. They were not mere fiery rabble-rousers, as the government charged, although nearly all of them—especially Scholte and Van Raalte—were so eloquent in oral harangue that they held thousands in the hollows of their hands by virtue of their emotional appeal. But they were men of erudition as well, the product of a formal education remarkable in its extent and depth. And in terms of ecclesiastical learning, it is doubtful if any dissenting group in any land has ever been shepherded by men of greater intellectual attainments.

But the people were like people of any land, with only a limited amount of public schooling, men and women of good sense rather than of intellectual attainments; deeply versed, however, most of them, in the theological subtlities that constituted their breath of life. If the leaders were genuinely educated men, in terms of what was then considered a "liberal education," the congregations were composed in large part of people who in the narrow sense of theological disputation were far superior to the typical travelers over sawdust trails.

It was such leaders, and such people, that the Dutch government subjected to a decade of persecution. Barred from the pulpits of the state church, the fiery dissenting ministers preached in private houses, in barns, in the open fields. The government, through the village authorities, applied the Code of Napoleon and arrested the preachers and the owners of the buildings where the services were held. Repeatedly meetings were broken up by the police or the military. Haled into court the offenders were fined as heavily as the law would permit. Just as often the people paid the fines, and the congregations gathered somewhere else the next Sunday to hold another service, only to have the weary sequence enacted all over again. The fines were sometimes so heavy that the congregations were unable to raise the money. The ministers—Van Raalte and Scholte among them—were more than once cast into common jails and forced to associate with criminals and vagabonds. Scholte later testified that in addition to serving terms in jail he had been forced to pay fines, during a period of about a decade, of $3,200. If they had kept books on the government's persecutions, several of the other leaders might have produced similar statistics.

As always happens in such cases, persecution merely served to increase the number of dissenters. A few fiery key individuals had aroused congregations, and throughout many sections of the Netherlands foci of infection—from the government's point of view—had developed. But during the early years of the movement most of the groups were small. A wise government would have taken care not to stir the disease into activity; or if it had become active in a big way a just government would have let it take its normal course. The chances are at least even that the growth of dissent would have been small. Persecution served to fire the hearts of thousands, and when the government was finally forced into reluctant compromise, toward the end of the period, the fat was in the fire. The hearts of thousands had been conditioned to the idea of emigration; moreover, the people could not trust a government that had shown itself unworthy of their confidence.

But not until some leaders had made one last attempt to save for Holland the human material entrusted to their care. A plan to direct the migration to Java, in the Dutch East Indies, was seriously considered. But once more the government revealed its inadequacy. It could not bring itself to guarantee the liberty of conscience that the dissenters demanded, and without that pledge migration would have lost one of its motivations. Thereafter, fearfully and reluctantly, the decision was made to settle somewhere in America. One of the remarkable facts of the story is that when the first waves of the migrating people had arrived in America neither their leaders nor they knew where they were going to light on this vast and to them unknown continent. The Michigan group stood poised for a time in New York, and the Iowa group in Baltimore, before they decided on a destination.

But Dutch governmental ineptitude was not confined to matters ecclesiastical, and it would be less than realistic to seek the causes of the migration exclusively, or perhaps even primarily, in theological tensions. There are not a few who feel that the principal cause was economic, not religious, that the insistent demands of Dutch bellies had as much to do with the trek to America as the real or imagined needs of Dutch souls. Who is wise enough to decide that they are not right? It would be natural for people driven by hunger to rationalize their motivation as spiritual, when after the lapse of years hunger had been appeased and not only physical needs had been supplied but com-

forts and the graces and amenities as well; and it would be natural
for their descendants to follow them in this line.

They would not have to be conscious of rationalization; it is much
more attractive to dare all for the cultivation of immortal souls than
for the nourishment of mortal bodies, much more dramatic to suffer
for an intangible idea than for bread and meat and raiment. Walt
Whitman's pioneers, in sober reality, were responding to physical and
biological urges that could hardly form the subject matter of the great
poet's ode, but that does not prevent the poem from being truer than
the facts it celebrates. And though the village folk of Holland were
driven by hunger to uproot themselves and migrate to an unknown
world, that fact does not prove that their subsequent rationalizations
were not more real than the physical realisms that confronted them
when they made the irrevocable decision "to take up the task eternal."
In making that decision they understood that they would never see
their home land again; they would die somewhere on a vast continent,
and they did not know the approximate location within two thousand
miles. Whitman, who was even then at work on his great task, would
have responded to their type of courage and might have said of them:
"conquering, holding, daring, venturing as they go the unknown
ways." And he would have had perceptiveness enough to understand
that such words might be true of men and women who left their home
land because of pinched bellies.

In any event hunger—in a quite literal sense—had a great deal to do
with their decision. Had there been a chance for them and their children in Holland, it is very well possible—perhaps probable—that they
would have fought it out with their own government on the spot and
challenged official stupidity to a showdown. As a matter of fact they
had virtually won their battle for freedom of worship. Government
persecution was ending about the time the migration began in earnest.
The last time the authorities tried official coercion on a congregation
was in 1846, the very year Van Raalte and his co-religionists left for
Michigan. And in 1848 a new liberal ministry finally put an end to
persecution.

Hard economic common sense has always been a Dutch trait, incongruously coupled though it is with theological transcendentalism, and

the village subjects of the House of Orange understood that the alternative to migration was slow starvation for many of them, and what was harder to bear, that there were no prospects for their children. In one sense they did not make the decision, it was made for them by the grim necessities of their lives—aided and abetted again by a government that had learned little from the French Revolution and shifted the main burden of taxes to pay for the recent war with Belgium onto the shoulders of the farmers and artisans and village laborers, from which classes the emigration drew most of its strength. It was the eternally familiar story of the taxing power in the hands of privilege. So large a proportion of the people's meager earnings went to the government that many of them lived most of the time on the edge of want, and a startlingly large proportion of the population fell below the subsistence level. The statistics of the number of people kept alive through government grants or organized public charity or the semi-private charity of church assistance would seem rather appalling even to a generation that has gone through the great depression of this century. Holland, indeed, had been in its own depression since Napoleon had left it stripped, and the burden, as usual, bore down most heavily on the little men who were likely to have the largest number of mouths to feed.

Also, accident stepped in to help push the Dutch folk out of their familiar village shelters to seek log or sod huts in an unknown America. Or was it accident? The Four Horsemen of the Apocalypse never run singly, always as a team in tandem; where there is hunger over a long period of time disease is a certainty. After Napoleon there was hunger not only in Holland but throughout Europe, as there was after Hitler. And in the mid-nineteenth century, as in the mid-twentieth, plagues found easy prey in cramped bellies or in the children that sprang from hungry loins. Perhaps the only accidental element in the situation in Holland was that disease reached a crisis stage at a time when other elements had for a decade or more been trying to force a decision. Cholera took a heavy toll in Holland, as it did throughout Europe, and added to the general sense of insecurity. And during 1845 there was a disastrous visitation of "potato rot," which destroyed the staple food of the poorer classes. It has been estimated that out of a

Dutch population of some two million about 700,000 had to be given support in one form or another.[1]

A curious difficulty confronts those who try to engage in objective research of the records a century after the emigration. The reports of poverty, disease, financial depression, starvation wages for labor, ruinous taxes are so numerous that there can hardly be a doubt of their reality. And yet, when the shiploads of Hollanders arrived in America —or at least some of them—those immigrants usually gave the impression of a reasonable prosperity. The leader of the Iowa migration, Scholte, gives some color to this impression when in an early report he blasts American confidence men who tried to exploit the immigrants. They were, he wrote, "so accustomed to see incoming ships filled with half-starved Irishmen or ill-smelling Germans that the rumor of the coming of so many Hollanders, with money in their pockets and clean looks besides, goaded their zeal anew to give chase after what people here have already generally learned to call 'Willempjes'" (a Dutch coin).[2] A twentieth century author writes that "the rumor of the coming of so many well-to-do Hollanders preceded Scholte."[3]

The difficulty is more apparent than real. Poverty is comparative, and to Americans of that day, accustomed to the pauper conditions of steerage immigrants, the self-respecting appearance of the Hollanders may have seemed like comparative prosperity. Cleanliness and a decent regard for the amenities of life are Dutch racial traits; many of those immigrants doubtless denied themselves necessities to make a decent appearance, and all reports agree that those shiploads of common people won the admiration of the port officials by the passengers' provisions for maintaining health and cleanliness.

Some groups, moreover, were more prosperous than others. The immigrants came from widely scattered sections of the Netherlands, and some communities had been less hard hit by economic depression than others. The impression is unconsciously given by the records, for instance, that in general the congregations that made Iowa their objective were financially better off than those who went to Michigan or Wisconsin.

[1] The Rev. Jacob Vander Meulen, *Hollanders*, p. 16.
[2] Jacob Vander Zee, *The Hollanders of Iowa*, p. 49.
[3] *Ibid.*, p. 60.

But even in the same group there was likely to be considerable variation. Thus in the Michigan contingent Jannes Vander Luyster, one of the founders of what later became the city of Zeeland, was, relatively speaking, a man of some wealth. When he had decided to emigrate, he had sold his farm in the Netherlands for 60,000 florins, about $25,000.[4] He was able to advance passage money for indigent emigrants, buy land for others, and meet expenses that only a prosperous man could have coped with. There were a few other men of means, but many more had spent their lives just above the subsistence level, and others had been accustomed to life below that line. The fact should not be lost sight of that this was a migration of communities, not of individuals or families—communities organized for the most part as church congregations. The movement preserved the characteristics of real communities; hence the variation of prosperity and poverty.

[4] Anna Kremer Keppel, *The Immigration and Early History of the People of Zeeland*, p. 26.

XII

The Long Journey

THE MIGRATION OF seceders from the Dutch state church was not an isolated phenomenon. The movement has to be seen in its proper setting—national, even continental—to be justly appraised. Throughout Europe the idea of emigration was in the air during the forties. The Hollanders of that decade who made the plunge were only a handful compared with the total of European emigration. The movement of Hollanders was most active during the second half of the decade, but only a little over twelve thousand left the Netherlands for America during that period, as compared with nearly half a million Germans and nearly a million Irish for the same period.

And of those who made up the total of Dutch emigrants the seceders from the state church were actually in the minority. For the year 1847, for instance, the peak year of the movement, there were nearly twice as many Dutch emigrants who were members of the state church—that is, the persecuting ecclesiastical body—as there were members of the seceding church—that is, the persecuted. During that same year the number of Roman Catholic emigrants was nearly two thirds as many as the number of seceders. Catholics and state church members combined added up to considerably more than twice the number of persecuted seceders.[1] These figures for the peak year are fairly representative for the whole period while the emigration was at its height.

The first contingent reaching Michigan was fairly small, but before the end of the first year the number exceeded that arriving in Iowa.

---

[1] Bertus Harry Wabeke, *Dutch Emigration*, p. 90.

Late in 1846, Van Raalte and his family, and fifty-three followers (some authorities say fifty), arrived in New York. Then by Hudson River boat, Erie Canal open flatboats, and by lake steamers, they traveled to Detroit. There they paused while their leader pushed on by rail to Kalamazoo, the rail terminal, and thence by primitive means of travel to the area of what is now Macatawa Bay and the city of Holland. There he purchased nearly a thousand acres of wooded land from the government, which tract was later greatly enlarged.

The men of the party meanwhile had taken jobs in the shipyards of St. Clair, to support their families and provide some ready cash for the winter. The whole party presently traveled to Kalamazoo by rail, and thence over Indian trails to the site of their future home. During December of 1846 several hundred more immigrants had arrived in New York, to be routed during the next few months to Michigan; and in March of 1847 five more vessels arrived in New York. Census figures show that Michigan's Dutch population in 1860 had grown to 6,335.

In the initial wave of Iowa immigrants there were over eight hundred persons. Carrying along with them from their homes in Holland such articles, domestic and personal, as they could transport, they landed in Baltimore, then traveled overland by rail, canal boat, Ohio River packets to the Mississippi, to St. Louis. Pausing there they waited for Scholte, their leader, to purchase land for their occupancy, many of them taking jobs while waiting and thus supporting their families. When title to some eighteen thousand acres of rich Iowa land had been acquired for them from private owners and the government, they pushed on to the area of which the city of Pella is today the center and began their life on the American frontier. Other waves of immigrants followed quickly. Census figures show that by 1850 the foreign-born Dutch population of Iowa was 1,108, and by 1860 the number was 2,615.

Chronologically the Dutch settlement in Wisconsin antedated those of Iowa and Michigan. So early as 1845, two years before the Van Raalte group arrived in Michigan, a Hollander named Albert Meenk settled in Alto, Wisconsin, and the following year ten more families arrived to make it a Dutch settlement. The initial wave—perhaps it could more accurately be called a wavelet—can hardly be described as a mass migration, at least not in its early stages. The Dutch colonists erected a log church, however, and extended a call to the Reverend G. Baay of Het Loo, the Netherlands. He died in 1849. Other ministers carried on, and in time the little settlement occupied a place of some importance on the Wisconsin Dutch frontier.

So early as 1850 Dr. Van Raalte considered the community in Wisconsin important enough to pay the people a visit.[2] Van Raalte, in fact, had considered Wisconsin as a first choice for settlement, and his party might have gone there if they had not arrived in Detroit after the close of navigation on the Great Lakes. He had been attracted to Wisconsin not because of the presence of a handful of Hollanders but because the state had become the scene of large-scale German settlement.

Almost at the moment Van Raalte was establishing his settlement in Michigan—but arriving a little later in the spring of 1847—a party from the province of Zeeland, under the leadership of the Reverend P. Zonne, settled some twenty miles south of the present city of Sheboygan, Wisconsin, on land purchased from the government. The leader gave the name of Cedar Grove to the settlement. The congregation became affiliated with the Presbyterian denomination. Their leader built a church on his own land and gave it to his congregation. But some of the group formed a new congregation and affiliated themselves with the Dutch Reformed Church.

Such were the modest beginnings of the Dutch Protestant settlement in Wisconsin.[3]

What amounted to a more pretentious mass migration of Hollanders headed for Wisconsin was the departure from the Netherlands early in 1847 of 120 Dutch Catholics under the leadership of a lawyer named C. Verwagen. Their announced intention was to found a new state to be called "Disabdera." A second contingent was to sail a month later, to make up a much larger company. On paper, and in terms of impressive public ceremonies, this migration was the most ambitious of them all. The second group did not sail, however, and the first wave appears to have been dissipated along the American travel route from the port of arrival to Wisconsin.

A more important mass migration of Dutch Catholics was conducted

[2] The Rev. J. H. Kregel, "History of the Reformed Church of Alto, Wisconsin," p. 9.
[3] Sipko F. Raderus, "The Dutch Settlements of Sheboygan County," *The Wisconsin Magazine of History* (March, 1918), p. 256.

under the leadership of Father Theodore J. Vanden Broek, O.P., who
had served as a missionary to the Indians in the Green Bay region for
more than a decade before he became an agent of immigration. In the
spring of 1848 three vessels were chartered by him to carry congregations of Dutch Catholics to Wisconsin. They followed the usual route.
One of the ships made port in New York, the second in Boston, and
the third in Philadelphia. The company arriving in New York, including Father Vanden Broek, reached Wisconsin after eighty-three
days of land travel and settled in Little Chute. The others soon followed and founded a community fifteen miles distant, to which later
the name of Hollandtown was given.

Thus Wisconsin became the third Dutch frontier in America. Although Dutch immigration to the state took on impressive proportions
in the years that followed, during the early stages the settlement there
was less dramatic than on the other two frontiers. By 1860, however,
Wisconsin had 4,906 Holland-born residents, as compared with Michigan's 6,335, and Iowa's 2,615. In actual numbers it had become the
second Dutch frontier at the time of the Civil War, but in the consciousness of the Dutch people it remained third.

In addition to those three waves, thousands of non-Separatist Protestant Hollanders settled in various communities in America, as single
families or as individuals, and they are a part of the picture of Dutch
immigration. Hollanders attracted to America by the contagion of
emigration were found in many cities and farming communities all
the way from the Atlantic seaboard to the Mississippi, at least in the
Northern states. The Michigan-Iowa-Wisconsin mass migrations had
in them elements of drama that kept the spotlight of immigration
history directed on them. The thousands of scattered Hollanders have
been more or less forgotten. But that was inevitable.

Whether they migrated as individuals, as families, or as whole congregations, the Hollanders who pulled up their ancestral stakes faced
a journey that to most of them must have seemed like Jules Verne's
trip to the moon. It is probably impossible for the twentieth century
to get a realizing sense of what it meant. Most of the humble Dutch
villagers or farmers had never been much more than a dozen miles
distant from home. They had been born into the tradition of remaining rooted in their native spot from the cradle to the grave. The people

of a village ten miles distant seemed somewhat strange to them, those of another province almost alien. The very dialects spoken in different provinces were so different that it was not very easy for a native of Overyssel to converse fluently with one from Zeeland. Amry Vanden Bosch, in a doctor's dissertation about Dutch immigrants in America, asserts: "A Dutch lady was heard to remark about another who did not hail from the same province as herself, 'She is not a Hollander, she is a stranger.'" [4]

It was people like that who started upon a journey that would first of all carry them across three thousand miles of ocean, then over a thousand or two thousand miles of land. They knew that it was a journey from which there would be no return. True, the technique of emigrant ocean travel had become more or less standardized. The leaders of a congregation chartered one or two or three vessels, and the passengers had the moral and physical support of one another; they remained among neighbors and friends. But they knew that the hazards were great. The death rate during a passage of six or eight weeks was several times that of a similar period at home; and there was an added poignancy about burial at sea, especially the burial of little children, who were often the first victims, that meant terror to the emigrants. Of the original Van Raalte party, for instance, consisting of the leader and his family and only fifty-three (or fifty) others, six had to be consigned to the ocean during the seven weeks' voyage. The death rate was proportionally as large for many of the other passages.[5]

Those who went in the initial waves enjoyed the bliss of their ignorance of the hardships of land travel in America. They naturally believed that their troubles would end when they reached an American port. Usually the real hardships began there. River packets, Erie Canal flatboats, primitive railway coaches, lake sailing vessels, ox-carts, and finally travel on their own weary legs—all of them, with hardly an exception, tested courage and endurance to the breaking point. As many as eighty-three weary days of travel from debarkation port to final destination—most of the immigrants must have felt at last that there had never been a settled life for them and never would be again.

[4] Amry Vanden Bosch, *The Dutch Communities of Chicago*, p. 80.
[5] Louis Adamic, "Americans from Holland," in *A Nation of Nations*, p. 105.

And they left graves all along the endless route; the death rate was appalling. And while the members of the initial groups did not suffer the full terrors of anticipation, later emigrants knew from letters home what they were facing. Yet they faced it with hardihood, thousands of them.

Such a journey would almost certainly have ended in disaster if it had not been for unusually intelligent leadership. The part those leaders, most of them, played in the success of the long journey itself, aside from later success of settlement, is illustrated by Van Raalte and Scholte. Both of them give a strong impression of business acumen coupled with a messianic fervor that marked them as spiritual shepherds of their flocks. The latter quality—evangelistic enthusiasm—is not surprising, rather to be expected and taken for granted. These particular leaders and other Separatist ministers had led their people, whole congregations numbering many thousands, into a secession from the state church. They could hardly have done so if they had not been zealous religious propagandists who could sway large masses of people with the fire of their eloquence.

Much more astonishing it is that such men proved to be good business leaders, to whom their people looked for guidance in the enormously difficult problems of making the long journey and establishing an orderly community in a raw new land. Both Van Raalte and Scholte taught themselves a smattering of English during the journey to America, enough so that they could represent their people in dealing with the governors, congressmen, land agents, American church authorities. They displayed considerable skill in negotiations with American officials in New York, Albany, Boston, Baltimore, Washington. Later Van Raalte, in Detroit, and Scholte, in St. Louis, met and conferred with influential citizens and political leaders, and through them made provisions for the welfare of their followers. On the actual frontier they converted themselves into real estate agents and mastered the intricacies of land office routine and title deeds. When it is remembered that the chances were enormous that ecclesiastical leaders educated in the scholasticism of Dutch universities would be babes in the woods in the practical affairs of a mass migration, it is nothing short of astonishing that both of them proved successes.

Their temperaments rather than their logical faculties seem to have led them to select the two widely separated localities. Van Raalte, who arrived in America before Scholte, chose Michigan, after rejecting the Southern states for fear of yellow fever and other tropical diseases. He chose that location partly because of plain cold water. At least that impression is left by the records of his elaborate rationalizations. Coming from a land of canals and intricate waterways, and with pictures in his soul of the Zuider Zee, he felt the need of water for his people. That need appears to have been an intuition with him. When he found good land almost within sight of Lake Michigan, drained by a bay then named Black Lake and its river running into it, he seems to have fallen in love with the region. There also was heavy timber on the land, that could be used as building material and fuel; and there were many other advantages—at least he rationalized them later as advantages. But the word *water* recurs constantly in his reports.

He would hardly have been himself if he had not tried to persuade the Scholte wave, following a little later, to settle in Michigan. There would be plenty of room for all who might wish to come; the larger the settlement the stronger it would be. All the migrating communities and their leaders were of one mind on the main issue, to carve out for themselves a place of security and freedom in the economy of America. What could have been more natural than that they should combine their forces and resources, all for one and one for all?

But Scholte was a man of somewhat different temperament. His intuitions caused him to reject Michigan, with its *water,* its woods, and other advantages, and to select Iowa. Perhaps rationalizing in his turn, he saw all Van Raalte's advantages as liabilities, except perhaps water. The Hollanders, he argued, came from a flat, open land. Timber was for them an obstacle; they were not accustomed to clearing woodland, and stumps would be a nuisance. He believed that Van Raalte had made a mistake and that his settlement might come to grief as a result. What he was looking for was the open prairie that would yield crops as soon as the sod had been broken. There is a note of near-irony in his observation that he does not wish to detract "from the pleasure of hearing the warble of birds in the cool shade of virgin forests." He almost says that Van Raalte's poetical pictures are all well enough but that they will butter no parsnips for his Hollanders in their seriously practical endeavor of getting farms established. The practical bent of his nature is shown in his characterization of Hollanders coming to America as "more prosaic than poetic" and thinking "not so much of pleasing their eyes and ears as of buying suitable land for farms, the easier to cultivate, the better." [6] So he rejected timber and chose prairie. Strong-willed, he appears to have arrived at his conclusion solely on his own initiative, as had basically been true of Van Raalte also, although the latter tries hard to give the impression of having leaned heavily on the counsel of others; in reality he usually knew what he wanted.

In fact, the suspicion will not down that those two men of God were engaging in a rivalry of wills and temperaments. Beneath all the fraternal well wishing there is a note of competition for leadership. It is possible, probable even, that their instincts caused them to settle hundreds of miles apart. In the early days of the secession in the Netherlands Van Raalte had been a kind of Scholte disciple, a member of a group called the "Scholte Club." In America they were two independent leaders of the people, and Van Raalte had stolen a march on his associate by arriving in America first with his followers. Was there perhaps a sense of jealousy in the older leader's heart, and did he reject Michigan—without knowing it himself—for the simple reason that there he would have to share his rule with a former disciple? And did Van Raalte, on his part, stand by his decision so tenaciously because—it was his decision?

Who shall say? Such intuitions can be apprehended only intuitively. Official documents are of no help in arriving at an answer.

[6] Jacob Vander Zee, *The Hollanders of Iowa*, p. 59.

XIII

Life on the Michigan Frontier

IN A RECORD intended to tell the story of a culture's march across the continent a detailed account would be superfluous. In most respects the experiences of the Hollanders on the frontier in America were not different from those that fell to the lot of all migrating groups, including the Yankees. The half-legendary Daniel Boone, the more than half-mythical Davie Crockett, the startlingly real Andrew Jackson— they and their associates and followers had met with virtually the same experiences that faced the Hollanders, and their story has become so familiar a chapter in the folklore of America that its repetition under cover of mere Dutch names would be tedious. All of them had wilderness to clear or tough prairie sod to break; wolves and bears and, earlier, Indians were a problem for all; disease and quick death on the frontier with its inevitable dearth of doctors, fill the daily records of all pioneers; lack of transportation, resulting in periods of scanty food supplies, visitations of forest or prairie fires, plagues of grasshoppers— all that is part of the almost too familiar story of any American frontier at any time during the nineteenth century. Fiction has come to the aid of sober history, and there can hardly be a literate American left who is not, even if only unconsciously, familiar with the main details of American migration.

There remains for that reason only the story of what was unique on the Dutch frontier. In some ways the Hollanders were confronted with difficulties that the general frontiersmen did not share with them; in some ways also they left footprints on the American scene such as only they could have been expected to make.

Most of the American pioneers were experienced woodsmen; the Hollanders who settled in Michigan were so ignorant of the ways of forest life that they literally did not know how to cut down a tree. Coming from a land of tiny little flat farms that had been under cultivation for a thousand years, they were so unskilled in forest lore that their early hardships were multiplied many fold because of it. When they cut down trees for the first log hut, the ax men nibbled around the trunk like beavers, but without the shrewd skill of those animals. They had no conception of directing the fall of the tree and were likely to get killed or maimed—until given instruction by the American squatters of the region.

In time they learned to become skilled woodsmen. They built log huts in the woods, solving the problem of roofing by using hemlock bark and other similar material, and they filled the chinks between the logs with clay and grass. Accustomed to stoves in the Netherlands, the women learned the knack of cooking in an open fireplace. And they learned all the other domestic arts necessary for survival on the frontier—candle moulding, soap making, spinning, weaving. The men learned not only the art of cutting down trees, they found out how to transport them to the home site locations without the use of oxen or horses. When every pound of weight had to be lifted by sheer human muscle power, the difficulties were enormous and the labor was prodigious. The workers from the little garden-like farms in Holland had to re-educate themselves in frontier techniques to raise crops among trees and stumps. Most of them, at first anyway, had not learned the art of girdling trees, known to the Indians and the American frontiersman, killing the trees with the least trouble to let in the sunlight for crops. But they quickly adapted themselves to the extent of growing wheat and corn and potatoes among stumps, and showed their good sense in cultivating the clearings abandoned by the Ottawa Indians, who had been transferred by the government to the Grand Traverse region.

The Hollanders' diet on the frontier was monotonous the first year or two, and sometimes scanty; supplies often had to be carried on the backs of husky Hollanders for a distance of twenty miles or more through the woods, from the little settlement of Allegan or the village of Grand Rapids. At other times flatboats were used to carry supplies from the settlement at Grand Haven at the mouth of the Grand River, along the Lake Michigan shore to the mouth of Black Lake. There the boats frequently had to be unloaded because they could not cross the sandbars that choked the outlet; the supplies had to be re-loaded on other flatboats in Black Lake and hauled the six-mile length of the bay to the settlement.

That annoying and expensive reloading of supplies resulted in a display of typical Dutch self-reliance. Van Raalte and other leaders attempted after a time to enlist the aid of the federal government to get a proper channel dug, under the direction of Washington engineers, but failed. So the people on the Dutch frontier called a meeting—which, as with all meetings, they opened with prayer—passed the usual portentous-sounding motions and resolutions, and made a brave show of taking action in spite of Washington. All in the familiar pattern—with this material difference: they followed talk with action, shouldered their shovels, carried their tools and their supplies the length of the six miles of the bay to the outlet of Black Lake, and began their molelike job of biting out a channel to Lake Michigan, shovelful after weary shovelful.

Today a channel deep enough for the passage of the largest freighters in the world, and built by the government at the costs of millions, connects Macatawa Bay (Black Lake) with Lake Michigan, and a coast guard station protects the entrance, and a system of piers and breakwaters provides an artificial ante-harbor, and a lighthouse blinks intermittently through the night, and a foghorn blasts its warnings when spindrift sweeps the lake. A century ago bare Dutch human hands holding only shovels and picks cut a channel to Lake Michigan to solve the settlers' simple navigation problems. It was but a poor shallow channel, only deep enough to accommodate their flatboats, but it was a labor of Hercules to the frontiersmen. They did for themselves what cried out to be done, without waiting for the government to wake up. And they were simple and undramatic about it.

In odd contrast is such an episode with incidents growing out of the religious life of the Dutch Puritans. Writers about the Netherlands in Michigan never miss the point that a log church was one of the first buildings erected, before many of the families had a domestic roof over their heads or even food for their makeshift cupboards. But that was

DUTCH PIONEERS

Typical group photographed in 1887, forty years after founding of Zeeland, Mich

Netherlands Museum, Holland, Michigan

THREE LEADERS OF THE DUTCH MIGRATION
Top left: Scholte of Iowa.
Top right: Van Raalte of Michigan.
Bottom: Vander Meulen of Michigan.

almost to be expected from them; at least it is small reason for surprise. Nor is the incident usually scanted that certain federal engineers who had come to have a look at the harbor, arriving on Sunday, found the settlement almost literally deserted, except for a few persons too ill to leave their log huts; all the people—literally all—were in the log church, which was located about a mile from the bay. When the visitors arrived within hearing distance of the church the strains of the long-metre Dutch psalms reached them among the trees, as the frontier folk lustily gave lung and voice to the praise of the Lord.

But that too might be taken for granted. Those simple pioneers— channel diggers, tree choppers, house builders, raisers of wheat and corn and potatoes among the stumps—were in a sense ecclesiastics as well, often surprisingly subtle in theological disputation, who did not hesitate to withhold from the pastor-leader himself the hand of fellowship after a church service, in token of agreement with the points of his sermon, if actually they did not agree. Van Raalte, in fact, graduate though he was of the famous university of Leyden, and skilled theologian as the result of many years of study, was now and again subjected to censure by some of the members of his flock when they took exception to his preaching. The grotesque incongruity of this is more apparent than real. Doubtless there was in it sometimes the self-willed pride of the narrow learning of little minds, but within their own limits those Dutch frontiersmen had a certain specialized skill in theological dialectics that sets them apart, miles apart, from the traditional woodsman of fiction and history.

That fact makes their almost endless theological discussions credible —disputation to which both ministers and laymen gave themselves with fanatical zest at a time when the problems of getting enough to eat were still pressing upon them. The great basic doctrines that had been discussed, and presumably settled, at the famous Synod of Dort in 1618-19, were threshed over again endlessly in the forests of Michigan not by the leaders alone but by the laymen as well. For the Dutch folk, even some of the most illiterate of them, were theologians by instinct. They knew the various points of their ecclesiastical doctrine as intimately as savages know their tribal taboos, and they were ready to maintain them almost to the death. It was not necessary for them to have had a college education to discuss in great detail and at great length the solemn questions of predestination and free grace.

But sometimes their discussions were concerned with highly practical affairs, even with intimately personal matters. The ecclesiastical governing body on the frontier was known as Classis Holland, made up of pastors and laymen representing various churches of the settlement. This body met twice a year, and the minutes of those gatherings, fortunately for history, have been preserved. They constitute perhaps the most valuable document in the record of the life of the Hollanders in Michigan. In 1943, the minutes for the years 1848 to 1858 were translated and published in a single volume, a book that is almost worth its weight in gold for the light it throws on the life of the people.

Thus on April 23, 1848, barely a year after the first ax blow was struck to fell the first tree, the following entry is made:

Art. 7. In the congregation of Rev. Ypma, there is a widow who wishes to get married; but since her former husband died only three months ago, some of the brethren object; and wish her to wait a while.

Answer: Whereas the assembly knows of no regulation on the subject in the word of God, it cannot place any obstacle in the way of this marriage; but advises that the parties who contemplate it be instructed; in order that we may seek that which is lovely and of good report; and that no offense be given to decency, honor and natural human feeling.

The unctuousness of the language of that decision is more than half redeemed by its good sense. There was as yet no civil government in the community, and even had there been, the people were accustomed to submit their most private problems to the adjudication of the church authorities. The community was ruled by a near-theocracy, almost to the same degree as had been true of the New England Puritans. Such an action as this—and it was but one of many—makes the true character of the people flash into incandescence. Unlettered most of them may have been, hardhanded and sometimes uncouth, but they had a strong regard for the decencies of an ordered life. There were from time to time cases of adultery and other sex irregularities—as anywhere, in any age under any conditions; biology is never adjourned, whatever the race or creed or level of social development—but they were not ignored. Those Dutch frontiersmen considered themselves civilized, the custodians of a true culture.

When a citizen of one of the outlying communities wanted to marry his brother's widow, the church authorities withheld their consent. Unconventional and rare though a union of that kind may be in an established society, such things have always been fairly common on most frontiers, where the supply of women was necessarily limited. The authorities read the eighteenth chapter of Leviticus to the would-be husband when he "could not acquiesce in the judgment which the assembly had pronounced," and that settled the matter as far as the church—which was the government—was concerned. And there were teeth in the church law: "in case of contumacy [that is, if the man should persist in his intention] he is to be excluded from the church, because we cannot look upon such a marriage in any other way than as incest." The Dutch folk on the Michigan frontier had a high regard for the decencies of orderly life even if the physical conditions of their existence were crude and their institutions primitive. They were transplanting to a wilderness the domestic and community mores developed in a thousand years of living.[1]

Nor did the ecclesiastical teeth hesitate to bite when the application of disciplinary action seemed necessary. There was nothing soft about the Dutch Puritans on the Michigan frontier. They were quite as capable of plucking out their own eye if it offended them as the English Puritans had been two centuries earlier. They did not, and of course would not have been allowed to, carry it to the length of executions; the world had moved for them as for all others in the course of two hundred years. But they had the stamina to act on their convictions and would have dealt with the principals in *The Scarlet Letter* quite the same way the English colonists did. Their sometimes grim adjudications of the all too human cases of sexual irregularity can hardly help winning a reluctant admiration a century later when life has become more tame. Policy and privilege and favoritism obviously played their part, but the Dutch Puritans clung to discipline as an evidence of their culture.

There was in one instance an Arthur Dimmesdale among them who appears to have been quite as prominent, and in some ways quite as saintly, as the lover of Hester Prynne. On the Dutch frontier a minister, especially a popular minister, was regarded with an awe that in

[1] *Classis Holland: Minutes 1848-1858*, p. 26.

terms of today has in it a touch of the grotesque; ordination was almost literally looked upon as changing the very composition of a man's mortal flesh. Yet, like Hawthorne's character, this minister had "fallen into sin" and had to be dealt with, first by his own congregation, then by the ecclesiastical governing body, Classis Holland.

There the case first makes its appearance in the minutes of the meeting held on October 14, 1851—four years after the founding of the colony. The man's prominence may be gathered from the internal evidence contained in the voluminous documents of the case, and also from the fact that nearly a century after the event the translators of the *Minutes,* "under instructions from the Classis of Holland," considered it necessary to represent his name, and the name of his church, by dashes. In a footnote they explained that "it was at first proposed to omit the article altogether, but that it was finally decided that it was too valuable to be omitted, on account of the light it sheds upon the Christian spirit of all parties." [2]

The first entry reads:

Art. 7. The overseers of the church of ———— communicate the sad news (which was already a general public rumor) that their minister, Rev. ————, has fallen into the sin of adultery. This sin being suspected, it was at first denied by him, but when, after long continued admonition, the woman confessed, it is said that thereupon he also came to the point of confession. Thereupon this was made known to the congregation, and deposition and excommunication were decided on. After public confession he was again received, not as a minister but as a brother; with regard to which circumstance it is now desired to obtain the judgment of Classis. For further explanation it is stated that the reverend gentleman had lived in that sin. Another complaint is also presented, that he had solicited yet another woman, which was looked upon by him as merely a frivolous joke, which was taken by the woman in another sense.

That communication dragged the incident into the full glare of the pitiless publicity of the whole settlement. The documents covering the case are voluminous—official letters written by order of the Classis to the "brother," to the congregation; reports, judgments, comments. But they can be only a small part of the word-yardage, oral and written, that came out of the incident. So far as can be gathered from the documents extant the "Christian spirit of all parties" claimed by the trans-

[2] *Ibid.,* p. 70.

lators appears to have been real. The church authorities displayed the grace of tempering justice with mercy and evidencing a "Christian spirit." Oh, they were not soft or sentimental. "Rev. ——" remained "deposed," apparently for all time, but the excommunication was lifted when he confessed his sin and he was accepted as a "brother." What kind of a job he turned to, or what his later history was, does of course not appear in the records.

In its main lines the incident is creditable to "all parties" from the point of view of human relations, without regard to the ecclesiastical issues involved. The only doubts that obtrude themselves arise in connection with the unction of the language employed in the letters that grew out of the case. There is in them no note of sentimentality, as might be expected—sentimentality is not a Dutch trait—but the sentences ooze "piety," the kind that has to be enclosed in quotation marks. In all fairness it should be added that that kind of phraseology was characteristic of the middle of the nineteenth century—English and American as well as Dutch.

There was never any occasion for "vigilantes" on the Dutch frontier; during their century of life in America the members of the Michigan-Iowa-Wisconsin migration and their descendants have usually been defenders, not disturbers, of order. The feature of frontier life that has furnished most of the drama of American settlements before the coming of the law was wholly wanting among the Holland immigrants. They would not easily qualify as material for movie scenarios; their instinct for law and order was so strong that conditions could hardly be imagined developing among them that would call for the gun play and the hanging parties familiar to frontier fiction. The few writers who have attempted stories of Dutch frontier life have been reduced to exploiting material that the producers of pulp serials would not look at.

Not that crime was absent even in frontier days, and there has been a fair amount of it since, but hardly the type or the amount of crime that lends itself to dramatization. In the early days such "vigilantes" as the community produced were ecclesiastical policemen, and they were identical with the leaders of religion, the ministers and church overseers who saw to it, not that the people obeyed the civil laws—that was hardly necessary—but that they kept walking the narrow line of a religious orthodoxy that meant everything to the leaders. And in the main those guardians of religion had the spontaneous support of the mass of the people. To men and women who found their very recreation in theological dialectics the most venial departure from orthodoxy was a matter of passionate personal interest.

Hence schisms and secessions occupied what from the point of view of today was a disproportionate amount of the time and attention of the ecclesiastical leaders during the early years while they exercised most of the functions of civil leaders as well. During the ten years for which the minutes of the Classis of Holland have been published, Van Raalte and other ministers were constantly plagued by troubles of this kind. At first glance it appears somewhat surprising that a community of persons whom religious persecution had forced out of their homes should so quickly fall out on questions of theological differences. But they came from many sections of the Netherlands and had many different backgrounds. And they took even trifling ecclesiastical matters with a passionate seriousness that would be incomprehensible to many; those were things on which compromise was not possible.

Moreover, their human nature was not adjourned when they came to the Michigan frontier. Bullies remained bullies, saints remained saints; the proud were proud still, and the opinionated continued to worship at the shrine of their own ideas. Some of the leaders who were in the seats of power took delight in exercising their frontier authority; some of those who were "outs" aspired to be "ins." In lieu of the preoccupation with the ordinary small-town civil affairs of the average Americans, the election of a ward alderman or a township highway commissioner, the Hollanders played religious politics with a zest that leaves the reader of their century-old records a little breathless.

Thus so early as 1853, the charge was lodged against a certain minister named Smit: "that he promotes factions, acts arbitrarily, thrusts aside and oppresses the former leaders of the church and promotes to office those who are ignorant. Also, that he has tried to make the church secede, under pretext that we are sold to the Old Dutch Church by Rev. Van Raalte for a good purse of money." [3]

The Smit case runs through many pages. In the end Smit was deposed, one of the curious counts in the article of deposition being that "you, in addition, permit in your congregational meetings the most

[3] *Ibid.*, p. 117.

shameful outbursts of disorderly yelling, under pretense of having to tire them out in such a way." [4] With a solemnity that is impressive even a century later, and that must have seemed doubly so at the time, the "brothers" felt that they were in duty bound, "in the sight of the Triune God, before the flock of the Lord throughout the world, and before our own consciences, to forbid you, in the name of our Lord, the ministry of his word and sacraments." [5]

The church in Michigan, on its part, had qualms about the orthodoxy of the churches on the Iowa frontier. Classis Holland had of course no jurisdiction over the Western communions, but it could at least worry about the purity of religion in Iowa. Van Raalte reported to the Classis his "cause for sorrow, arising chiefly from the total neglect of these fellow countrymen and the lamentable divisions of the Hollanders at Pella, caused by worldly difficulties and the spirit of ecclesiastical anarchy." [6]

Such were some of the major problems that agitated the "brethren" on the Michigan frontier. The number of minor questions of regulation and discipline was legion. To a degree that today would seem fantastic to the descendants of said "brethren," and that must at that time have seemed astonishing to non-Dutch citizens of Michigan who were cognizant of it, the ecclesiastical authorities regulated and ordered the lives of the people in many of their most personal affairs. Such amusements as dancing and card playing were not merely frowned upon, they were prohibited quite as effectually as they had been two centuries earlier in New England. And during the early years on the Michigan frontier a theatre would have had no more chance to obtain a charter than an icicle would have to survive in a blast furnace.

Indeed the interdict on theatricals has not yet entirely lost its force. The larger communities of Dutch descent have their movie palaces, but many of the people in such places, and many others in hamlets and villages, still consider it almost as inconceivable to enter one of them as it would be for them to enter a saloon. The city of Zeeland, with a population of three thousand, has never in its history granted a charter to a theatre or movie house of any kind. "The last proposal to license a

[4] *Ibid.*, p. 135.
[5] *Ibid.*, p. 136.
[6] *Ibid.*, p. 221.

movie house was turned down early in 1945." [7] It doubtless has the distinction of being the only city in America without a movie "palace." In every respect it is a progressive community, its citizens possessed of a culture that compares well with that of other cities of comparable size and age, an unusually large number of them successful in business or in the professions. The traditional hostility toward the theatre developed on the frontier a century ago dies hard. It is only fair to add that the movie "palaces" in neighboring towns, only a few miles away, are liberally patronized by the people of this unique community.

[7] Louis Adamic, *A Nation of Nations*, p. 112.

XIV

Dutch Growth of the Soil

Not to go into too many confusing details, the geography of the Dutch settlement in Michigan was determined by three rivers. The Grand, with the present city of Grand Haven at its mouth and the furniture city of Grand Rapids some twenty miles to the east, may be taken as roughly forming the northern boundary. The Kalamazoo river, with the present resort town of Saugatuck at its mouth and the world's celery capital, Kalamazoo, some forty miles east, makes the southern line. In between these two waterways, Black Lake, now Macatawa Bay, served as a six-mile arm of Lake Michigan, fed by a little river, now hardly more than a brook that meanders through today's pleasant meadows and among corn and wheat and sugar beet fields of a prosperous people whose ancestors cleared the primeval forests along its banks. The settlement therefore is an area that extends for some forty or fifty miles along Lake Michigan's shore, with a depth eastward into the state of another forty or fifty miles.

Approximate distances are dictated by the fact that the geography itself has been in a state of flux. At first the area covered was hardly more than a pin-prick at the head of Macatawa Bay. The Dutch folk spread over much of the territory as the years passed, and spilled over sometimes into areas that lay beyond the imaginary boundaries. But throughout the century many people of non-Dutch stock seeped into the Dutch territory, so that today the population of so typical a city as Holland, the center of the Van Raalte settlement, contains a considerable admixture of non-Dutch stock. All together are Americans, the descendants of the Van Raalte Hollanders indistinguishable from those

137

whose fathers and mothers may have come from New England or Virginia or Mississippi or Ireland or Cornwall.

While the first contingent of Hollanders numbered only fifty or so, besides the leader and his family, the community had a fast growth. The advance guard that arrived in the woods of Michigan in February of 1847 could not erect log shelters quickly enough to accommodate other waves that followed almost immediately. Throughout the next few years whole congregations kept arriving, most of them in orderly phalanxes, each with a minister at its head and carefully organized into a socio-religious group, all the proper officers and overseers at their posts of duty to ensure order and decorum and to fix and enforce health regulations and rules of cleanliness and godliness.

They bought up tracts of land in the area, and straightway proceeded to occupy them in an orderly way, building homes and churches and schools. During the first year the population grew to about 1,700, and in 1848 there were 4,000 inhabitants.[1] Almost invariably the settlers gave to the area they occupied the name of the province or village in the Netherlands from which they came: Holland, Zeeland, Drenthe, Overisel, Vriesland, Graafschap, Noordeloos, Harderwijk. Place names such as those dot the map of the area today.

One of those settlements—Zeeland—deserves more detailed description, for its own sake and because it will serve as a sample of all. The province of Zeeland, in the Netherlands, is made up of an intricate system of islands just above the present Belgian border. The name literally means Sea-land, for the province is almost as much sea as land. It was in that region of complicated waterways that the famous "Sea Beggars," in the time of William the Silent, had their origin and hideaway so they could successfully thumb their noses at the mighty fleet of Spain. It was from Zeeland that the progenitors of the various branches of the American Roosevelt clan emigrated three hundred years ago to make New Netherland on this continent their home; today not a single Roosevelt remains in the province.[2]

Out of this province, in 1847, came the most numerous and the best-organized group to join the frontier adventure of the Van Raalte emigrants. Their emigration was to be an experiment in near-communism

[1] Aleida J. Pieters, *A Dutch Settlement in Michigan*, p. 90.
[2] Hendrik De Leeuw, *Crossroads of the Zuider Zee*, p. 155.

until the voyage should end and they should be established in their individual homesteads. They formed an association for the purpose of pooling funds and resources, the well-to-do providing for the poor and indigent; and most of them were poor. To make the scheme work they drew up what in their language was called the "Zeeuwsche Reglement," a Dutch "Mayflower Compact," which, in idea at least, may have been copied from the Pilgrims. At a convention held in the Netherlands in February, 1847, the month the Van Raalte party arrived on the Michigan frontier, an organization was affected of which any Zeelander of "good Christian character" could become a member, whether he had funds or not; all the money that was needed was one guilder (about forty cents) as a membership fee. The association assumed the responsibility for all necessary arrangements and promised to erect a communal building for cooperative use after the location of the settlement had been selected, as well as individual temporary shelters for the members. Resources were pooled, under the terms of the compact, the funds to be used for necessary public works, which would be decided upon by a majority vote of the members.

The emigrants, coming from many communities, organized themselves into a new congregation with a complete set of ecclesiastical officers, who for the time being were to serve as civil officers as well. They chose as their pastor and spiritual leader the Reverend Cornelius Vander Meulen, and chartered three ships to carry the members of the association, together with their families and gear, to America. The decision on a location was to be left to the leader of the first ship to arrive. When the first of the three reached New York there was a spirited contest between Van Raalte and Scholte for these highly desirable recruits. The former finally won, and the group, on his advice, settled on a tract of land some five miles to the east of his own community. They arrived in midsummer of 1847, and promptly called their settlement "Zeeland." There were 425 persons in the fully organized mass migration; others of course followed, and individuals have continued to arrive for a century, as has been true for many of the other communities in the settlement as a whole.

Allowing for differences in detail, the story of all the Dutch settlements in what came to be known as the "Dutch coast" in Michigan was very much the same. In most of them the people had pooled their funds and their matériel to transport their families and their gear, their lares and penates, to the distant shores of America. Theirs was the first mass migration of its kind since the Pilgrims landed on Plymouth Rock, and their methods, their motivations, their attitudes so closely resembled those of the seventeenth century New England colonists that the name "Dutch Puritans" is hardly a figure of speech.

And the Dutch frontier grew in numbers and area, and presently its metamorphosis into an American community began. The vast majority of the emigrants were emigrants in spirit as well as physically. They tore themselves up from their home roots for keeps. They sailed for America to become Americans. Certainly none of their responsible leaders entertained any illusions on that score; from the beginning they advised their people to look forward to American citizenship. The law required two and a half years' residence before preliminary papers could be taken out. At the expiration of that period of probation those future citizens invited the county clerk to come to them instead of their journeying to the county seat—a display of good horse sense, to save on transportation. In this wholesale naturalization the clerk made out citizenship papers for 440 persons in one day. Because this was a bonanza for him, and doubtless also because the new voters were worth cultivating, the clerk cut his fee in half, and still went home at night with $70 in his pocket.[3]

When the Civil War broke on the country only a little more than a dozen years after the Hollanders' arrival they had developed into good enough citizens so that they sent more than four hundred of their men to the front.[4] The issue of slavery was one they could understand, and their passion for freedom was ancestral, centuries old. It is odd to think of their reading Lincoln's inaugural address in Dutch, as many of them of necessity did, and later the Emancipation Proclamation and the Gettysburg Address; but that did not prevent them from fighting for the Union, some of them dying for it.

The early Hollanders on the Michigan frontier were like Isak in Growth of the Soil. In the beginning they had only axes with which to build houses. They had no horses or oxen, no sleighs and wagons. Bit by bit, item by item, their soil grew—an ox acquired at astonishing

[3] Aleida J. Pieters, op. cit., p. 158.
[4] Ibid., p. 96.

sacrifice from a settlement twenty miles away; or perhaps two or three hens to start a flock, or a sow with her litter to become the pig parents of the community, or a calf to be nursed almost as a member of the family.

The story of all this is not unfamiliar; it is common to the history of any pioneer community that starts from scratch, and only the imagination of a great novelist has succeeded in telling it as it should be told. There was this difference between Knut Hamsun's folk in the Norwegian wilds and these pioneers on the Michigan frontier, that here thousands of Isaks and Ingers were matching the adventures of those two in their "growth of the soil." There was public rejoicing when a primitive sawmill was added to the community's equipment, liberating the people from the toil of cutting planks by hand. Well they might celebrate. The coming to a community of a circular saw driven by steam may be as great an event as laying of the cornerstone of a skyscraper.

And coming as they did from a land of canals and inland lakes, it was natural that the Dutch frontiersmen should early turn their thoughts to a lake vessel. It was a sailboat they called the *Knicker-bocker,* and it was used to get supplies from Chicago for a cooperative store the people were trying to operate. But the store failed, and the vessel had to be sold.

Other enterprises were attempted: an "ashery," to utilize for soap and lye the ashes of the trees ruthlessly burned to clear the land; a windmill to furnish power for flour grinding, but it failed because Michigan wind lacked the constancy of the breezes from the North Sea over the flatlands of Holland; a stage service, a mail service, and later a railroad; a survey of their harbor through the efforts of Van Raalte; a brickyard to utilize local clay for building material. Industries, enterprises, most of them dictated by the needs of the community, and such as would have developed no matter what the nationality of those who occupied the land. Some were successes, others failures; all were a part of the growth of their soil.

As the years passed they adapted themselves to their American environment, sometimes with astonishing success. Thus the comparatively modern innovation of celery on the dinner table of the world is commonly associated with the Dutch farmer. Properly so, because without his molelike industry it is doubtful if celery would have become a must in American diet. But the Hollander did not discover celery, he adapted it. The original idea belongs to a Scotchman named James Taylor. Taylor imported some celery seed from England—dried celery leaves had, in a limited way, been used in soups in Europe for a long time; Taylor seems to have hit on the notion that the stalks themselves could be developed into an edible vegetable. The celery he grew in his backyard in Kalamazoo was included as an item on a local banquet menu, but the guests did not take to the novelty. This was in 1856, and for a decade celery was forgotten.

Then a Kalamazoo Hollander named Marinus De Bruin took it upon himself to become its grower and promoter. He calculated shrewdly that the muck he owned might be made to pay dividends if such a vegetable could be popularized. Not only did he develop the best celery produced up until that time, he tied it up into neat bundles and sent his children to sell them from door to door. The initial sales resistance came from a fear that the celery was a poisonous weed, because it slightly resembled the hemlock plant. But Marinus De Bruin persisted, and presently other Dutch owners of worthless swamp lands saw their opportunity.[5]

Since about the close of the Civil War celery culture has become big business, annually adding millions of dollars to the national wealth. It has spread from Michigan to all sections of the country where nature had through millions of years deposited the rich black sediments known as muck. Many of those water-bogged swamps had long been a nuisance and sometimes a terror to settlers. The root-infested bogs were usually considered fit only for a scanty pasturage for cattle, and not very fit for that, because in wet weather the cows were likely to get fouled in mud up to their bellies. When other Michigan farm land was worth from $50 to $100 an acre the muck bogs were scarcely worth holding for the taxes. Drained, and cleared of roots and developed into celery farms, they later brought all the way from a thousand dollars an acre and up. If the Emersonian dictum is correct that he is a benefactor to man who makes two blades of grass grow where only one grew before, then the Dutch celery farmer is a benefactor indeed; he turned land that was a nuisance, or at best worthless, into a wealth-

[5] *Michigan:* Michigan Writers' Project, pp. 322-23.

producing garden, and he added an important article of food to the dinner table of the world.

But not without a struggle that was physically back-breaking and that called for psychological stamina. Ditching a mosquito-infested swamp in the heat of July was bad enough; clearing out of the drained soil what seemed like millions of hydra-like roots, the accumulation of centuries, was worse. Worst of all was the growing illusion that the roots annually reproduced themselves, for after clearing the soil during ten successive years, the farmer always found additional stubborn roots that broke his plowpoints, or sometimes his horse's leg. It was never easy to believe that some time the last root would be cleared out.

And all the time he had to stand up to the amused skepticism of his American neighbors; and worse yet, of grain- or corn-growing Hollanders. To try to make anything out of that swamp! It was a laugh! Grubbing on hands and knees in the black ooze; who but a fool would think of such a thing? And later, when a few square yards had actually been cleared for a crop, to crawl antlike over the ground setting each individual plant with his fingers, pressing down the muck around it—a man must be balmy to do such a thing. Later—years later—many of those same fools might overtake the skeptics walking along the country highway, threadbare and unable to afford even a horse—overtake them in an eight-cylinder Buick and give them a lift to town. But that fact did not help them in the early days when they had only faith and shrewd Dutch common sense to keep them going.

Celery has been grown by all kinds of nationals in many of the states. But the citizens of Dutch descent have continued to hold the lead in this industry. In time the Iowa district became almost as famous as the Kalamazoo area for celery growing, and wherever Dutch farmers have settled, if they found swamp land, they have promptly converted it into money-making celery farms.

But Dutch "growth of the soil" was not agricultural alone. In the course of the years the Hollanders built cities and took their place in the commercial and industrial life of America. Or they developed skills of craftsmanship that gave them a kind of guild standing. Thus, to take a single example, they compose a high percentage of the furniture craftsmen who have made the city of Grand Rapids almost the best-known furniture center in America. Something of the skill that lodged in the fingertips of their distant ancestors in Holland's Golden Age appears still to find expression in various ways.

Within five years after the first tree was cut down the little hamlet of Holland had seven stores, two hotels, a bakery, a tin shop, a jeweler's shop, a tailor's shop, and various other business establishments that provided for the needs of the people of the village and the farmers. Not that there was anything phenomenal about that, or anything unique. It is likely that as good a record, or in many cases a better one, could be shown for not a few American frontier settlements; mushroom growths have always been common as civilization marched across the continent. Such uniqueness as there was in the growth of the Dutch frontier in Michigan lay in the people's audacity in trying to induce a kind of hothouse cultural growth to parallel the physical growth of their soil. They built a log church before many of them had roofs over their heads. Within half a dozen years they erected, at enormous cost in proportion to their needs, a new church that is still doing service after nearly a century and the beauty of whose architecture still makes it a subject for picture postcards.

In erecting their churches the Hollanders displayed on a smaller scale something of the devotion of the medieval cathedral builders; through it they expressed the culture that chiefly characterized them. In one community—not in Michigan, but that is irrelevant; it might have been there—the Hollanders decided to erect a church. As was often the case, they only barely had roofs over their own heads, and they certainly were not embarrassed with excess funds. Although the congregation consisted of only five women and three men, a church was built with a seating capacity of six hundred! It was constructed entirely of black walnut, the exterior covered with shingles of walnut painted white.[6]

Such fantastic audacity was matched by many schemes and plans on the Michigan frontier that often had something splendid in their basic structure even when they ended in futility. Practical though they were in most things, the Hollanders were not incapable of near-apocalyptic visions. They sometimes dreamed dreams that were never realized, but that fact did not shake them in their conviction that it is good to dream even if only for the sake of dreaming. Practical though they have

[6] The Rev. Jacob Vander Meulen, *Hollanders,* p. 11.

always been, they have also been infected with a certain transcendentalism that might have appealed to Emerson and Thoreau. Usually religion was the motivating force for the exercise of this trait, and sometimes the sublime was not far removed from the ridiculous.

Some of them, when the frontier was still young and raw, conceived the audacious notion of building and maintaining a missionary ship. The idea itself they had brought with them from the Netherlands, where they had been too poor to translate it into tangible form. But seventeen years later, although still poor, they felt rich enough to build such a vessel. It was to be used to carry their type of religious faith all over the globe, transporting missionaries and their families and mission supplies to China and Japan and India and Arabia, always keeping Black Lake as the home base and returning to it after each sortie into the strongholds of the devil. Before the keel was laid they enthusiastically worked out on paper what the first route would be, and then they laid about them with a will to make their dream come true.

But as the event turned out, only in rhetoric. Normally Hollanders are even more eager to make speeches and listen to them than the average American type. The missionary ship idea was too golden an opportunity for speechifying to be overlooked. Someone—it may have been Van Raalte—thought of the phrase, "The Laying of the Keel,"—like the title of a poem. On June 24, 1864, the solemnly impressive ceremonies were held on the shore of Black Lake, in the little village of Holland, that were to initiate a global enterprise, an enterprise that was intended to be perpetuated throughout the centuries; for the people had no doubt that their ship would develop in time into a fleet, and that the fleet would in turn grow into a missionary navy which would evangelize the world—converting it of course to the faith of the Reformed Church.

The printed program of "The Laying of the Keel" has been preserved. There was in it almost a touch of the fantastic, worthy though the ideal was that inspired it. The program began at three o'clock in the afternoon and it must have lasted until the stars came out, for there were nineteen separate and distinct numbers! Since Hollanders are seldom brief even in public prayer, the ecstasy of many in that audience, and the sufferings of a possible few, may be imagined.

Dr. Van Raalte (he had by this time become a D.D.) pronounced the invocation, and none of the accompaniments of Scripture reading and psalm singing were omitted. There were two main addresses, one by a secretary of the board of foreign missions and the other by a missionary to China. Those speeches were in English, and in each case the words had to be translated for the benefit of many in the audience. Between the two addresses the people revived themselves with a missionary hymn by the children, and after the second address and its translation all sang lustily "From Greenland's Icy Mountains."

But that was only a starter, a kind of hors d'oeuvre, as it were. After a lengthy prayer by one of the leaders, there were addresses by at least two representatives of the Classis of Holland; "and others," the extant program informed the audience and posterity—how many others does not appear, but the number would quite certainly not be few, nor their addresses brief, if experience of such things is a safe guide.

That worked off, a breathing spell was called, with psalm singing to prevent what today would be called "dead air" on the program. Then, when the people had been fortified by song, the speaking began again. This time two more speakers, from the Classis of Holland, are mentioned by name, followed by the notation "and others." Those who had not yet been reduced to numb immobility could then enjoy a missionary ode by the Academy Choir. And then at long last the ceremony of the laying of the keel—an actual keel of an intended vessel, laid down in an actual lake—was held that was the tangible excuse for all the rhetoric and all the eloquence. This ended, there remained only hymns and a benediction, and the people were free to go home to milk the cows and feed the hens and hogs.

The contrast between the sublime and—well, its opposite, was pointed up by the fact that that keel so eloquently laid never became more than just—a keel. The community's idealism had outrun its common sense. After their spree of speeches and songs and prayers they lost interest, the preoccupations of practical living crowding out the dream. Year after year the keel lay clamped by cables to the shore, a reminder of an ecstasy remembered in tranquility, which as everybody knows is the beginning of poetry. Finally it rotted and passed from the ken of the people.

But it is fair to add that the Hollanders continued to be a missionary-producing and missionary-maintaining race. Throughout the nineteenth century, and the twentieth, men and women of Dutch stock have served as missionaries in many lands. A few of them—Dr. Samuel M. Zwemer as an example—won international reputations in statesmanship, geographical research, anthropological discovery, philological investigations, and authorship of books that were additions to scholarship.

And so the Dutch "growth of the soil" proceeded, a growth in geographical area, in population, in equipment, and in American knowhow buttressed by ancient racial skills. Clusters of individual farms grew into organized rural communities, hamlets and villages became cities, Hollanders turned imperceptibly into Americans while retaining their basic racial traits. The community had learned to stand firmly on its own feet and instead of asking help from others was extending it. It had sent its young men to the battlefields of the Civil War, and it was dreaming of sending other young men and women to what in the community was always quaintly referred to as the "foreign field." The Dutch Sellanraa had ceased to be a frontier in the true sense by the end of the Civil War.

Newcomers were still arriving from the Netherlands in large numbers, however, and were to continue to come until well on into the twentieth century, but they were no longer arriving in organized groups. The period of mass migration was at an end, and only individual families came from Holland. Those people, as well as some of the earlier arrivals who had clung to the mores of their youth, perpetuated the Dutch language on the Dutch frontier, making its use a necessity in many churches, and they were the reason for the prosperity of the Holland-language newspapers that competed successfully for many years with the English-language papers. In many ways the community was settled and prosperous, the pattern fixed for a consistent development that would parallel the growth of other frontiers of different racial strains. At the close of the Civil War the "Dutch coast" was an established community.

Then disaster struck with a suddenness that was bewildering. To this day the Great Fire of 1871 is always referred to in upper case letters. It was to the Michigan Dutch people what the San Francisco earthquake was to the inhabitants of that city, what the Chicago fire at about the same time as the Holland disaster, was to Chicago. Those other calamities have been dramatized much more competently and they have found their places in American fiction and drama. To the general public the Dutch settlement in Michigan was only a minor detail in the story of America's frontier, and its Great Fire could hardly hope to win a place in public consciousness. But to the Hollanders of that day, and to their descendants, the Great Fire of 1871 deserves its capital letters. To them it seems much bigger than those other disasters, and the anniversary of the holocaust is seldom allowed to pass without reminiscent descriptions in the newspapers, even now that many of those papers are owned and edited not by Hollanders but by men of Anglican American stock.

The fire broke out in the city of Holland in October of 1871, after a summer of heat and drought that had converted the western Michigan forests into firetraps. Considerably more than half of the city was completely wiped out, and many people lost all they had slaved for during nearly a quarter of a century of back-breaking pioneer life. Fire-fighting equipment was necessarily primitive, and a system of insurance had not yet been established. There was a finality and a completeness about the devastation that could hardly find a parallel anywhere today.

But after they had recovered from their stunned despair, the people set about the work of rehabilitation with an energy that was in part dictated by necessity. They had to have roofs over their heads and they had to erect temporary shelters where the necessaries could be bought and sold. They displayed no greater courage than did the people in other disaster-ridden communities—in Chicago or San Francisco, or in many places the world over hit more recently by the bombs of global war. But neither did they show less courage or enterprise. They had come to America to stay and grow up with the country; disaster could not drive them out. Temporarily they accepted help from other communities, among other donations $2,500 from the Iowa Hollanders, but for the most part they did not depend on charity. Practicing their gospel of self-reliance, they rebuilt their city largely through their own exertions and with their own funds.

The Great Fire was the end of an era for them. The community had come of age.

XV

Life on the Iowa Frontier

THOUGH THEY WERE of one blood, and came from the same small land
in Europe, the Hollanders of Michigan and those of Iowa showed distinct marks of dissimilarity. This may have been due in part to the
difference in frontier backgrounds. If the North Wind made the Vik-
ings, the forests and swamps of Michigan conditioned the Van Raalte
pioneers, just as the rich soil of the prairies determined to some extent
what the frontiersmen of Iowa would be like. One group was not
more heroic than the other, the two developed different temperaments
and different ways of life.

All things considered, the Iowa Hollanders were more secular than
the Michigan Dutch. Scholte, their leader, himself gives color to this
judgment. He wrote a pamphlet during the early months on the
prairies of Iowa, *Eene Stem uit Pella,* that was published in Amsterdam
in March, 1848, in which he expresses the opinion that "nearly all
appear to be taken up with their new social and worldly condition—so
much so that they are lost in it."

The Hollanders of Michigan had immediately become a cog in the
machine of the Reformed Church; Scholte resisted affiliation with that
national ecclesiastical body, and to the day of his death he remained
an independent. Not a few of the Iowa Hollanders tried to force him
to affiliate the community with what they thought of as a parent
church, but they did not succeed. Congregations in many communities
later joined in spite of him, not through his leadership. The uneasy
doubts of Van Raalte and other Michigan leaders as to the orthodoxy
of the Iowa churches were due to their ecclesiastical independence.

Some of Scholte's followers, after his death, expressed the conviction that his attitude of independence had been a mistake, because it had split the community on the Iowa frontier into two religious factions.[1] Quite certainly it was a mistake as a matter of policy; whether it was in terms of the man's own soul is another question that only he could answer.

Immediately on his arrival in America he was courted by the Reformed Church leaders and formally invited to affiliate his community with that denomination. But he had suffered at the hands of organization in Holland, and he appears to have been temperamentally an independent. Was there, perhaps, also a touch of personal arrogance in his decision? He was a man of strong will and he did not suffer gladly regulation by others. Yielding to the will of authority was distasteful to him; at any rate, to the end of his life he maintained his independent ecclesiastical status. His own rationalization of the attitude was: "Boldly and cheerfully do I profess that God's Word is my only regulation in the affairs of God's church on earth."[2] His independence had shown itself in Holland some years before emigration had been decided upon; friction had arisen between him and his fellow Separatists on questions of doctrine so that he had been forbidden to preach the gospel under the auspices of the organization.

His immigrants in Iowa formed a religious society of their own, under Iowa law, that took the name of "The Christian Church of Pella," claiming in their constitution that their church was "founded upon the one, entire and indivisible Word of God as revealed in the Scriptures of the Old and New Testaments." The language is almost certainly Scholte's. He associated freely with adherents of various church denominations, and when the Baptists founded a college in Pella he promptly consented to serve on the board of directors.

Some of his people were confused by this attitude of independence, others were antagonized by it. The human mind normally loves authority and does not rest at ease without it. Perhaps Scholte aspired to be the authority himself that is usually represented by a denominational governing body. The trouble was that, great though his eloquence and intellect, strong though his will ("convictions" must have

---

[1] Leonora Scholte, *A Stranger in a Strange Land,* p. 53.
[2] Jacob Vander Zee, *The Hollanders of Iowa,* p. 294.

been the word he employed), he was after all a man of flesh and blood, not a mystical idea such as an organization invariably becomes. It is hard for ordinary people permanently to maintain an ecstatic faith in a man who wears pants. In any event, he had to admit sadly: "To be frank in what I say, I must admit that religion does not flourish, because there is no evidence in daily life that seeking God's kingdom and righteousness assumes a foremost place, but rather the things of this world." [3]

Many of his countrymen in Michigan had similar doubts about the spiritual life in Iowa, as shown by the discussions reported in the *Minutes of Classis Holland*. In addition to the fact that some Iowa churches found a place in the fold of the Reformed Church, by which act they repudiated the ecclesiastical if not the civil leadership of Scholte, not a few members of his own independent communion finally rose in a kind of revolt. So early as 1851 there was a split, with a later reunion. The details involved ownership and the sale of land for secular purposes that had been set aside for the church. There was a secession, some members cleaving to their leader, many others refusing to follow him.

He promptly built a new church, in which his eloquence—there is no slightest doubt about the power of his oratory—continued to move the people to ecstasy or to tears, in sermons that often were three hours long but that seemed brief to his listeners, because to them they were a substitute for drama and poetry. The wife of one of his descendants, years later, testified: "Sectarian lines meant nothing to him, for a child of God was his brother as long as he believed in the orthodox faith of Christ and his life." [4] Some of his people evidently were not convinced that he alone should be the judge as to the meaning of "orthodox faith." The same writer came to the conclusion: "Some, however, remained faithful to him. We, who came after him, think he made a mistake, for when he died his congregation was divided. His was a one man movement which seldom if ever lasts. When the leader dies, the followers are scattered." [5]

Scholte's uneasiness about the growing secularization of his people

[3] *Eene Stem uit Pella.*
[4] Leonora Scholte, *op. cit.*, p. 53.
[5] *Ibid.*, p. 53.

was shared by many; some in fact, among them some Hollanders in Michigan, were much more uneasy than he was. There were those who did not hesitate to attribute it to his attitude, a judgment that he could not reasonably be expected to share, when twice each Sunday, and sometimes during the week as well, he whipped himself into the fervors of two- or three-hour sermons, or when he prayed so ecstatically with repentant sinners that his own wife—who was considered a "worldly woman" by the folk—confessed that it brought the tears to her eyes. A preacher who can make his own wife weep must of necessity believe in his own divine mission.[6]

The secularization on the Iowa frontier hardly admits of the easy explanation that some who were hostile to Scholte gave it. There is reason to believe that the general tone of the Iowa group was from the beginning different from that of the Michigan pioneers, that in fact the choice of Iowa was to some extent conditioned on their desire for "success" in the American sense. Quick returns were to be had in a prairie land that could not be expected in hardwood forests. To a far greater extent than the Hollanders of Michigan the Iowa immigrants saw their migration as an investment in material prosperity. They were perhaps less illusioned than their fellow migrants; they saw the adventure more in terms of farms and towns, less in terms of philosophical ecclesiastical verities.

They came for the most part, nearly all of the more than eight hundred who made up the original Scholte migration, from the Utrecht district in Holland. The society of Utrecht Separatists, whipped into ecstasy by Scholte's preaching, at one time numbered 1,300 members, of whom more than eight hundred actually went to America, in four sailing vessels. They were not, generally speaking, poor; there was a good deal of prosperity among them, in many cases not a little wealth. Scholte himself was well off; his personal revolt was philosophic rather than economic. In the Michigan congregations wealth was a rare exception, even reasonable prosperity was not common; in Iowa, although wealth was rare, prosperity was quite the rule.

Some of the people carried furniture and plate and household goods from Holland to the prairies that must have seemed incongruous there in the early days. They did not carry provisions on their backs to the frontier, they traveled from Keokuk to the site of the future Pella as a kind of cavalcade. Each family bought its own conveyance for the five-day trek into the prairies. There were those who piled their goods on a horse-drawn cart. Some depended on ox teams. There were even some who acquired two horses and a wagon. In addition to buying conveyances for their gear, some hired carriages for their families; among them Scholte himself, and in his case the carriage was a coach for his family of five and a maid. When one man bought a wheelbarrow to transport his belongings he was singled out for commendation as one who was really roughing it. Think of the early Michigan pioneers having so much as a wheelbarrow to trundle; they were more often Isaks carrying their gear on their backs. On the Iowa ox- and horse-drawn wagons there were often "large beautiful chests" in which the pioneers carried their precious belongings. Scholte had moreover provided a wagon, drawn by an ox-team, for the transportation of the community strongbox, an iron chest that held all the guilders of all the pioneers. It was guarded day and night by two armed men.

No, the folk on the Iowa frontier were not paupers, and from the beginning they were without the mental attitude of paupers. They were men and women who were confident they could make their migration pay.

Scholte himself came out of a background of wealth, and so did his wife, who as a girl had spent two years in an exclusive school for girls in Paris, where her father had been professor of astronomy. She had taken courses in painting, she had given a piano recital at the Grand Opera House in Paris. Some years later, after she had married the eloquent Separatist clergyman and had followed him to America, she had a considerable social success in the hotels in Albany, New York, and Baltimore while her husband was busy with his colony.

Mareah Scholte was distinctly not a pioneer woman, and she never developed into one. In her frontier home she was devoted to the latest fashions, imported her gowns, was among the first to adopt the hoopskirt when it came into fashion, gave herself up to music with a passion of devotion that must have been disconcerting to the practical-minded people of the community. Her husband had promised her a house in Pella that would be as nearly as possible a replica of her beautiful home in Holland. When at first there was only a crude hut to come to she cried her eyes out for weeks at a time. The doting husband made it his business to redeem his promise within a year after the arrival, even installing a fine piano in what, in her European way, his wife called the drawing room. Mareah had brought many chests of precious Delft dishes—all of which, with four exceptions, were found broken when they were unpacked. In the end the couple paved a garden path with the fragments, to remind them of Holland. Many of the other possessions had also been damaged, but not so irretrievably. In time the Scholtes furnished the new home so that it became a show place of the community, and Scholte laid out a formal English garden that became famous throughout that part of the state. This leader of the people was not poor, and the people themselves were far from being paupers.

The people of necessity had to live primitively for a while, although from the very first they had the benefit of a frontier sawmill that a native resident had installed a few miles distant from the spot where the Hollanders settled. As they had some funds, they were not reduced to the stark primitivism that their fellow countrymen suffered in Michigan, but could begin erecting reasonably civilized homes as soon as they could set about hauling the lumber. But this advantage was more than offset by the scarcity of timber. Well might they envy the Michigan pioneers the oaks and beech and maple and hemlock and pine that were ruthlessly burned to get rid of them as a nuisance.

Many of the Iowa Hollanders, therefore, even though they had money in their pockets, could not get a house of boards over their heads. So they did what many prairie pioneers had done before them; they dug a semi-basement in the firm Iowa soil, then built up walls of tough prairie sod as high as necessary, covered the walls with a roof that was reasonably watertight, and moved in such furniture as they had brought. Crude and primitive though they were, the sod houses served for a hardy and adaptable people. "Straw Town" the community of sod houses was called. For some people such homes had to serve for a year or two.

The Hollanders on the Iowa frontier were by training and inclination distinctly agricultural. Most of them had been fairly well-to-do farmers in Holland; others adapted themselves quickly to that way of life, because it was there that money could be made, and they were for the most part hard-headed, practical people. Scholte recognized this fact when he observed that "the Hollanders who were coming to North America were more prosaic than poetic, and consequently they thought not so much of pleasing their eyes and ears as of buying soil suitable for farms, the easier to cultivate the better." [7]

They plowed up the prairie as soon as they arrived, some of them before they had a roof over their heads, so eager were they to get on with the job of raising a money-producing crop. Perhaps their pedestrian imaginations were not up to visualizing what their fellow migrants in Michigan had to contend with—clearing away trees, grubbing out roots, draining swamps before they could so much as seed a small field of wheat or plant a patch of potatoes. If they could imagine it they must have marveled at the obtuseness of those countrymen for failing to select Iowa, where a simple turning of the sod gave the farmer a soil of unrivaled fertility ready for seed. More probably, human nature being what it is, they envied the Michigan frontier its inexhaustible supply of lumber.

But meanwhile they sowed their crops, turned cattle into the lush grass of the untouched prairie, and laid the foundations for modest fortunes in wheat or corn or in dairy products. Iowa cheese soon found a place for itself in the St. Louis market, because some of the Hollanders in the Pella area had been skilled cheese makers in the Netherlands and they exploited skills that had been in their families for many generations. Cattle raising was an inevitable development, given the prairie grass of the great meadow that was Iowa. And the Hollanders were adaptable enough, and shrewd enough, to become hog raisers as well. That was a skill they had not brought with them from Europe, because in a relatively cornless land the hog had not found an important place, certainly not on the grand scale it had been developed here. Like all people in the corn belt the Dutch farmer quickly learned to solve the equation: corn plus hog equals pork and ham and bacon and lard, which in turn mean cash in the bank.

In the early years the Hollanders on the Iowa frontier had a luck that the more pious among them attributed to the special care of a Providence watching over them as a reward for their serving the Lord.

[7] *Eene Stem uit Pella.*

The first winter was so mild that they came to the conclusion the reports of American cold had been greatly over-exaggerated. Inadequately provided as they were with frame or sod houses, this piece of luck was more than twice welcome. And in 1849, just after they had harvested their first lush crops but had little or no market for them without near-ruinous transportation costs, the market came to their very doors and gave them a harvest of unfamiliar American dollars that must have made them a little dizzy with the excitement of the unexpected bonanza. Again the pious gave proper credit to Providence, and of course to their own virtue in making themselves worthy of Heaven's special favor. But all took advantage of the opportunity; they would hardly have been Hollanders if they had failed to do so.

Gold had been discovered in California, and Pella was in the direct line of march of the treasure hunters. They came by the Dutch farmers' doors in flocks and droves, and they desperately needed all the stuff the Hollanders had to sell. Moreover, they were in a reckless mood of being willing to pay almost any price asked, without quibbling over nickels and dimes. In fact, the Dutch farmers had as yet hardly learned the value of the American coins. But they all knew what a silver dollar was worth. So they adopted a form of "dollar diplomacy" that must have astonished such gold seekers as had the time to think about it at all. Did a covered wagon need a bushel of wheat? O.K., or rather it Dutch vernacular equivalent of that time, that would be a dollar. Did another want to buy a bushel of oats for his horses? Again O.K., that would be a dollar. Or a bushel of potatoes, or a ham, or a chicken, or a cheese, or a pot of butter? Anything and everything cost a dollar—no more, no less. No making of change for the frontier salesman. They gathered in their harvest of silver dollars, and when the cavalcade had passed on, or all the farm stuff had been bought up, the primitive strong boxes were bursting with dollars that would presently become the basis of the community's banking system.

There appears to have been less mysticism on the Iowa frontier than among the Michigan Hollanders. There was less isolation, and as a result there was little more theocratic government than on any American frontier, whose governmental institutions of necessity can't quite keep pace with the life of the people. Ruling over a divided church, and one that was on its own and did not share in such sanctions as grow out of affiliation with a historic parent body, Scholte could hardly have hoped to establish a theocracy, even if he had desired to do so. There is a relative absence on the Iowa frontier of those exemplifications of church discipline that give the flavor of drama to ecclesiastical life in Michigan.

Doubtless the Iowa folk were as human as the Hollanders of Michigan, but it is difficult to associate a *Scarlet Letter* with that frontier; or some of the sexual purple patches that turn what would normally be a dull set of printed minutes of long-forgotten meetings into a book almost as exciting as a twentieth century realistic novel. There probably were comparable sets of ecclesiastical documents on the Iowa frontier. If they were published, it is doubtful if they would be worth reading today. There was a flavor of "God intoxication" among the Michigan pioneers that was lacking in Iowa. After the lapse of a century it is hard to avoid the conclusion that life must have been more exhilarating in the forests of Michigan, more profitable on the prairies of Iowa. It is not easy to imagine a comparison between the Iowa Hollanders and the Puritans of New England. In large measure they avoided the more unpleasant aspects of a theocratic organization of society, but in doing so they must have missed some of the ecstasies that go with such a system. The Puritans must have had a good time while they were hanging witches to the glory of God, and in the milder days of two centuries later such theocratic disciplines as the Hollanders of Michigan applied to the people, also of course sincerely to the glory of God, must have been stuff for an ecstasy that mere getting and spending can never know. Not that the Iowa Hollanders were without their idealisms, and certainly they were adept in the phraseology of piety, but there is a relativity in such things, and on the whole the Iowa folks' tone was inclined to be more secular than that of the Michigan Dutch.

Such an incident as the program for "The Laying of the Keel" is not easy to imagine on the Iowa frontier, not because there was no water there in which to lay a keel but because there was a lack of the transcendentalism that inspired the Michigan episode. Moreover, such things can be truly successful only in isolation. When there is a mixture of races, with its inevitable uncertainty of the patterns of living, a crystallization of community opinion is too difficult to achieve. For in such a community an unconscious censorship is constantly being exercised, the eccentric portion of the population always under observation and subjected to community criticism and evaluation. And while a people of strong convictions may be stiffened in their point of view and follow their own line in very defiance of opinion, they don't remain unaffected by it. If the Massachusetts Puritans had not lived in an isolation that was so complete as to be unattainable anywhere today, they could not have established their theocracy, at least not without a self-consciousness that in itself would have modified it. If the Michigan Hollanders had not lived in such isolation as was only possible in the middle of the nineteenth century, their social patterns too would have been different.

Now the Iowa Hollanders did not live in that type of isolation. Separated they were in a frontier economy, but almost from the start the people of the Pella area were composed of Hollanders and native Americans both. By 1860 so many of the latter had chosen to cast their lot with the community that the population of the city was fairly evenly divided between Hollanders and Americans. The American element would inevitably exert a strong influence on the total public opinion of the community, and a sense of folk humor would make itself felt. For the ways of an alien element in a population always look queer to those who are normally at one with the ways of life of the nation as a whole. A mere burst of laughter, even if kindly, at such a manifestation of otherness as "The Laying of the Keel" would have affected that ceremony and many others like it. On the Iowa frontier, it is reasonable to assume that the non-Dutch infiltration of the population served to modify the racial peculiarities of the institutions and habits of the people.

It is wholly inaccurate to assert that the people of the Iowa frontier were lacking in idealism, but it was an idealism that was markedly different from the type found in Michigan.

Their idealism was exemplified, for instance, in the people's early eagerness for American citizenship. Within one month after their arrival they invited the clerk of the district court to administer to them a kind of preliminary mass oath of allegiance. Two hundred men of voting age took part in the ceremony, making their responses in Dutch when they renounced their allegiance to the King of Holland. In Scholte's words: "we declared our intention to become citizens of the United States of North America, so that our status as subjects of William II came to an end once for all." The state legislature, at its next session, passed a special statute giving the Hollanders the right to vote in local elections and to run for township offices. There can have been few parallel cases in American politics of immigrants being given the right to vote and hold office before they had become full-fledged citizens of the United States.[8]

Dutch idealism in Iowa was further proved by the people's response to the Civil War. Only a little more than a dozen years had passed since those people had been subjects of an Old World king. Like the Michigan Hollanders, who flocked to the colors before some of them could read the call to arms in the language of their adopted country, the young men on the Iowa frontier responded with an enthusiasm that was certainly as spontaneous as that of the general American population. They were American citizens now, those frontier Hollanders, but it would have been reasonable to expect that they would be confused by the unfamiliar political issues that led up to the war. Although some of the enthusiasm of the young men may have been due to the compelling eloquence of their leader Scholte, who had attended the Republican national convention in Chicago as a delegate and had cast his vote for Lincoln, it was doubtless as spontaneous as such emotions ever are when masses of people are subjected to the impact of patriotic enthusiasm. Sixty-three volunteered from Pella alone, and some thirty Hollanders from other Iowa communities responded to the call. A number of them died in battle.

Scholte, the leader of the people, himself responded to the national idealism that motivated Lincoln. Starting as a Democrat he swung over to the new Republican party long before the campaign of 1860, suffering abuse on the charge of being a political turncoat, an abuse that he accepted and defied with his usual strong-willed self-assertion. Sent to the convention pledged to Seward, he voted for the New York candidate on the first ballot, then swung to Lincoln and advised the other members of the delegation to do likewise. Lincoln was politician enough to note and to remember the support of this Hollander

[8] Jacob Vander Zee, *op. cit.*, pp. 211-12

from Iowa; when Scholte went to hear the nominee's speech of acceptance Lincoln called him his "Dutch friend" and invited him—and of course many others—to come to the inauguration, if the Republicans should win. The "Dutch friend" went to Washington the following March. Some time later Lincoln asked Scholte if he would accept appointment as Minister to Austria, but before the appointment could be formally presented to the Senate the law was changed, making it necessary for Ministers to foreign courts to be American-born.

Before Scholte died in 1868 there was one little incident in which his idealism and that of his people met on common ground with their practicality and common sense. The King of Holland, not the ruling monarch of 1847 but a successor, sent a message to the leader on the Iowa frontier acknowledging that the government had done the emigrating congregations a great wrong. The message was sent through a learned Netherland preacher who was paying a visit to America. The King, after rather humbly acknowledging that "you and your colony were maltreated in your native land by my predecessors," just as humbly invited the emigrants to return to their European home.

The invitation was not met with contempt such as might have been justified. Time heals many wounds, and the people who in 1847 had refused to perpetuate the name of the Dutch royal family in their American home had lost their bitterness. Both Scholte and many of his people felt rather flattered by the royal attention and were confirmed in the Dutch idealism of their race. But they had also developed a new American idealism; they were American citizens; some of their sons had died for America. Besides, they were prosperous in their adopted country. No one but an impractical fool would have taken seriously the invitation to return to a land that could not maintain them in the condition to which they had meanwhile become accustomed. There is no record that anyone gave even a moment's consideration to such a proposal. Certainly the leader of the community did not. Both leader and people were practical men of hard-headed good sense.

NINTH STREET CHURCH, HOLLAND, MICHIGAN

Built by the Hollanders during the first decade, this church, unchanged, is still giving service after nearly a century.

AN AMERICAN MAIDEN IN NATIVE DUTCH COSTUME

XVI

Beyond the Horizon

The time came when the young men on the Iowa frontier began to wonder what lay beyond the horizon. The result was another mass migration that rivaled in numbers and importance the original emigration from Holland. In the local writings of Pella historians the movement is often referred to as the "swarming of the hive." The metaphor is apt. When the Iowa hive became so crowded that the excess population could not be taken care of locally, planned and organized steps were taken to find an additional location. The site for the new hive was on the whole more favorable than the old, and so in due time the new settlement matched in numbers and economic wealth the parent community. Today, more than half of the Iowa citizens of Dutch blood live in the section peopled by the second migration.

Pella is located southeast of Des Moines, in direct line with Keokuk, which is in the extreme southeastern corner of the state on the Illinois border. Sioux County, with Orange City as the central focus of Dutch settlement, is in the extreme northwestern corner of Iowa, not far from the South Dakota and Minnesota borders. It therefore lies diagonally across the state from the parent area. When the hive swarmed, the human bees made almost a beeline across Iowa, settling just before they arrived at territory which, from the point of view of the Iowan, was at that time an alien land; they just managed to remain on the Iowa frontier.

The swarming took place twenty-two years after the arrival of the Dutch in Iowa, in 1869 and the years immediately following. Some time before that, feeling the need of an outlet for excess population, some of the leaders of the Dutch folk had sent delegations to Texas and Kansas to look for a site, but those attempts had come to nothing. Finally a committee was delegated to find cheap good land somewhere nearer home. They found it in northwestern Iowa, and the Dutch "land rush" began.

The first wave was composed of seventy-five men and eighteen wagons. They had a trek ahead of them over the trackless prairies of some three hundred miles. The committee had taken possession of thirty-eight sections of land and had staked out a town site; tentatively they had given the location the name of "Holland," as the Dutch pioneers had done in Michigan in 1847. The land was secured, and the migration was made, under provisions of the United States Homestead Law. In accordance with the rulings of that act many took up homesteads, while then and later others pre-empted 160 acres of land each on which they secured the title rights after "proving up" and paying $1.25 to $2.50 per acre. After the first contingent of families made the long journey in 1869, other waves followed, and for many years after that the migration continued, until in time the new land was filled up and the new frontier had become merged with the general American scene.

This second migration did not leave the Pella area because all the available land there had been occupied, but because such soil as was left had become too dear. When during the fifties and early sixties the settlement of prosperous Hollanders gave promise of a big unearned increment in land values, American speculators bought up the excess territory and held it for rising prices. By the time Dutch boys and girls who had come to the community as children were ready for marriage and homes of their own, twenty-two years after the arrival, the cost of an available farm had become so great, in proportion to the prices of farm produce, that their Dutch economic sense told them it was a losing venture. Infected with their elders' eagerness for "success" in the American sense, they were unwilling to descend in the economic scale by becoming tenant farmers or saddling themselves with debts that would keep their economic noses pressed down indefinitely on the well-known grindstone.

Many other nationals on other western frontiers showed less good sense than the Hollanders. The results appeared in the eighties and nineties, in the conditions that led finally to the agrarian revolt and

the tragic deflation described in *Main-Travelled Roads*. The Iowa Hollanders were only slightly involved in any of those economic disturbances that were later dramatized by Bryan in his first bid for the
presidency.

When the land speculators had overplayed their hands and had let
greed motivate them to keep their holdings at prices that were economically untenable, the Dutch folk decided to face the hardships of
emigration as their fathers had done, rather than live a life in which
they could not hope to become their own masters, if ever, until they
had arrived within sight of the cemetery. It took courage to emigrate
twice in the same generation, but not a few of the original settlers did
so, and many of their sons and daughters faced and met the test.

Not that they understood the economic laws that underlay their
decision, at least not as a theory. But each young man in need of a
farm on which to raise his family had common sense enough to understand that untouched and unimproved prairie land that in 1847 had
sold for from $2.50 to $5.00 an acre was not worth from $40 to $60 in
1869, at least not to him, whatever the speculators might say. He knew
that he could not make such a farm pay, as his father had done with
the same type of land two decades earlier. What he did in joining the
second mass migration may not have been recognized by him as "good
economics"—he would not have known the meaning of the phrase—
but he knew it was good horse sense. And the event proved that he
was right.

The name "Holland" did not become that of the city that arose; it
survived as the name of the township. The town site of the new
colony was named "Orange City," in honor of the royal House of
Orange that had persecuted the earlier generation of emigrants. By
the time the settlement was made the old bitternesses had been largely
forgotten, at least by the children now grown to manhood and woman-
hood. Their language, however, was still largely Dutch, many of their
institutions were reminiscent of those under which their ancestors had
grown up in Holland, and the House of Orange that to many of them
had never been more than a name had taken on a sentimental meaning.

The nearest railroad connection was eighteen miles away, and about
all Sioux County had was a rich soil. For the rest it was almost liter-

ally an empty land; there was nothing save prairie grass, mile after endless monotonous mile of it, with a trail running through it here and there. In 1860 the whole county, as large almost as some Eastern states, contained a population of just ten, and when the Hollanders moved into it in 1869 the number had risen to 110. But fertility of soil was all the Hollanders needed; they were confident they could build their own civilization there, given that one thing indispensable. Since there were, again quite literally, no houses when they arrived, and no lumber with which to build them short of a weary haul of eighteen miles, most of the newcomers went without them. As some of their fathers had done at Pella, they broke the prairies' sod for seeding next summer's wheat crop before they bothered to get a roof over their own or their families' heads. Some camped in tents, others made shift to live in their wagons for a while.

When warnings of the coming winter began to arrive they once more did what had been done at Pella—they dug primitive rooms into the soil, built up walls of prairie sod above the floor plans, roofed the structure over, and lived snugly, if primitively, in their sod houses. They were not facing the anxious uncertainties the arrivals at Pella had faced; they were seasoned Iowans, familiar with all the idiosyncrasies of the Iowa winter; they could not be taken by surprise by western blizzards and knew that they could survive in any type of weather nature might elect to provide. They had even learned, as the original Pella immigrants had not, to erect their dug-outs on the eastern or southern slope of a hill to protect them against the prevailing northwest blasts.

How the new colony grew in numbers; how the village of Orange City became a city; how the Hollanders built schools and churches, even presently an institution of higher learning known as the Northwestern Classical Academy; how the railroad relieved them from their isolation; how the sod houses gave place to comfortable farm homes, and the temporary cattle shelters to red-painted barns; how men with money established banks; how Hollanders took part in the post-Civil War government of their state and learned to select and elect their own men; how from being a ragged-looking group of "Straw Town" dwellers they developed into a dominating force in northwestern Iowa

—all that, and much more, makes a fascinating story that has properly taken an important place in the local histories of the community.

But it is a story that is not unique to the Hollanders; it has been repeated over and over again on all the frontiers in America over a period of three hundred years; the details may differ somewhat in the case of the second Dutch frontier in Iowa, and the names certainly have the flavor of an alien culture, but in all essential characteristics the story is the same and it has been told too often to warrant its detailed repetition here.

When the community observed the twenty-fifth anniversary of its founding it had not only become well established, the new hive had more than rivaled the old. And that has remained the relative position of the two parts of the Iowa Dutch frontier. In the statistics of population, wealth, and economic importance the Sioux County settlement has maintained its place. The Pella district lays an unexpressed claim —not quite always unexpressed, however—to a certain prestige, based perhaps on its slightly older history and, also perhaps, on a certain imponderable "culture" that may date back to the time when the Scholte home and English garden made up the show place of that section of the state, and when an aristocratic woman who had given musical recitals in Paris presided over that home. Sioux County was a community of plain Dutch farmers, and towns like Orange City, Sioux Center, and others were inhabited by small-town merchants who catered to the needs of the farmers. They made little pretense to being anything more than they honestly were—sensible folk who understood on which side their bread was buttered, people who put on less front than they had a right to do, who almost invariably, like Hollanders on any frontier, were worth more in dollars and cents than appearances credited them with being. That, in fact, was an outstanding Dutch trait in America, and the Hollanders of northwestern Iowa had it to a marked degree.

One episode of the early history of the colony deserves mention, not for its uniqueness but because it was such a test of the stamina of the settlers as few communities in other sections have been able successfully to meet. After three years of almost unprecedented prosperity, with crops from the rich prairie soil that must have made the people heady with dreams of quick wealth, a period of disaster set in for several

years that made them the subject of charity b   gislature.
And it was small comfort to them that throu   ster they
were destined to enter American fiction; they   e known
the fact at the time, and even if this had been   can't eat
magazine stories. The dramatic but dreaded g   ne down
upon them year after year, beginning with the   873, and
stripped them bare.

Almost literally. Crops of wheat and corn an   in June
that they more than justified all the folk son   t them,
simply did not exist by the end of July. Hardl   rass left
for the cattle to nibble; fields almost as bare as, in the twentieth century, some western lands were left by the dust storms, except that the
richness had remained in the soil itself.

Hundreds of families lost everything they had, except empty farm
buildings, and they were saddled with expensive farm machinery they
had bought on credit on the strength of the first three years of prosperity; the grasshoppers could not eat steel discs and reapers, but that
was about all they did not devour, or so it seemed to the discouraged
farmers.

One such experience would be bad enough. The Iowa farmers had
to face it until the devastation had run its course by 1880. Not every
year marked a total loss, but the disaster was great enough even in the
years of milder infestation so that the people could hardly have been
blamed if they had thrown in the sponge. The Iowa legislature took
note of their plight and appropriated money for the purchase of seed,
grain, and vegetables; the grasshoppers had not left enough to plant
next year's crop. And help came from other sources, but at best it
was hardly more than temporary charity, and of course galling to self-
respecting Hollanders more accustomed to extending charity than
receiving it. Individuals became discouraged and abandoned their
land; one of them is reported to have sold eighty acres for $225, "throw-
ing in a span of mules, wagon, and cow."

But the community as a whole stood up under the repeated blows,
and in the end the grasshoppers, that had been coming down year
after year like the wolf on the fold, stopped coming as mysteriously as
they had started. The Hollanders of Iowa had no sea gulls to save
them through an act of Providence, and hence they had no occasion

like the Mormons to place the statue of a gull in a public park. However, they had the gumption to face disaster without the gull. But not without Providence, for they were naturally a religious people and they had been conditioned by the forms and institutions of the religion of their fathers that had been the occasion for the establishment of the entire Dutch frontier in America.

When they left for their second front in Iowa the Hollanders took their ecclesiastical institutions with them, in embryo at least. Not to make the story too complicated for the general reader unskilled in unraveling the tangled threads of the church relationships of the Hollanders in America, there were at Pella, at the time of the "swarming," three Dutch church groups—in addition of course to some of the better known American communions like Baptists and Methodists. One was "The Christian Church at Pella," an independent communion presided over until his death by Scholte, without remuneration, in a sanctuary he had built with his own money. When the hegira to Sioux County began in 1869 Scholte had been dead for a year, and for all practical purposes his one-man church died with him. Another church, made up of several congregations on the Pella frontier, was the Reformed Church in America. A third, somewhat less well known to the general non-Dutch citizen, was the Christian Reformed Church, whose organization represented a secession from the Reformed Church.

The independent Scholte church was not perpetuated on the new frontier, but the other two flourished there. Throughout the years of locusts and drought they played a not unimportant rôle in the maintenance of morale. The Reformed Church especially spread rapidly, so that in later years the Iowa stronghold of the denomination was in that area rather than in Pella. The Christian Reformed Church, since it was new in the early years of the second frontier, made its way more slowly, but later it displayed a vigor that has not abated to this day.

Whatever their doctrinal differences, all those churches had one thing in common, the tradition of phenomenally long sermons. Scholte is credited with often having pronounced three-hour discourses, incredible though such a statement may seem in terms of twentieth-century standards; and two-hour sermons, for him, meant that he had not properly wound up his pitching arm. The ministers of the Reformed and Christian Reformed churches in Iowa were often almost as prolix;

and in Michigan Van Raalte and many of the other ministers appeared to regard two hours as the norm for sermon length. In fact, brevity was associated in the Dutch public mind with unorthodoxy. A man of God who could not keep on talking almost indefinitely was regarded with an uneasy suspicion, as if the fountains of inspiration in him were shallow.

Sermons by the book were under similar suspicion; manuscripts in the pulpit were unheard of; the only concession public opinion made was the use of unobtrusive notes. A prayer read from a prayer-book— there were rumors of such goings on among the Americans—was regarded as sacrilegious. But the highest and truest inspiration was credited to the minister who could turn on the talk wholly extemporaneously and keep it flowing indefinitely. Since recording devices had not yet been invented, and taking a sermon in shorthand would have seemed irreverent, there is no way of knowing whether those two-hour and three-hour sermonizers took up so much time because they really had that much to say, or whether they just kept on talking because it was expected of them by the folk.

While the Hollanders on the frontier could take as much oratorical punishment as any other people have perhaps ever done, with the exception of the Nazi enthusiasts who were intoxicated by Hitler's prolixity, nature did now and then take its revenge. They were a hard-working people, those Hollanders in both Iowa and Michigan; they put in long hours of toil, from before sunup until far into the evening. They were not physically conditioned to sitting still in the confinement of a church, and sleep would overtake them in spite of their passionate interest in what the pulpit was dispensing. Various devices were adopted to overcome this weakness of the flesh. A janitor might be delegated to tap the sleeper on the head with an awakener at the end of a long stick, or the preacher might pause in his discourse and invite the sleeper's neighbor to recall him to his duty and his opportunities. Some sufferers, when they felt the assaults of approaching sleep, would arise in their pews and stand in silence until the attack had passed.

Women had their own devices for themselves and for small children who occupied the pews with them. For themselves they carried tiny hinge-covered silver boxes containing a cologne-saturated sponge.

These they passed along the pew to the other women, who, politeness dictated, must take a sniff. It was in some communities a nice question of protocol who should pass her cologne box, when, and how often. But it helped to keep the housewives awake in spite of anything the drone of the pastor's voice might do to put them to sleep. As for the children, they were given peppermint lozenges; the bite on the tongue of this candy was at least a help against sleep, if not a sure-fire preventive.

The settlement in northwestern Iowa represented the last mass movement in the march of Holland's culture across the continent. Up until this point migration had been organized. Scouts had been sent ahead to spy out the land, doing so under a community mandate that was definite and binding. In both the Netherlands and, later, on the American frontier when Dutch hives had begun to swarm, emigration companies had been organized. The most careful regulations had been adopted to insure the success of the ventures; not much had been left to chance or to the improvisations of the moment; the migrating Hollanders had trusted in Providence but, with Dutch common sense, they had also believed in keeping their powder dry, and if need be in passing the ammunition.

Now a new era had set in. Throughout the closing years of the nineteenth century, and during the early decades of the twentieth, the migration of Hollanders continued, but now they marched as individuals or as families. Ended were the migrations of masses of people whose movements and objectives had been planned in advance—communities of men, women, and children marching (or sailing) under a discipline that had many features of military regulation about it.

The time arrived when even Sioux County became too crowded for some who craved elbow room or whose land hunger was too great to be appeased by opportunities in a settled country. Such people pulled out first to neighboring counties, then to neighboring states, then to states more distant. South Dakota, North Dakota, Minnesota; and, finally, at about the turn of the century, the Pacific coast was reached— with settlements particularly in Washington and California. Montana attracted a few communities of Hollanders, but Wyoming was not attractive to them; nor were Utah and Oregon popular. In general they took the northern routes and kept more or less away from the Southern states.

Considerable concentrations of Hollanders developed in several states, but usually without prearranged action. A family might settle like Isak in the wilds, then send word to other land-hungry people at home to come and join them. A few scattered pioneers formed themselves into a community, and in time there grew up clusters of Dutch sections.

This was true not only of the excess population of the last organized Dutch frontier in Sioux County; individuals kept separating themselves from the herd in the Michigan communities, in the Pella area, in communities in states on the Atlantic seaboard that had been formed by individual immigrants from Holland, in Dutch settlements in Wisconsin, Illinois, and in other Midwestern states where Hollanders had lighted. Not infrequently such one-family immigrants faced an adventure quite as great as that of the mass migrations. A young couple pulling out from Michigan for Minnesota, or from Iowa for Washington, were often latter-day Columbuses, with no assurance that they would ever see home and friends again.

Quite a few never did. While some returned in triumph, many years later, after making good on the new frontiers, for others the normal hazards were too great; grasshoppers ruined them, or drought, or prairie fires. Almost every community on all the Dutch frontiers has its tragic legends of promising young men and their families swallowed up, their lives and deaths a repudiation of the illusion that pioneers always surmount all hazards. Family Bibles continue to list certain names, but they are names that are also listed in the records of neglected and forgotten cemeteries in Minnesota or the Dakotas or Montana or Washington.

But such things are true not only of pioneers of Dutch blood. For the most part the story remains unrecorded of the failures in immigration, whether organized or individual. No Whitman ever writes an "O Pioneers!" about the men and women who left their bones along the highway, whether through their own incapacity or by reason of accident or circumstance. Only those who become empire builders are noticed by history and poetry. Success justifies the risks taken, and failure is the unpardonable sin.

The Hollanders who did succeed and who organized communities on distant frontiers in the wilds carried their ways of life and their institutions with them—invariably their church, often both of the two main denominations, even though the settlement was too small to support two churches; their manners and customs that were gradually modified by their rubbing against the customs of the communities they occupied; their unremitting and beaverlike industry that often was their best passport to eventual success. In course of time, when success or at least security had come, they sent their sons back to the parent communities in Iowa or Michigan to be educated, and occasionally their daughters as well. In such ways links were forged between the frontier communities and the settled Dutch societies further east.

Holland had missed her chance in the seventeenth century to impart her culture to the whole of the American continent. But that culture itself, modified because of the inevitable and necessary assimilation of its carriers into the American host society, still had vitality enough to reach the Pacific at last, and in its passage across the nation to affect and modify the American culture it met on its way.

XVII

Life on the Wisconsin Frontier

NOWHERE ON THE Dutch frontier in America were the contrasts so great as in Wisconsin. In that state two types of Hollanders, with entirely different backgrounds, were found—Protestant and Catholic. Such places in Sheboygan and Fond du Lac counties as Cedar Grove, Alto, Oostburg, Gibbsville were settled by people indistinguishable as a type from the Hollanders of Michigan and Iowa. There was in them a messianic determination to make their life on the frontier a kind of racial Armageddon. At Little Chute, and at Hollandtown fifteen miles to the east, a type of Dutch immigrant settled far less fierce and stern, more genial, less puritanical.

Those latter settlers had been piloted to America by a kindly missionary to the Indians of the Green Bay region, Father Theodore J. Vanden Broek. No less sturdy than their Protestant countrymen, they were appreciably gayer. Because they were somewhat untypical, and because their number was small, their story has been largely ignored by those who have set themselves the task of writing the history of the Dutch mass migrations to America. But they clearly belong in the picture, and the contrast their life presents to that of the others gives their story an emphasis that their number would hardly suggest.

The temptation is great, however, to overemphasize the contrast between the Catholic and Protestant settlers on the Wisconsin frontier, to convert the Calvinists into unyielding Puritans and the Catholics into Cavaliers. In sober reality, the latter, like the former, were lower-class Hollanders, in terms of economics—farmers, villagers, artisans, laborers. There was not more education among them than among the

Protestant settlers; if anything, perhaps less. They were simple people, who emigrated to improve their lot. They went to Wisconsin with the intention of working hard to carve out a home there for themselves and their children; and they carried out their intentions quite as effectually as did the Protestant settlers.

But they came out of a different background, and their life on the Dutch frontier suggests a contrast to that of the Hollanders in general merely because a similar contrast had existed in Holland. A great many things that the Calvinists regarded sinful they accepted as a matter of course. They had loved their simple village dances in the Netherlands, so it was natural to try to mitigate the austerities of the frontier by indulging in them there.

Dances were not wholly unknown, after a time, among the Dutch settlers in other sections, but they were not attended by the respectable. When theocratic government there yielded to normal civic processes, it was no longer possible to suppress such things by force, but for many years ecclesiastical disciplines were quite effective, and young people who attended dances brought disgrace to their families. On the frontier at Little Chute and Hollandtown in Wisconsin dancing was as respectable as an ice cream social in a prairie village. If the Protestant Hollanders heard about such goings on they were doubtless scandalized. But there was of course nothing they could do about it.

My countrymen used to have occasional jollifications [writes Chrysostom Adrian Verwyst]. There was, for instance, the carnival entertainment just before Lenten fast. After mass was over they would betake themselves to the home of Mr. Vanden Berg. The house was a large building for those primitive days, and there they would dance—the younger generation, of course—all day till sundown, when they would go home. Night dancing was not carried on, and I believe the present generation [1916] religiously follows this custom of their grandparents; that is, they dance during the day, and every decent woman and girl is supposed to be at home before dark.[1]

The mild and primitive gayeties at Hollandtown and Little Chute were in no sense a "Merrie Mount" defiance of authority. For there was nobody who was trying to interfere with the merrymakers. The Protestant Hollanders in other settlements had no jurisdiction; there

---

[1] Chrysostom Adrian Verwyst, "Reminiscenses of a Pioneer Missionary," *Publications of the State Historical Society of Wisconsin, Proceedings for 1916*, p. 154.

was an impassable gulf between the Protestant and Catholic communities on the Wisconsin frontier. When the Hollandtown and Little Chute people went to a carnival-dance they did not do so with one eye cocked to see how they would shock the Puritans; they went unself-consciously because they wanted a little pleasure.

There were other pleasures they allowed themselves, to them just as innocent as a country dance but that must have scandalized their countrymen a few miles distant if they heard about them. In his "Reminiscences of a Pioneer Missionary" the Reverend Chrysostom Adrian Verwyst speaks of men playing cards at the home of a neighbor during the leisure of a Sunday afternoon, occasionally passing around a jug to add to the good cheer. Their women meanwhile had their tea or coffee, and cheered one another with such frontier gossip as might present itself; and the children indulged in games out of doors.[2]

The whole picture is that of innocent amusement to mitigate somewhat the austerities of frontier life. Tomorrow morning at dawn those pioneers would rise from their hard straw ticks to face another week of bone-wrenching toil; for the moment they were refreshing themselves with such innocent entertainment as they could devise. It had been like that back home in Holland, except that there the men had gone to the village pub instead of to a neighbor's house. On the Wisconsin frontier they were merely trying to reproduce the social life they had been accustomed to at home, sincerely blessing their guardian saints for that much surcease from the rigors of their frontier lives.

The people were accustomed to various simple sports and they tried to perpetuate them on the frontier. One was a community shooting contest, the target a "wooden bird, made of very tough material, placed at the top of a high pole like a flagstaff." Young fellows proud of their marksmanship might keep in condition during the Sunday afternoon leisure, to be ready for the annual shoot-festival, when the competition was sure to be spirited.

Occasionally we heard of a fight [writes Verwyst], or of some poor fellow becoming tipsy, but nothing more serious than that occurred. There was universal good will among all and toward all.[3]

The people were simple-hearted Catholics, sincerely devoted to their

[2] *Ibid.*, p. 155.
[3] *Ibid.*, p. 154.

religion, most of them, meticulous in attending mass. When a priest came to Hollandtown once a month, on foot from Little Chute, the people hastened to church with enthusiasm to make confession. The rest of the time they had to be content with improvised services, the reading of a sermon by a layman named Vander Hey. All the evidence points to their sincerity and simplicity, and a general wholesomeness that marks them as good material for the American stock into which they were to develop.

Father Vanden Broek, their leader, was not a man of many talents, as were Van Raalte in Michigan and Scholte in Iowa. He had been a simple and sincere missionary to the Indians in the Green Bay region, beginning his work among them in 1834. After a while he had made Little Chute his headquarters. There he had labored for more than a dozen years, with some success, but it does not appear that he set any worlds afire. He was getting along in years, was in fact almost at the end of his life. In 1847 it occurred to him to try to persuade those of his home friends and neighbors who were less than prosperous to come to Wisconsin; he saw opportunity beckoning them there. So he made a trip to Holland as the final vacation of his life, talked to the people at home, and persuaded many that America was the place for them.

He does not appear to have been a man of great eloquence, just a kindly missionary to the Indians eager to help his boyhood friends and neighbors to help themselves to a new life. He was not unlike the frontier priest of fiction; he inspired affection, not awed admiration.

Nor is unusual heroism associated with the people he conducted to America. They were just simple Dutch villagers, and they tried, with the encouragement and approval of their priest-leader, to perpetuate their native habits and customs, their amusements and Dutch village ways, on the Wisconsin frontier.

The beginnings of the Wisconsin settlements differ in one other respect from those of the Dutch frontiers in other states—a completely accidental difference. The Hollanders in Wisconsin began their life in America in an atmosphere of tragedy. When the three shiploads of Dutch immigrants in the Vanden Broek migration arrived in Little Chute the loss of the lake propeller *Phoenix* was so recent that it was still live frontier news. The Dutch victims of one of the worst Great Lakes tragedies were Protestants, and of course not personally known to the new immigrants; but they were countrymen, the number of victims was large, and their pitifully burned bodies were still lying under Lake Michigan's waters within sight of the Sheboygan shore. The story of the *Phoenix* became a Wisconsin Dutch saga that has not yet quite lost its tragic appeal there a century after the event. For that reason it deserves a place in the story of the Dutch frontier in that state.

On Sunday morning, November 21, 1847, the *Phoenix* steamed out of Manitowoc bound for Sheboygan, twenty-five miles distant. It was heavily loaded with freight and carried as many passengers as could be packed into what space was left, perhaps between 250 and 300—the exact number has always remained in doubt. A very large number of them were Dutch immigrants almost within sight of their new home. But the vessel reached Sheboygan only as a burned hulk; most of the immigrants sank below the waters of Lake Michigan after they had been burned to death like rats in a trap. One careful writer has expressed it as his opinion, based on the most painstaking research, that "the loss was not much below 250." [4]

Nor was the number of the victims the most tragic part of the disaster. The manner of their death was so horrible, and the fact that they died almost within sight of home was so fraught with tragic irony, that the disaster has become a Dutch folk legend on the Wisconsin frontier, and to some degree on the other Dutch frontiers as well. The victims have been commemorated in local poetry and song; a century after the event newspapers and history magazines of the area still occasionally retell the story, and grandchildren of friends of the victims read the accounts with a revived sense of the poignancy of the tragedy. For them it is a kind of Dutch "Wreck of the Hesperus"; but, of course, the disaster described in Longfellow's poem was almost trivial compared with the Lake Michigan holocaust that happened less than a decade after the schooner went down "on the reef of Norman's Woe" whose fate has been commemorated in one of America's best-known ballads. The *Phoenix* disaster did not have the luck to find its poet, and so it is remembered only on the Dutch frontier, while the tale of the wreck of the *Hesperus* has become the possession of the American

[4] William O. Van Eyck, "The Story of the Propeller *Phoenix*," *The Wisconsin Magazine of History* (December, 1923), p. 293.

people. Yet in refinement of tragedy the *Phoenix* story far surpasses that of the *Hesperus*.

The Dutch immigrants had boarded the vessel at Buffalo. It was to carry them on their last lap of a voyage that had begun many weeks earlier in the Netherlands. They were not an organized group but many families bound for various Dutch settlements—Wisconsin, Iowa, Illinois, Michigan. The long, hard, dreary passage of the Atlantic in a sailing vessel was behind them; also the still drearier journey up the Hudson on a river steamer and through the Erie Canal on open flatboats. At Buffalo, they knew, they would begin the last weary lap. Presently they would be "home"—at least among friends and relatives, to begin their new life in America.

By this time lake transportation had become standardized; the immigrants knew approximately how long it would take to reach their destination, and they were tidily getting their household belongings in order against the end of the pilgrimage. The sense of weariness and boredom and discomfort was yielding to happy thoughts of their new life in a new land—only one more day, or for some at most two, for others only a few hours. At the last some could actually see with the naked eye the shore where friends and relatives were waiting for them, but were burned to death, or if they escaped that fate, were swallowed up by the icy swells that were rolling over the surface of Lake Michigan. No mere *Hesperus* tragedy this; as tragedy in the grand manner its only lack was that it lacked a poet.

The owners of the *Phoenix*, a wood-burning vessel of three hundred tons burden, were understandably eager that it should make good time; the navigation season was closing on the Great Lakes, and dividends are dividends. The vessel's load was disproportionately heavy, the number of passengers probably too many. But shipping regulations were lax in those days, and the owners of this ship of death probably sinned no more than their competitors.

The reason why it is not known exactly how many passengers there were is that the ship's papers were of course lost, and the office of the company, in Cleveland, had only the list of those who sailed from that port. In those relatively unregulated days it was quite natural for a captain to yield to the temptation of taking on one more passenger, and yet one more, who could be stowed away somewhere. The officials of the *Phoenix* were merely doing what was common practice.

And the crew, the immediate agents of tragedy, were likewise doing what was usual. Making a record run was then, as now, something to talk about, to boast of in port. What actually happened was lost to marine history; most of the evidence was burned, and many who were immediately responsible expiated whatever may have been their blame in a death as horrible as that of their passengers. All that is known is that the boilers were pushed beyond the point of safety.

Most of the passengers were asleep, for it was three o'clock in the morning when the first intimation of trouble came. Captain B. G. Sweet was also in bed, laid up with an injured leg. That was the reason why the two or three Dutch passengers who had not gone to bed were forced to protest to the crew members themselves instead of to the captain, when they sensed that all was not as it should be. Quite naturally, because they were immigrants unacquainted with the ways of this strange new land, and having no knowledge of the crew's language, they showed greater diffidence than they might have displayed in their own country. But at least they protested that something was going wrong in the engine room. They were bluntly told to mind their own business. After the tragedy there were many accusations that the crew members had been drinking at Manitowoc. No direct proof was ever produced, but a survivor charged that the crew members had knocked down one of the immigrants who protested. The crew's attitude of irresponsibility suggests that the charge of drunkenness is at least plausible.

Less than an hour after the immigrants' attempt to look out for their own safety smoke began to come pouring out of the boiler room in such volume that not even the befuddled crew members could ignore it. But when the fire alarm was sounded the fate of the *Phoenix*—and of some two hundred and fifty human beings—was already sealed. Some semblance of discipline was maintained, and the passengers turned themselves into fire fighters. But even their unpracticed eyes told them almost immediately that the ship was doomed.

There were only two lifeboats—for some three hundred passengers! The injured captain took command of one, which was overloaded with twenty-two passengers. The mate of the *Phoenix* was in charge of the second boat, carrying twenty-one persons in all. So crowded were the boats that the crew members in charge faced the terrible choice of having the boats founder or letting victims in the water sink without any attempt at rescue. They faced something more terrible. One immigrant girl grasped the rail of the boat with a grip of despair. Her fingers were wrenched loose one by one and she sank as the lifeboat moved away. Of the forty-three rescued, twenty-five were Dutch immigrants.

In the excitement one of the boats had lost an oar, so that it had to be sculled all the way to Sheboygan, five miles distant. This resulted in shipping water beyond the point of safety for a craft so heavily laden. But two or three of the immigrants came to the rescue. Although most of the passengers were only scantily dressed, a few had had the presence of mind to step into their wooden shoes, which they now used as bailers. And one immigrant used a broom as an improvised oar. Both lifeboats reached shore—which was lined by this time with most of the inhabitants of Sheboygan anxiously watching the burning vessel only five miles away.

The schooner *Liberty* and the propeller *Delaware,* docking at Sheboygan, had begun making ready to go to the rescue long before the arrival of the survivors. But there was so little wind that the *Liberty*'s captain had to resort to his lifeboats, and it took the *Delaware* some time to get up enough steam. The lifeboats of the *Phoenix* also returned immediately, and many small boats hurried to the rescue.

But when they arrived only three persons were still alive. Most of the others had long since slipped from sight. Here and there bodies were floating on the lake's long swells, held up by a door or a chest or some other piece of wreckage wrenched loose from the deck of the burning vessel. But they were all dead from exposure to the bitter cold. The burning hulk of the *Phoenix* was still lighting up the scene of horror. All that the rescuers could do was take aboard the three survivors and tow the burning ship to shallow water.

When news of the disaster reached the Netherlands, it resulted in retarding emigration for a time. Most of the victims of the holocaust had been well-to-do citizens. They had carried all their property with them, most of it in gold coin. One careful writer, whose researches extended to Holland itself, records the claim that one of the families carried as much as $50,000 in cash.[5] The loss of Dutch property was very large, in addition to the loss of Dutch lives; the twenty-five immigrant survivors were penniless as well as bereaved. All but two settled on the Wisconsin frontier, where some of their descendants were still living a hundred years after the tragedy.

The relatives and friends of the victims, in the Netherlands, were not the only ones for whom the loss of the *Phoenix* meant personal tragedy. Nearly all the immigrants had come to America in response to urgings by people already living on the various Dutch frontiers. There was mourning among the settlers who had just passed their first difficult summer in a strange land and who were facing the bitter winter. Even those who had not suffered a personal loss felt the blow as a community tragedy. It sounded a note of disaster on all the Dutch frontiers that was extraordinarily untimely for the maintenance of morale. That it did not cause any of the settlers to yield to despair is a measure of their stamina.

As for the Wisconsin settlers who witnessed the tragedy that fateful Sunday morning, they could never forget to the end of their lives what this new land had done to countrymen of theirs. The moods of Lake Michigan are infinite in number and variety. Although the tragedy had not been caused by the weather but by human incapacity, the lake had been storm-swept for days up until the very eve of the disaster. Now as morning spread over the November sky the Dutch folk on the beaches turned sad eyes to a scene that reminded them of a quiet summer afternoon on their own Zuider Zee. Far to the eastward an ironical peace lay upon the lake—peace, and the memory of storm.

[5] *Ibid.*, p. 296

XVIII

Leaders and Motivations

WHAT MOTIVATED THE leaders of the Dutch mass migrations to America in the nineteenth century? The compulsions that drove their followers are not too difficult to understand. What impelled the leaders to exchange an ordered life in Holland for a precarious existence on the American frontier is less easily explained. The assertion often made that they were God's captains who yielded obedience to a divine mandate is mere rhetoric that explains nothing; it leaves the mystery as dark as before.

To arrive at an approximation to an answer it may be fruitful to look at a few typical leaders; there are many others whose spiritual logbooks might be examined with equally good results. Three—Albertus Christiaan Van Raalte, Hendrik Pieter Scholte, and Cornelius Vander Meulen—are perhaps best known, and they offer opportunity for studies in motivation that make them at least somewhat typical. Were those leaders, and others like them, almost disembodied spiritual abstractions as some of their biographers like to portray them, or does an honestly objective view suggest that their motivations were at one with those of other men, great or small?

First Van Raalte—first for no other reason than that he was the earliest arrival. In marble, on a community commemoration tablet, he is characterized as "a man mighty in words and deeds." That has become his official legend on the Dutch frontier. His best-known American biographer, Dr. Henry E. Dosker, who knew him personally, twice asserts in his *Levensschets* that there was "something Napoleonic" about Van Raalte. When proper discount has been made for chauvinistic racial enthusiasm, and the scale has been reduced from the international to the parochial, the characterization is not inaccurate. The biographer means it as the highest praise he can bestow; but there are implications in it also of Napoleonic traits that are not so highly regarded today. Van Raalte possessed many qualities of parochial statesmanship, and of almost military talent, but like Napoleon he was inclined to be arbitrary and dictatorial.

His admirers point out that the migration could not have succeeded if the leader had been democratic. The people were mostly a simple folk, peasants or villagers with little education and with less conception of what the American frontier demanded. Moreover, they were by nature and training a contentious people, always threatening to fly apart, almost fanatically individualistic, with a low degree of cohesiveness. Their religion was the strongest force that kept them united, and even that was not strong enough to prevent a major split in the community within ten years after arrival. For such a people, Van Raalte's admirers contend, an iron hand was required; without the leader's personal force the community would have fallen apart and would probably have disappeared.

That contention is almost certainly true, but an objective analysis suggests that the seeds of "Napoleonism" were in this leader from the beginning, that he became the generalissimo of the people because he felt himself destined to rule, and that he succeeded because he had the ability to do so. He was by nature an empire builder, in the best sense of the term. He felt in the marrow of his bones that he belonged in the driver's seat, and to his credit it should be added that he did not use his position for self-aggrandizement. Grandiose schemes were hatched in his imagination, of which the migration to Michigan was the most conspicuously successful. Those projects were the born ruler's way of expressing himself.

Some of his plans did not succeed. A decade after the arrival on the Michigan frontier his people fell apart ecclesiastically, and not even the force of Van Raalte's leadership could put Humpty-Dumpty together again. That was a major failure for the frontier Napoleon. During the last decade of his life there was a sudden flareup of empire building zeal in his soul, and he tried to establish a second settlement of Hollanders, this time near Richmond, Virginia. The attempt was a total failure, and the cluster of settlements he established disappeared completely from the map. That, too, was a major defeat for the Dutch leader.

His biographer, reflecting personal contact with his subject, testifies that there was in Van Raalte's life, toward the last, a period of extreme pessimism, when he felt that he was seated amid the ruins of his career. That often happens to a man whose plans have been too grandiose. The too sanguine becomes the too hopeless; thus Mark Twain, to take an entirely different type, became one of America's greatest pessimists.

Van Raalte was born early in the nineteenth century, the son of a clergyman in the state church of Holland. Little is known about his early aspirations, except that his first choice of a profession was medicine. But later, to the joy of his father, who was a fairly prominent but uncritical cog in the Dutch ecclesiastical machine, he decided to be a minister.

At the famous University of Leyden he fell under the spell of Hendrik Pieter Scholte, a slightly older man and a leader of a discussion club that went under his name. The two young men, and some others, debated whether church and state should be separated, an idea that was dynamite to the civil powers and, generally speaking, to the state-supported clergy. They discussed many other subjects, and gradually became convinced that the church in Holland was in a bad way and ripe for a revival.

Scholte acted on the conviction soon after he had been licensed as a clergyman, and his revolt gave all the members of his club a black eye. When Van Raalte came up for the final examination, although his scholastic record was highly satisfactory he was refused a license to preach in the state church, on what he considered a technicality. So he was a clergyman without a charge, or the possiblity of getting one. His father meanwhile had died and he was on his own. It was natural that he should join the seceders; there was little else he could do.

All the indications are that he was a man of surpassing eloquence, a spiritual spellbinder who could bend large masses of people to his purposes. All indications likewise are that he was a man of unusually strong will, so much so that a kind of holy arrogance characterized some of his acts. There can be no question of the man's sincerity; he was so convinced of the rightness of the things he wanted to do that it did not seem incongruous to him to force men and women to become the instruments of his sacred purposes. Nor can there be any question that he led a devoted life, dedicated to the service of God and his people, giving himself without stint to both.

But there was little chance in Holland for the free exercise of the powers he possessed. As the minister of a conglomeration of dissenting social outcasts he could never hope to occupy a position of leadership that would satisfy his instincts for command; he would always be in the presence of the comfortable, well-paid, socially approved clergy of the state church, himself a kind of pariah, laughed at and without standing except among the outcasts. In America he could be a truly great leader, take his rightful place on a spiritual pedestal, and at the same time be be a blessing to the masses of the poor people who in Holland were less than paupers but who in America might be self-respecting and substantial citizens. He could be an empire builder in a new land, with the eventual rewards of the prestige of an empire builder, and at the same time a spiritual and material blessing to thousands. Philanthropy and a very human ambition may have met in the same man, without his being even conscious of the latter.

There is no indication that love of money or personal material advancement played a part in his motivation, as almost certainly they did in the case of some other leaders in his migration, and as they are likely to do in almost any group no matter what the nationality. The man appears to have been free from that very human trait, to a marked degree. All his life he drove himself without mercy for a much smaller remuneration than his talents deserved or than he could reasonably have claimed.

But it is not at all certain that love of leadership, the desire to be looked up to as the greatest man in his parochial world, was not at the root of his final decision, after ten years of hesitation, to lead his people out of the Egypt that was Holland to the Canaan he and they conceived America as being. Coupled with that was a messianic fervor, a feeling that the Hound of Heaven was at his heels. In the days when the world was young, he might have heard a Voice that gave him specific instructions what to do and where to go. In the atmosphere of the sophisticated Holland of his day that would hardly have been possible; and he was an honest man, honest even with himself, a some-what rare trait. But he was the kind of man who could honestly have persuaded himself—if the nuances of the atmosphere in which he lived had been right for it—that Divinity spoke to him directly. Which is another way of saying that he believed passionately and sincerely in his own mission.

But there was also a streak of practicality in his nature. In preparing for the migration, in Holland, and later as he faced the very real diffi-culties in America, he showed himself a man of resourcefulness, one who had the only right any man has to lead, the ability to do so. The people trusted him and looked up to him, even though they sometimes, very humanly, found fault with him when things went wrong. He was highly respected, but there is little evidence that he was regarded with warm human affection; he was not that kind of a man.

Hendrik Pieter Scholte's was a still more complex nature. An intel-lectual aristocrat and a man of wealth, he had the temperament of an artist. He was the architect of the house he built for his aristocratic wife, erecting it the very first year on the bleak prairie; and he made it a thing of beauty not by the standards of the frontier but by those of an Old World civilization. And he erected a church at his own expense that was not merely utilitarian in its architecture, as frontier churches are likely to be, but that satisfied his craving for beauty. He laid out for himself a formal English garden in an Iowa that considered a potato far more important than a rose; and he paved a garden path with broken Delft china because his soul gloated over the beauty of even its fragments.

In his young manhood he studied in the Academy of Arts in Amster-dam, intent on becoming a painter. Although he is said to have shown promise, did he feel in himself a want of talent and did that fact cause him to give up the idea? It was not want of money. When his wealthy, factory-owning father died, young Scholte, then sixteen, grad-ually tore himself loose from the world of painting. Finally he abandoned the Athenaeum entirely and began philosophical studies at the University of Leyden, where he soon became a leader in under-graduate disputation. Although he had entered the university as an art student, he ended by concentrating on theology. His interest in this subject seems to have been largely intellectual and philosophical, at least at first.

And throughout his life there was in him a pride of intellect such as is usually not associated with the arts of a spellbinder, of one who today, with some slight show of reason, might be called a rabble-rouser. It is well to remember that the rabble he roused in Utrecht were people who, at least in the field of theology, were, many of them, capable of intellectual subtlety. His pride of intellect was fully justified. His was a subtle mind, and he used it with an artistic finesse that wins admiration even a century later.

Such a man might have been expected to fill a university chair or to hold a place of honor in the comfortable and respectable state church. Instead he championed the dispossessed, threw in his lot with social if not economic outcasts, went cheerfully to jail on repeated occasions, lived the life of a hunted man whose hand was against authority. What was it that drove him?

There are often many facets to a human soul, and one of Scholte's appears to have been a somewhat unexpected love for his kind, an artist's appreciation of their sorrows coupled with a human desire for artistic expression of his own nature. As in the case of Van Raalte, there is no slightest doubt of his sincere sympathy with the poor and the oppressed. But there is also a very strong sense of a desire in his heart to play upon the keyboard of human souls, not primarily for those souls' welfare but for his own artist soul's satisfaction. The two emotions are not at all incompatible, nor is the second necessarily more ignoble than the first.

He gives the impression of having been a man "wrenched with a woeful agony" to tell his tale somehow. Instinct or want of technical skill may have warned him that he could not find expression in painting. But an artist can express himself sometimes quite as well in argument and harangue, and this Scholte did in the university and later as a clergyman. But art is a jealous god, impatient of restraints. And the fact that Scholte loved his fellow men was not incompatible with his leaving the conventional church because he felt an irresistible need to express only himself.

Always also, there was the delight of the artist in playing on the emotions of large masses of people. In the Netherlands he found in that a means of self-expression, even if he had to stand on a farm wagon for a pulpit. The theatricality of that, together with the drama of the attendant danger of arrest, may have appealed to his artist heart, even when he attributed all he did to the love of God and His people. Later in America the fact that he preached three-hour sermons contains a hint of what the man was doing without perhaps his knowing it. His love of pictures, of art in general, had been transmuted into a love of words, particularly when they were his own. Most real orators are self-intoxicated, and they taste greater delight even than those who hear them speak.

But that alone did not satisfy him; he might have found an outlet for his eloquence in Holland itself. His was a restless, complex nature that needed many avenues of expression. For that a frontier society, where his was the master voice, was best suited. He may have known this, he was a man of keen perceptions, or he may have turned to this solution of his problem instinctively. All that can be gathered from the record is that he spoke with many voices, in many tones, that he used many techniques of self-expression. In accounting for his alleged loss of spiritual power at a later stage in his career one writer gives a partial catalogue of the activities of the man:

He was a gentleman farmer, owner of sawmills, brick-kilns and lime-kilns, land agent, notary, printer, broker, banker, dealer in farm implements, attorney, editor, owner and publisher of a weekly.

In addition to all that, and while continuing to preach three-hour sermons each Sunday, he became very active in politics, so much so that Lincoln called him his "Dutch friend", and invited him to his inauguration.

And he engaged in still other activities. Some of them were doubtless forced upon him by virtue of his position as leader of the people, but can anyone doubt that he chose most of them, perhaps unconsciously, to satisfy the craving of his nature for expression? How could he have found so many outlets within the framework of the rigid social structure of the Holland of his day? Or even half or a fourth of that number of outlets? He might have been a great orator there, and perhaps also at the same time an intellectual leader. But there was not much opportunity for him to be anything more. In a new land, if the conditions are reasonably favorable, a man of many moods may hope to find expression for them all. It was not perhaps primarily the love of power that drove him, although that was not absent, but the need for expression, and this led naturally to power, or power was a means of its attainment, and the love of God and of men was a part of it.

The man's domestic life was in tune with such a nature. He loved not only beautiful things, he doted on the beauty of the hot-house flower of a woman that he carried with him to the prairie. Fantastically unsuited to the life of a pioneer, she mystified and scandalized the people throughout the years she lived among them, incongruously preoccupied with her music, her painting, with flowers, in a community that was up against the stark realities of the frontier. Scholte expressed a part of himself through her, leading with her a kind of double life— that of the Old World domestic amenities, even frivolities, and that of his public character as the leader of a pioneer people. Not nearly all men could successfully have combined the two rôles. To the end of his life he remained the lover of this exotic bird of rare plumage, and at the same time the civic and spiritual leader of a people who were wholly out of touch with her and completely incapable of understanding her.

How much stranger life is than fiction is shown by this Dutch pioneer's story. No responsible novelist would have dared to interweave the incongruous threads found not only in his own complex nature but in his domestic relationship as well. A novelist is under the necessity of being believed. Not so life; it nonchalantly ties together strands that a man's mysterious biological or spiritual needs seem to require, and leaves the mystery where it finds it, without so much as attempting an explanation.

Quite a different type was the Reverend Cornelius Vander Meulen, the "Apostle of Zeeland." The book of his life is somewhat easier to read, and its perusal leaves fewer doubts of its having been read aright than in the case of the other two. His heart and his mind were not in conflict; he had attained to an equilibrium in his nature that must have generated peace in his own soul. In the hearts of others it inspired an affection that leaders rarely enjoy. While the other two were looked up to and venerated, he was worshiped and loved by his people.

In the records of the Dutch immigration of the nineteenth century his name is usually bracketed with that of Van Raalte. The latter was the first to arrive, but the two settlements of Holland and Zeeland were established side by side, the town sites about five miles apart. The portraits of the two men often appeared side by side in the same frame, and the familiar print had a place of honor on the walls of many houses in both Holland and Zeeland colonies, so that to many people they seemed like joint leaders of the immigration.

Vander Meulen did not start life as a member of the dissenters from Holland's state church doctrine. His business was that of a government contractor, and he was a deist in religion. The death of two greatly loved children on the same day, during a cholera epidemic, caused an emotional upheaval that altered the face of life for him, so that he abandoned a profitable business and dedicated himself to evangelism. After a brief period of theological study he was licensed as a minister of the dissenting church.

When the seceders in the province of Zeeland had formed an organization for the purpose of emigration to America he was invited to become their minister, and that was how he found himself in Michigan in 1847. Almost in spite of himself, because so late as 1846 he had warned the people against emigration, in a "Call to Thanksgiving and Prayer." But he had changed his mind, or perhaps his sympathetic heart had impelled him to cast his lot with the people he loved. He was not their civil or political leader, as were the other two, and in matters of economics he was inclined to be delightfully childlike. The practical affairs of the settlement were handled by two business leaders, Jannes Vande Luyster and Jan Steketee. Although each of the three was supposed to be in charge of one of the three vessels that carried the Zeelanders across the Atlantic, Vander Meulen had associated with him a man named Kabboord, who probably handled the practical arrangements. The "Apostle" of Zeeland was quite literally that, a spiritual leader. And that type of leader he remained to the end of his days.

There was about him a sweetness of temper that inspired not only affection but a confidence in the singleness of his motivation; in its presence people found it difficult to maintain their very human hostilities. He quite honestly found it hard to understand why men and women of the same blood, isolated in the wilds of Michigan, should go in for philosophical dialectics that invariably led to bitterness and controversy. His single-hearted nature saw no incongruity in asking the lion to lie down with the lamb, contrary though the practice was to all the laws of nature.

The surprising thing about his career was that frequently, partly through his eloquence but probably more through the unconscious influence of the life of a man who was without guile, he succeeded in getting lions and lambs to associate. Not a leader in the usual practical sense, he yet exerted mystic powers that kept him out in front of his people; there was about him a gentle transcendentalism that did its work without conscious volition on his part. No pride of intellect betrayed him, but he had a large share of the sagacity that is hidden to the wise and prudent but is revealed unto babes and sucklings.

Perhaps his most engaging trait was tolerance—not the mere charity of heart that is willing to let men search out other roads to heaven than the one he himself was following, but a mind-set that instinctively respected the opinions of others in secular as well as in religious affairs. Born leaders often have a low specific gravity in this particular virtue; they are so passionately convinced of the rightness of their own attitudes and convictions that they find it hard to tolerate gladly any opposite points of view. That is frequently why they are leaders; in their very weakness lies their strength; they can keep well ahead of the crowd because they are not lured by their own hearts into fascinating byways. Vander Meulen kept ahead in spite of his tolerant nature.

And many people followed him who did not have this virtue themselves. By reason of this trait, and from his own choice, he became a kind of ecclesiastical trouble-shooter on the Michigan Dutch frontier. When the spiritual inflexibilities of others had betrayed a group into controversy, he was sure to be called upon to straighten out the tangle; or if not called upon he was likely to nominate himself for the job. Undoing human snarls became a kind of profession for this rather untypical leader of the Dutch folk.

There were plenty of such tangles. The people on the Michigan frontier were Dutch Puritans, about as much given to an uncompromising defense of their own ecclesiastical points of view as had been the Massachusetts Englishmen who prosecuted Thomas Morton for indulging in innocent Maypole dances, and who drove Roger Williams into the wilderness for preferring the dictates of his own conscience to theirs. The Hollanders were as inflexible in maintaining what they sincerely believed in as their convictions, and compromise in ecclesiastical matters was likely to be regarded not merely as a weakness but a sin.

Vander Meulen trusted largely to emotion, whereas they were likely to exalt logic. His sermons were evangelistic in character—a remarkable fact when it is remembered that he was speaking for the most part to a folk who set more store by the head than by the heart. But in addition to tolerance and gentleness of heart Vander Meulen had the grace of humor, a trait that is almost impossible to associate with the other two leaders.

What drove him to join and lead a migration against which he had warned only a year earlier? The answer is not far to seek. The title of "Apostle" was applied to him with an inevitability that leaves little room for doubt. He did not aspire to satisfy through migration a secret craving for the all too human will to lead, for the very simple reason that he was free from such cravings. He was almost certainly what he purported to be, and what both he himself and his followers believed he was, the bearer of a message of goodwill to men. He did not hobnob with statesmen, and he did not aspire to be a statesman himself; but he could enter wholeheartedly into the sorrows of his granddaughters whose kitten had died and he could hold a funeral service for their deceased pet without a feeling of condescension or incongruity. He was one of the meek who shall inherit the earth.

Such were some of the leaders of the Dutch people in the nineteenth-century migration. There were many others, at the head of many groups from most of the provinces of Holland. And they were of many temperaments. In the parochial history of the settlements they are sharply individualized, as of course they should be, for there is no common pattern of human hearts and minds, and there is no such thing as generalizing human character even in units of the same racial strain. Hollanders, like members of any other race, are "good" or "bad," kindly or hard, tolerant or inflexible, simple or subtle, saints or sinners. And leaders are in the main not different from the people they lead.

Those three samples may come as near to constituting a generalization as it is possible to achieve.

Whether or not Van Raalte was driven by an unconscious will to power, certain it is that some of the leaders of the Hollanders responded to this very human trait. This was so clear that it was now and again recognized by the people themselves. Whether or not Scholte was motivated by a similarly unrecognized need of an artist to convert men and women into the instruments of his art, there is no doubt that some of the leaders felt this need and sought to satisfy their hunger. Clearest of all is the type represented by Vander Meulen—leaders whose hearts were single, who were free from conflicting motives and purposes.

XIX

A Civil War Without an Appomattox

ALTHOUGH THEY HAVE won the reputation of being phlegmatic, the Hollanders have proved many times during their century of life in America that there is plenty of dynamite in Dutch nature. The resulting explosions reverberate with thundering echoes through their local annals. They have now and again counted the world well lost—if not for love, then for a cause that was far dearer to them than the sentimental affections of the heart. They have often fought at Armageddon with an abandon that had something splendid about it. To many non-Hollanders, however, those battles of ecclesiastical titans usually seemed incomprehensible, even somewhat comic.

Keeping clear of ecclesiastical complexities, the person who wishes to see the issue whole must understand, as a minimum, that there are two main Dutch church denominations. One is, as of today, called the Reformed Church in America; the other is the Christian Reformed Church. Historically the former dates back to a period in Holland long before even the seventeenth century migration was thought of. The latter developed on the Michigan-Iowa-Wisconsin frontier. Ignore the endless ecclesiastical hairsplitting over the contention that such a statement is inaccurate, that the organization of the Christian Reformed Church in America represented a *return* to the "True Church," and that the Reformed Church on the frontier was permeated with "abominable and church-destroying heresy and sins." That way madness lies, at least for average minds not conditioned by Dutch ecclesiastical dialectics from the cradle onward. It is only necessary to know, for purposes of seeing the main outline of the picture, that these two major denominations developed in America during the past century on the Dutch frontiers. That last word should be plural, for there is hardly a village in any state in America where Hollanders or their descendants have settled that does not contain churches of the two denominations side by side.

The first explosion of ecclesiastical dynamite came in 1857, in Michigan, just ten years after the Hollanders arrived; in Iowa the so-called Secession developed somewhat later. Some pastors, in Michigan, developed scruples of conscience about continuing their allegiance to the Reformed Church in America; some others may very humanly have rationalized personal ambitions or irritations into scruples of conscience. There would be no point, in a record like this, to try to arbitrate the differences of opinion on that score. Endless books and pamphlets and newspaper and magazine articles—endless in number and sometimes in word-yardage—have been published in two languages, with sometimes a liberal addition of Latin for impressiveness, to prove that one or the other was "right" or "wrong." It is not necessary, for purposes of this story, to bring in an indictment or to apply whitewash. The story is just as dramatic if the assumption is adopted that both sides, and all persons on both sides, acted in good faith.

Nor is it important for the general reader—though of life-and-death importance to the people involved—to understand in full detail what questions were at issue. One writer hostile to the seceding groups speaks of their "opposition to hymns, to funeral services, to dead bodies in church during a funeral, to flowers on a casket, to church organs, to fire insurance, to lightning rods, to flowers on bonnets, to white dresses, to Sunday Schools, to the English language, to the suffocating gas of Methodism, to foreign missions, to Christmas trees, to vaccination, and to picnics."[1]

There is animus in this catalogue. While most of those apparently trivial reasons for secession became a part of the discussion, many of them were on the lunatic fringe of the debate. The seceding congregations set forth their reasons in terms of impressive doctrinal questions and in terms of ecclesiastical practices that they considered, no doubt honestly, as being "abominable and church-destroying."

The bitterness generated in those controversies is likely to seem out of

[1] William O. Van Eyck, *Landmarks of the Reformed Fathers*, p. 34.

all proportion to its cause, at least nearly a century later. When after a year or two of wrangling the first explosion came in 1857, whole congregations, through their church officers, gave notice to the higher ecclesiastical authorities that they could no longer "hold ecclesiastical communion" with them, usually listing formal charges of unorthodoxy, irregularities in church practices, and so on. Sometimes a seceding church carried only a part of the membership along, resulting in bitterly contested controversies over ownership of church property. In most cases the initiative came from the ministers, and their eloquence persuaded their people to leave the parent denomination in a body. Some of those secessions inevitably became tangled up in personalities, so that after a century it is next to impossible to undo the snarl and determine how much was sincere searching of the heart for conscience' sake and how much was pride of opinion.

Often the language of the letters of notification was unctuous, rich in expressions of sorrow that the parent demonination was continuing to live in its sin and degradation, and of hope that it would some day see the error of its way and come to repentance. Such language always seems hollow and insincere after a long lapse of time, when the passions that inspired it have cooled. It may have been, it probably was, an expression of genuine emotion, and it is fair to remember that the defense also applied rhetorical unction to the replies. Rhetoric has a way of betraying those who employ it; phraseology often is hollow and yet at the same time an evidence of true emotion.

One minister wrote: "Brethren, I exhort you in love not to lose this joint character. The Church, the Bride of Christ, is a garden enclosed, a well shut up, and a fountain sealed. The Lord open your eyes, that you may follow your calling." He subscribed himself: "Your affectionate brother in Christ."

Another one, after giving detailed reasons for withdrawal, and rejoicing that even "our dear little children" were whole-heartedly in the movement (the "dear little children" almost certainly did not know what it was about), added the devout wish: "And oh, we should rejoice still more if the king of the Church should bring you to this conviction. This is the duty of us all."

Still another concluded the notification: "In the hope that God, who alone is able to make a roaring sea calm and smooth, may also make your hearts so calm and smooth that you will walk with us in the way of our fathers, is our heartfelt desire and prayer."

Not quite all used the language of ecclesiastical unction. At least one was blunt, even brutal. He did not subscribe himself "Your affectionate brother in Christ" or anything else; he simply signed his name and indicated the office he held. In his letter he spoke of "abominable heresy and sins" that were "rampant among you," and then he added: "I hope that your eyes may yet be opened to see your extreme wickedness, to take it to heart, and to be converted therefrom."

These things were written, not to prodigal sons or to people who had spent their days and nights in revelry, but to men and women, ministers and laymen, who were almost fantastically pious, who preached two-hour sermons or gladly listened to them, who felt uneasy when they so much as laughed on Sunday, who were not behind the Puritan Fathers of New England in strictness of religious observances. The arguments used were often highly legalistic and technical, in an ecclesiastical sense. They have been defended and denied for nearly a century in an enormous number of documents that have generated a great deal of heat. But whether they displayed bluntness, as some of them did, or unction, as was true of by far the majority, they were the record of an explosion that was devastating in its effects. Here was a relatively small group of aliens making their desperate fight for existence, but falling out among themselves over philosophical concepts, split into two hostile camps, losing sight of the need for presenting a united front to the world.

It was not merely an unimportant family quarrel, it was much more like a civil war on the Dutch frontier; a civil war moreover that would never have an Appomattox. For although one writer so late as 1922 called for reconciliation and reunion, the very tone in which he did so proved that it would never happen. That civil war has lasted nearly a century; during the past several decades there has been a kind of armed truce. The two ecclesiastical branches of the Dutch people in America live on terms of a sweet reasonableness and mutual respect, but the cleavage is too deep, and has continued too long, to suggest that the chasm can ever be bridged. If nothing else would prevent it, a complicated institutionalism, with investments of millions in church property on both sides, with colleges and theological seminaries, would make reunion highly improbable.

For the original explosion of 1857 was followed by another of even greater intensity a quarter of a century later, in 1882. During those twenty-five years more congregations, in Michigan, in Iowa, in Wisconsin, and in nearly every community where Hollanders had settled, had joined the movement and the Christian Reformed denomination had become firmly established. It had founded what is now a full-fledged college and theological seminary, and it had entered upon an aggressive line of action in nearly every community on the Dutch frontier. But the intensity of the original bitterness was dying down, when a second mass secession, on a bigger scale than the first, struck the Dutch people—on a single issue this time, and one that most non-Hollanders found still more difficult to comprehend than the original points of difference. Was there an irreconcilable conflict between membership in a Masonic order and affiliation with the Reformed Church? Large numbers of people, again led for the most part by their ministers, felt that there was, and said so with force and decision.

For two years, roughly from 1880 to 1882, the Dutch ecclesiastical hosts fought a kind of battle of Gettysburg on this issue, with no quarter asked or granted. The files of the church papers for those years and many years later, as well as those of the secular press—though, strictly speaking, no newspaper on the Dutch frontier was entirely secular— present a picture of the life of the people so fantastic that if a reader did not fall back on his creative imagination and on common sense, he would be sure to experience a sense of intellectual vertigo. The people who were the subjects of, and participants in, this battle had far more good sense than the rhetoric employed would indicate. On both sides they were kindly husbands and fathers in spite of their seeming fanaticism on a point of church practice, they were shrewd businessmen or farmers, they were good neighbors even though they fought one another in opposing ecclesiastical camps. In short, the documents in the case tell only a part of the story.

Such was the history of the Great Secession as it developed mainly, at first, on the Michigan frontier. In Iowa the story was similar, with only the dates of explosion different and with somewhat milder repercussions. The first mass secession there took place in 1866, nine years after the period of crisis in the Van Raalte settlement. Forty-two members of the First Dutch Reformed congregation of Pella withdrew at that time, on virtually the same grounds as those by reason of which the Michigan Hollanders had seceded; but there appears to have been less bitterness and drama, less recrimination, and on the whole the war was more decorous.

But from that date on the process was one of progressive separations until in the course of time most of the Dutch communities in Iowa, and indeed throughout the farther western states, were split into two separate local communions so nearly alike in fundamental ecclesiastical doctrine that the non-Hollander invariably had difficulty distinguishing between them. But that did not prevent each from maintaining his own point of view with a tenacity, sometimes with a bitterness, that made cooperative action difficult most of the time, sometimes impossible.

Since the split had come three years before the second Iowa mass migration, the one that settled Sioux County, the settlers in northwestern Iowa carried at least the germs of secession with them on their hegira. Activity in church organization in Sioux County was a little slow in getting into its stride during the first raw, unsettled days, but as early as 1874 a Christian Reformed demomination took its place beside the Reformed Church communion in Orange City, and after that the movement spread rapidly, although somewhat less dramatically than in Michigan.

What this sensational split in the ranks of the Hollanders in America did to the daily lives and the psychical attitudes of not only those who initiated and joined in the civil war but also of their children and grandchildren is impossible to estimate with any degree of confidence. For many of the members of the second generation most of the issues involved lost some of their compelling significance; to still more of the third generation they seemed largely academic, all the more so since the polemical literature on the subject is largely in Dutch, and the third generation had ceased to be bilingual. But for the greater part of a century the split in the ranks of the Hollanders had social, to say nothing of sociological, consequences that have become the theme of novelists but that have never been subjected to adequate scrutiny.

The force of the impact of Dutch culture on the American scene and on American institutions was almost certainly much smaller than it might have been—not specifically in an ecclesiastical sense but in social forms and in the total American way of life. The process of assimilation of the Hollanders into the general American blood stream was probably retarded by it, and because of it the American public has developed a conception of the racial traits of the Dutch people that does them an injustice. Hollanders are often thought of as clannish and unprogressive, and are accused of living within their own social shells. Their ecclesiastical split, which turned out to be a social split as well, has compelled them to present two fronts to the general American scene, the two of them feebler than one combined and united front would have been; and that has diminished their influence in the communities in which they have lived, even when they constituted the large majority there.

But the social and psychical consequences in the lives of the individual sons and daughters of Hollanders have been greater still, often more personally disconcerting. Generalizations on this score are unreliable. Almost any statement that might be made about the social relations of the two ecclesiastical divisions would be true. Some men are convinced—their own experience tells them so—that the adherents of the two rival communions have lived together in the same community on terms of friendship and cooperation. Others have asserted that the rivalry between them was bitter, embittering the lives particularly of the young people whose biology impelled them to fall in love without regard to church connections. It would be easy to prove both statements, depending on the communities involved, or even to prove them for the same community. Surface facts do not by any means always reveal inner conflicts or tensions.

The generalizations here made are therefore tentative, almost experimental. Any Dutch "Middletown," particularly if it was a village or hamlet, would have at least two Dutch churches, even though in terms of economics the people could not adequately support more than one. Or if it was a farm settlement, there would be a Dutch church of one ecclesiastical complexion on one corner and a church of another complexion across the road or a half a mile distant. The two would not dream of an exchange of services. The son from one family might stroll to meeting with the daughter of a neighbor, the two separating at the church door to attend rival services which were yet essentially similar. The results were often unfortunate, especially when biology came into conflict with that intangible force earnest people thought of as religion but which was only institutionalism.

Not infrequently biology was the winner and then there were endless complications, and sometimes compromises of a kind that could not even be imagined by other young people who were not victims of a divided social structure. Psychologically it was often a serious thing for a wholesome young man, or for an equally wholesome young woman, to develop an imperfectly understood guilt complex for no more serious reason than that an ecclesiastical Montague had fallen in love with an ecclesiastical Capulet. The development of such a complex, of course, became rare in the third generation and it probably faded completely in the fourth. But meanwhile many men and women of Dutch blood had been domestically more unhappy than there was any necessity for their being, and had lived under tensions that had been artificially induced. Their elders took such things more seriously than they did, and often there was friction between parents and children for no other reason than that the latter were biologically wise enough to make their choices in terms of biology, not in terms of ecclesiastical connections.

If the young people contracted one of those "mixed marriages" in spite of the wishes of their elders, there might be further complications. In accordance with local public opinion, the male was the head of the house, which meant that he dominated his wife's spiritual life also; she was supposed to join his church and forsake her own. But she had been brought up in the conviction that her people were, ecclesiastically speaking, "right," others "wrong." Love might persuade her to chance the hazard, but even at best such family life often resulted in unspoken conflicts that were likely to take their revenge in needless irritations.

The relationship of good neighbors was affected by the split in ways equally subtle. In all the surface contacts next-door neighbors from the rival ecclesiastical groups acted like—next-door neighbors. Farmers did their threshing together as a matter of course, driven by necessity and their own common sense. No distinction was made, when there was a barn-raising bee or any other communal activity. In the village a citizen might trade at his neighbor's grocery store, even though the neighbor "belonged" to the rival church—especially if there was only one grocery store. Socially neighbors would intermingle, displaying a certain tolerance dictated by the exigencies of community living, but a tolerance that was sometimes not far removed from an only half-recognized condescension. And that is not a wholesome feeling to maintain among good neighbors, especially not if they themselves are incapable of analyzing it. There was likely to be a want of frankness in their neighborly interchanges, which is certain to make for artificiality in such a relationship. In some communities such things were of course the exception, in others they were likely to be the rule. Hollanders, like all other nationals, are individuals, not a mere type; no blanket formula will fit all cases, or even a majority of cases.

Perhaps the most curious, and in some respects the most disturbing, consequences of ecclesiastical bisection revealed themselves in the life of the individual family unit. The father, perhaps, had come under the spell of the eloquence of a fanatical preacher back there in the crisis of 1857 or later in that of 1882. He had honestly come to the conclusion that the separation of himself and his household from the familiar ecclesiastical communion was the most important thing in life —like that of Christian in *Pilgrim's Progress* dedicating himself to getting rid of the burden on his back. His wife and small children had just naturally followed him. In the course of the years he might come to feel that the Voice he had heard so clearly had faded into a mere whisper. But by that time he was an officer in the new church and frankly proud of his position of leadership and prestige. Also, habit had gotten in its work. He himself had no doubts of conscience; and although he was less clear than he had once been that that first fine careless rapture was the fruit of a mystic compulsion, he yet remained convinced that he was walking the one and only road to heaven and that all who were not of his communion were on bypaths.

But his children, now grown up, did not always share in his assurance. Sometimes this resulted in bitter conflicts, especially if neither parent nor child was blessed with temperamental tolerance. There can be no way of exposing to the light the bitter battles fought within the seclusion of the family, and there can be no way of finding out how widespread were such domestic conflicts. There are data enough, however, to prove that they existed and that their consequences were sometimes disastrous both to parents and to sons and daughters.

For the elders did not by any means continue to carry the young people along with them ecclesiastically. A son might insist on becoming a minister in the rival denomination, or sometimes even—*horribile dictu*—in such a communion as that of the Methodists or Baptists. A father's pride in having his son assume the cloth would be clouded by the fact that it was after all in an alien communion; and the son, aggressive though he might be, would still be left with a humiliating sensation of having engaged in spiritual desertion. Or occasionally— something that was rare—two sons in the same family would choose the cloth, one in his father's faith and the other in that of the rival church. Then there might develop a kind of three-cornered tension that even unusual tolerance could not cope with.

Or children of the same family would make various other combinations, even when taking the cloth was not in question. There might be business or professional relationships that were made by sons or daughters who were, quite normally, thinking more of economics than of ecclesiastical affiliations. Their elders might not always have mental flexibility enough to understand, or accept, their reasonable point of view. At least on the Dutch frontier family relationships frequently suffered from want of a fundamental unity that had grown out of issues which, from the point of view of the oncoming generation, had been obsolete before that generation had been born but which the older people regarded as being dictated by eternal verities.

So the Secession with a capital *S* turned out to be not merely ecclesiastical, not perhaps mainly ecclesiastical, at least from the point of view of the grandchildren of those who had set off the bomb and who were hit by it. Happily—again from the point of view of the grandchildren —the separation itself belongs among the "old, unhappy, far-off things, and battles long ago," and the worst of the social and psychological hazards resulting from it have faded out for them. For they are not so much grandchildren of Hollanders who split ecclesiastical hairs as they are Americans whose union with their grandparents is that of a blood stream, not of a given set of ecclesiastical rules. The sequence is biological, and it has biology's strengths and weaknesses. Important among the former are wholesomeness of germ plasm and a capacity for work. One of the latter is a certain mental rigidity that is, however, becoming more flexible through hybridization.

It is necessary to add, by way of almost an afterthought, that the explosions of 1857 and 1882 did not end secession on the Dutch frontiers. So late as the twentieth century there was further dissent—this time secessions from the Christian Reformed Church that had separated itself from the Reformed Church. The number was negligible, but the neo-Separatists often made up for this in ecclesiastical drama. A few of those cases in Michigan are so famous in local history that the names of some of the ministers involved have come to be symbols of revolt. Up until this moment, it seems doubtful that those latter-day explosions will ever be anything more than sporadic.

XX

And Gladly Teach

IN EARLIER DAYS in Europe, and during the past century in America, Hollanders have been a college-founding race. When the siege of Leyden was lifted, in 1574, after one of the most heroic defenses in history, William the Silent offered the people the choice of a remission of taxes for a period of years, or a university. It would not have been entirely to their discredit if a hard-pressed population had chosen the former. Or some people might have clamored for an imposing monument. In the midst of a great war involving their very existence, the Dutch chose an institution of peace that took final victory for granted and that was to be an instrument of rehabilitation. A biographer of William comments: "Significantly one of the first acts of the Nazis on occupying Holland in May 1940 was to close the University of Leyden."[1] During the seventeenth century the University of Leyden was the most famous institution of higher learning in Europe, and its prestige has continued to the present day. But the manner of its founding was more symbolic than its later success; the very fact that it came into being as it did was characteristic of the Dutch race, proof of its respect for and interest in higher learning.

Perhaps still more significant, although less dramatic, was Holland's interest in what may be called lower learning. For her common school education was truly democratic at a time when, in England and throughout Europe, such training was largely for the privileged few. But that type of education has little bearing on the story of the Hollanders in America, for the natural reason that the immigrant masses

[1] C. V. Wedgwood, *William the Silent, Prince of Orange* (Yale University Press, 1944), p. 168.

during the early years after their arrival simply adopted the American grade school system; but that system itself had originally received more of its inspiration and impetus from Holland than from England.

Later still, in the twentieth century, a system of grade schools was established by Hollanders in many cities. Known as "Christian Schools," those institutions cover the same ground that is occupied by the American grammar schools. Their purpose is that of providing a distinctively Christian education for the pupils from kindergarten through high school. The system has drawn its strength largely from the Christian Reformed Church, and its growth has been rapid in many places throughout the United States where that denomination is strong. But the vast majority of people on the Dutch frontiers have always used the public schools and do so today.

The story of the Hollanders' efforts in higher education in America begins in 1766, when Governor William Franklin of New Jersey, son of Benjamin Franklin—he was to become a Royalist during the Revolution—issued to the officials of the Dutch Reformed Church a charter, in the name of King George III, "to erect a college called Queen's College in the Province of New Jersey, and a Corporation of Body Politic, together with all the privileges, powers, authorities and rights belonging thereto as is customary and lawful in any College in His Majesty's realm of Great Britain."

Like most of the institutions of higher learning in America at that time Queen's College was founded primarily as a training school for ministers. In 1766 the language in most of the Reformed churches was still almost exclusively Dutch. For a hundred years ministers had either been imported from Holland, graduates of such universities as Leyden, or else American young men had been sent to the mother country for collegiate and theological training. There was a sprinkling of men who had received their college and theological instruction from ministers, much in the same way in which other men were admitted to the bar after reading law in an attorney's office. Not one of these systems of keeping Reformed Church pulpits filled was satisfactory. When Queen's College was founded it announced as its purpose: "Study in the learned languages and in the liberal arts, and in the philosophical sciences; also that it may be a school of the prophets in which young Levites and Nazarites of God may be prepared to enter upon the sacred ministerial office." The name of the institution was later changed to that of Rutgers College, in honor of Colonel Henry Rutgers. Today the institution is known as Rutgers University.

The year 1784 marked the beginning of a theological seminary in connection with the young college, today known as the Theological Seminary of the Reformed Church in America at New Brunswick, New Jersey. It started in New York but found a permanent home in New Brunswick in 1810. By that time the Dutch language had of course lost out in America. Washington Irving had just published *Knickerbocker's History*. The congregations of the Reformed churches were no longer distinguishable from those of other churches in language, in mores, in manners and customs. A considerable infiltration of the membership was of other than Dutch descent.

And that might have been the end of the story of Dutch activities in higher education in America if the mass migrations from Holland in 1847 had not added another chapter, or perhaps several chapters. For the record of the educational activities of the Hollanders of the West is more dramatic than that of their predecessors in the East a century earlier; or perhaps it merely seems so because it is nearer to our own time.

On the whole, however, it was more distinctively a matter of *Hollanders* founding colleges. When Queen's College was founded New Netherland had been in British hands for almost exactly a century, and the people had become Anglicized to such a degree that the founding of the institution was to some extent an American activity, although people of Dutch descent were principally involved in it. The academies and colleges of the West were organized by people born in Holland, at a time when their national manners and customs were still strong upon them and when many of their supporters spoke no other language than that of their ancestors. They gave their dollars to develop institutions which, they knew, would eventually help to rob their children and grandchildren of the language and national mores they themselves loved. There is something inherently dramatic in that situation itself.

Van Raalte, the Michigan leader, began talking of founding a college almost before the echoes of the first ax blow had died. Within four years he had succeeded in establishing an academy—which remained as the Preparatory Department of Hope College until after the first

World War, serving as a substitute for a high school. But he did not so much as pretend that that satisfied him. He dreamed of an institution to be known as "Hope Haven University," and he later suggested its establishment to the General Synod of the Reformed Church.

Although nothing came of that too ambitious scheme, Van Raalte did succeed in establishing his college, whose first class was graduated in 1866, nineteen years after the community was founded. Speaking of the projected school—first an academy, then a full-fledged college—Van Raalte often used the slogan, "This is my anchor of Hope," when he addressed the congregations of the community to try to loosen their purse strings for higher education. The name "Hope" came quite naturally to be associated with the college itself, and when formal articles of association were filed it was that name that was given to the institution. To this day the college newspaper is called *The Anchor*, a name distilled out of the same slogan.

But meanwhile, for about a dozen years, the high school known as "Holland Academy" had served the needs of the Dutch frontier boys who were looking forward to college, and for the most part to a theological seminary course. In raising money for this infant institution Van Raalte was not above resorting to what, in the colloquialism of today, would be called a "squeeze play." When he wanted money for a building at a time when the people displayed apathy toward the project, he hit on a technique of inducing liberality.

One day a "call" came from a church in Pella; the Iowa Hollanders were inviting Van Raalte, who had visited them more than once and had even served for a few weeks as temporary pastor, to become their minister. Now a "call," to the Hollanders of Michigan, was much more than the mere offer of a job; it was a mystic invitation in which identity was assumed between the voice of the people and the voice of God. It was not to be lightly regarded by either a minister or the congregations involved, the one he was serving and the one he was being invited to serve. But practically and objectively considered, there was a great deal of religious politics in such things, and the practical Hollanders saw no incongruity in injecting financial salary clauses of the most material and specific kind in a "call" that was supposed to be wholly mystic and transcendental.

Van Raalte was a practical man as well as a mystic. Was the Iowa "call" engineered by him? The record is of course silent on that point. It may be that it was not necessary, that he had the wit to take advantage of a coincidence. At any rate, he straightway indicted a letter to his consistory, speaking through it to his people, setting forth the urgent need for the academy building. Then he issued an ultimatum. He gave the people twelve days—no more—to respond with real dollars. He would wait until that deadline; if the money were not forthcoming by that time he would take it as a sign that the "call" from Iowa was the voice of God!

The consistory, in a panic, convened a meeting of the congregation; as soon as the letter had been read to the people they subscribed $250 in cash, a considerable sum for their purses, and signed pledges for more—$12,000 within the next year or two.

The institution that eventually grew out of this academy did not have an uncheckered financial or academic history. Hope College had its ups and downs, like most of the small colleges of the state. As was the case with many others, its primary purpose at first was that of serving as a feeder to the denomination's theological schools. For a good many years its curriculum emphasized heavily a classical education, because a knowledge of the classical languages was held to be indispensable to an educated clergy. For the same reason the Dutch language was one of the branches of study until well on into the twentieth century; enough churches continued the use of that language to make an acquaintance with it desirable.

But in the main the school's curriculum, from the beginning, was not basically different from the curricula of other liberal arts colleges in America, and except for the study of Dutch as a language, instruction was in English. The college was an American institution of higher learning established by Hollanders and descendants of Hollanders. And it is such today. Its students learn far more about the Puritans of New England than about the Walloons of New Netherland; they become much more intimately acquainted with the writings of Shakespeare and Milton than with those of Vondel and Bilderdyke. Quite properly so; they are Americans, not Hollanders, and American literature, although no longer an integral part of English letters, grew out of the culture of England. Holland missed her chance three hundred years ago, and the men who established such institutions as Hope

College intended from the beginning that they should be wholly American in character.

At about the time of the graduation of the first class, in 1866, a theological seminary was started in the little city of Holland, which remains today under the name of Western Theological Seminary. So great was the enthusiasm for higher education that the people dared almost anything, under the spur of the eloquence of their leaders. It was not considered fantastic to establish a post-graduate school the moment the college turned out its first class. The whole system—academy, college, seminary—was thought of as one training school. So great was the people's zeal that at one of the early commencement exercises six hundred persons assembled to listen to the oratory. The program that faced them, and that apparently they absorbed with relish, began at eight o'clock in the evening and continued till two in the morning! Then huge bonfires were kindled to light the people to their homes.

But as far as the seminary was concerned, enthusiasm had raced ahead of reality. The Michigan community was hardly large or wealthy enough to support it in competition with the institution maintained by the same denomination in New Brunswick. After seven years it was compelled to close its doors, but they were reopened in 1884. Today the institution is vigorous and prosperous.

Although not strictly in chronological order, this may be the place to speak briefly of Central College, at Pella, on the Iowa frontier. Its story is given at this point because Central College is at present maintained by the same denomination that founded Hope College and Western Theological Seminary, and its history is therefore a part of the sequence that brought those institutions into being.

It was established at Pella so early as 1853, but not by the Hollanders who had founded the community. A good many Baptists had thrown in their lot with the Scholte immigrants, and it was their denomination that founded the school, giving it the somewhat grandiose name of "Central University." The establishment of a college in his infant community six years after the first sod was cut for the first sod house delighted the soul of the Dutch leader Scholte. He had affiliated with no church denomination but was operating as an independent. He would probably have preferred an independent college of his own; but that was out of the question, so the establishment of an institution by a non-Dutch church communion was the next best thing. At least he welcomed it with enthusiasm, and agreed to serve as one of the members of the original board of trustees. One other Hollander served on that board, named J. Smeenk. Scholte expressed his opinion that he cared little "about differences of opinion regarding the less important points of religious worship."

At the time when the first class was about to graduate from Hope College, Van Raalte made some plans to establish a similar distinctively Reformed Church school in Pella, but the project was abandoned because by that time Central College was well established and two institutions of higher learning in what was hardly more than a prairie village were out of the question.

Central College remained a Baptist institution until 1916, when it was taken over by the Reformed Church. It was given up by the Baptists at that time because its constituency had become largely Dutch in racial descent, and it was located in an area dominated by people of that stock. Perhaps the most picturesque fact in its history is that at the outbreak of the Civil War all its students and faculty members enlisted in the Union Army to a man! For the duration it had the unique distinction of being a college without students or faculty—an institution in a legal and organizational sense only. But it reopened after Appomattox and has enjoyed a continuous existence ever since.

When a section of the church on the western Dutch frontier seceded in 1857 the leaders of the new denomination almost immediately began to think in terms of higher education. For many years there was no thought of a college; the people were interested in a school where future ministers could be trained in accordance with the tenets of the church. But the denomination was far too weak in numbers and finances to achieve even that limited objective. It consisted of only a few churches in a Michigan wilderness, and a few on the Iowa prairies; they had to be served for a time by ministers imported from the Netherlands. But it was often hard to persuade those Europeans to pull up stakes in their settled home and emigrate with their families to the American frontier. The desirability of training men at home was obvious if the new denomination hoped to prosper. Temporarily the problem was solved by turning certain of the parsonages of the incumbent ministers into classrooms for one or two students here and there.

This plan had been followed with some success a century or more earlier in New Jersey and New York, and it served in the West.

This went on until, in 1871, fourteen years after the first secession, there occurred one of those "leadings of Providence" that Dutch Puritans, like their English prototypes, have always been fond of discovering. In that year the idea had occurred to some of the leaders to send a young man from Michigan to the Netherlands to be educated. Soon after he arrived in Holland to enroll in the Kampen School of the Christian Reformed Church he died of the smallpox. A recent historian of the church comments: "Some considered this a hint of divine Providence indicating that training at home was the natural way of procedure in this case." [2]

Whether that feeling was immediately responsible or not, steps were soon taken for the founding of a school. It began its career in 1876, in Grand Rapids, Michigan, in rooms on the second floor of a grade school, and hence it came to be known as "The Upper Room." Incorporation under the laws of Michigan occurred in 1878. Some years later a building was erected and preparatory courses were added to the curriculum. By 1896 the school issued a catalogue, and it was decided that the teachers should henceforth be addressed as "professors." By that time the foundation had been laid for a future college where the young people of the denomination, women as well as men, could be educated in the usual liberal arts courses. This institution, Calvin College in the city of Grand Rapids, went through the stages of academy, junior college, three-year college, and finally four-year college offering an A.B. degree.

The process was complete by 1920. The institution has grown rapidly since that time in numbers and equipment; it had an enrolment of about a thousand students in 1947, the centennial year of the Hollanders' arrival on the western frontier. Like the other institutions of higher learning established by the Hollanders, it has placed great emphasis on scholarship; its students have won the respect of graduate schools, and not a few of them have found places on the faculties of colleges and universities. It draws its recruits largely from the denomination that maintains it, but during the past two decades many from

[2] The Rev. G. D. DeJong, "The School in Parsonage and Upper Room," in *The Theological School and Calvin College, 1876-1926*, p. 23.

other communions have looked to it for a sound liberal arts education.

In addition to the colleges, Hollanders in America have from time to time established "academies," schools of pre-college grade. Several of these were maintained for many years by the descendants of the New Netherland citizens, and several more by the mid-nineteenth century immigrants and their descendants. Of the latter group some are still in existence, but they are gradually losing their reason for being, their functions taken over by the high schools of the American school system.

As for the colleges established by the Hollanders in America, they are not better nor are they worse than other liberal arts colleges in their area, scholastically or academically. They reflect the Hollanders' deep respect for intellectual training, and they turn out a product that can well hold its own in comparison with that of other institutions of their class. Some of their old-grads, of course, give the impression that these schools are intellectually superior to all other colleges. But that is the way of old-grads of any college.

They are unique in one respect; or if not unique, at least somewhat unusual. Their student bodies, at least those of the colleges in Michigan and Iowa, are made up of young men and women some of whom have traveled from a thousand to two thousand miles to attend a particular college. A very large percentage of them have been almost predestined to do so. For them there has never been even the shadow of a possibility of going elsewhere. They may live in a university or college town in New Jersey or New York or Illinois or Minnesota or Washington; when the time arrives for entering college they will travel to Holland, Michigan, or Grand Rapids, Michigan, or Pella, Iowa, without so much as consciously making a choice. The student personnel is as highly homogeneous as that of many other institutions of their class is heterogeneous. A young man or young woman living in the city of Grand Rapids may leave home to matriculate in Hope College, in Holland, twenty miles away, doing so as a matter of course; anything else would be unthinkable. A young man or young woman living in the city of Holland may travel the same twenty miles to matriculate in Calvin College, in the city of Grand Rapids, equally as a matter of course; to do anything else would be equally incredible. Or one young man from, say, the little city of North Yakima, Washington, may travel two thousand miles to Grand Rapids to enter Calvin College, the idea not so much as occurring to him that it might be possible to obtain a comparable education, scholastically speaking, in his own state. Another young fellow living in the same block, even next door perhaps, may leave home on the same day to travel to Holland, Michigan, and enter Hope College; he too would be likely to do so because he had not imagined any other choice of school. The student bodies of the colleges established by the Hollanders show a geographical distribution that is out of all proportion to their size. For the descendants of the Hollanders have spread through many states, and this fact is reflected in the home addresses of their college-going sons and daughters.

XXI

Dutch Nose for News

A PATRIOTIC "LINE" of the first World War, revived during the second, was that the foreign-language press in America was subversive and hence should be suppressed. Whatever may or may not have been true of the other foreign-language newspapers, it was certainly not true of the Dutch-language press. Leaders of the mass migrations, men like Van Raalte and Scholte, urged their followers to become Americans in spirit as well as in language, and that in the main was the tone of the Holland-language press from the very beginning. At the time of the second World War the Dutch-language press had largely ceased to exist, but during the first of the two global conflicts it was still a going institution. As such it tilted its considerable influence whole-heartedly toward the side of the Allies. It is doubtful if even a single exception could be found.

While the leaders looked forward to the Americanization of their people, and understood that in the process the American language must crowd out the Dutch tongue, they also had good sense enough to understand that such a cultural process must of necessity be slow. All the more so because recruits from Holland would be appearing on the Dutch frontier in America for many decades, and those people could hardly be expected to read an American-language newspaper at first. The papers in the Dutch language served as an important instrument of Americanization. In the native tongue of the readers they introduced the immigrants to the ways and ideas of America, and served them as a training school in American politics.

One of the weaknesses of the Hudson Valley immigration, from the point of view of the spread of Dutch culture, had been that a printing press was never established by it on American soil during the whole of the four decades of occupation. A reason why English culture supplanted that of Holland may have been that the English were quick to establish print shops. And while newspapers had not yet been invented, those wilderness printers became the Daniel Boones of publicity for English culture. The Hollanders of the nineteenth century were quick to see the value of the printed word; they had been a newspaper-reading race in Holland; their leaders had been in the habit of appealing to them through the newspapers at home. And frontier papers did not fail to appear very soon.

But not, as might have been expected, first in Michigan or Iowa. The first Dutch-language newspaper that came out of the nineteenth century migration appeared on the least important frontier, Wisconsin. There the *Sheboygan Nieuwsbode* began publication in 1849. But although it aspired to become the official organ of the Hollanders in America, it was absorbed after a time by the German weekly, the *Zeitung*.

As between Michigan and Iowa, the former was the more active in Dutch journalism during the early years. So early as 1850, three years after the founding of the settlement, a paper was established at Allegan called *De Hollander,* at first half English and half Dutch. Soon it became an all-Holland paper, and its office of publication was moved to the village of Holland in 1852. For many years it was a very influential organ of Dutch information and opinion not only in Michigan but in Iowa and Wisconsin as well. In Iowa a Holland-language paper was not established until 1861.

Quite naturally, in a near-theocracy, freedom of the press was hardly to be expected, and thereby hangs a tale of early journalism on the Michigan Dutch frontier. Although *De Hollander* was published as a private enterprise its editor and publisher usually kept in mind that in such a community there were ways of disciplining a newspaper. One was through the church; a newspaper publisher was a church member, and if his paper could not be touched legally, he himself was subject to discipline as an individual. The editor of *De Hollander* discovered this early in his paper's career.

Van Raalte had been successful enough in squelching opposition to certain of his policies by rather arbitrary methods. There had been controversy over the question of affiliation with the Reformed Dutch Church in America, over the liquor question, and over Americanization techniques. The clamping down of the official lid had had its usual result—unofficial gossip and criticism. Van Raalte was accused of leading the "people around by the nose"; and finally an anonymous writer contributed an article to *De Hollander* under the caption, "The Pope and his Cardinals," that caused an explosion. Since the identity of the writer was unknown the editor was "put under discipline" for printing such matter. Van Raalte himself was intelligent enough to understand that public opinion cannot be suppressed by arbitrary methods; the disciplinary action was initiated and carried out by the church consistory. But the time soon came when such things could no longer happen on the Dutch frontier.

The next secular newspaper in the Michigan area was *De Stoompost* *(The Steampost),* established, in 1858, in the city of Grand Rapids. But the two papers with the greatest influence and popularity, aside from the strictly denominational press, were *De Grondwet,* founded in 1860, and *De Standaard,* which began its career fifteen years later. Both papers continued to hold an important place in the life of the Hollanders not only in Michigan but throughout the United States, until the period between the two World Wars, when they were killed by the fading out of the Dutch language in America.

Of the two *De Grondwet* was the more popular and had the larger circulation, advertising patronage, and influence. Its name, literally, means "fundamental law," hence *The Constitution.* Published in the little city of Holland for three quarters of a century, it was during all that time one of the most widely circulated organs of the Hollanders in this country. In its prime it was a very valuable newspaper property, printing as many as thirty-six pages to an issue. Each Monday, publication day, it went out to thousands of homes in a dozen states. In later years, while it was slowly and inevitably dying, some of its subscribers kept taking it for sentimental reasons, when they were losing interest in its contents and their children could not read it.

De Grondwet was Republican in politics, not because it inevitably favored that party but because the paper had been established in that tradition. When editors were imported from Holland, as they sometimes were, they might have difficulty at first adjusting themselves to the demands of American partisan politics. But usually it did not take them long to become infected with the passionate conviction that the "party of Lincoln" had a monopoly on political purity and that by and large the Democrats were rascals who should be kept out of office at any cost.

Like many Holland American papers *De Grondwet* differed from comparable English-language journals in the fact that it carried copious reprints from Dutch exchanges. Even those subscribers who had been born here appeared to take enough interest in the land of their fathers to warrant giving space to such news. The people on the Dutch frontier were interested in such things, and readers anywhere usually get about what they want. Nor did the Dutch journalists wholly neglect fiction; the serial reprints of Dutch stories—often with a background of the Eighty Years' War—were read around the evening lamps in lonely farm homes with a passionate interest that would seem incredible to a later generation.

De Grondwet, as a newspaper, labored under one difficulty that was not only inherent in the peculiar position it occupied in American journalism but one which was shared by many other foreign-language papers. It had to draw most of its advertising patronage from a very small local trading area, and the vast majority of its far-distant readers could never be expected to patronize the business houses that paid for much of the space. The merchants of the little communities of Holland, Zeeland, and a few other places in western Michigan bought advertising space year after year; they could not expect subscribers in New Jersey, New York, Iowa, Dakota, or Washington to buy their goods; yet many of the papers went to such subscribers. In spite of that fact the paper was a money-maker; some advertisers, like some subscribers, may have continued their support for sentimental reasons long after it had ceased to be good business to do so. Both advertising and copy were handset almost to the last. Until a decade before its natural death the paper remained a paying property.

The end came in November, 1939. Quite naturally there was no fanfare of any kind at the passing of this or similar journals. They had outlived their usefulness and usually the end came quietly. It was not in Dutch nature, not even in the nature of the third generation Hollanders whose fate it was finally to close the eyes of the journalistic casualties in the war of the languages to be melodramatic about the obsequies. *De Grondwet,* like other journals in its class, had served the Dutch people well for three quarters of a century. It had made the path to a difficult Americanism a little smoother for thousands of immigrants as they kept arriving from Holland through the decades; in its own undramatic way it had occupied a place of some importance in the American scene. But there was no point in keeping it alive when the life had gone out of its journalistic function. Most of the other Dutch-language journals arrived at their "thirty" in much the same way.

The history of *De Grondwet* was in the main that of its best-known competitors on the Michigan frontier, such as *De Standaard,* published in Grand Rapids, and *De Hollandsche Amerikaan,* a tri-weekly issued from presses in Kalamazoo, beginning in 1889. Another early Dutch weekly published in Kalamazoo was called *De Nederlander;* it began publication as early as 1850. At times there have been other Holland-language papers in such places as Muskegon and Battle Creek.

Such secular papers, and some others of briefer life and lower vitality, all had about the same objectives, they appealed to the same type of subscribers and advertisers, and their function was the same—that of bridging over the transition from Hollander to American. It is hard to see how the job could have been done without them.

Of course, the church press served the same purpose in a limited way, but only indirectly so. There were a great many of those religious journals on the Michigan frontier, some of them short-lived. Several were monthlies. Often they carried religious news to a limited extent, seldom news of a strictly secular character. The articles were often polemical and controversial, the papers of one denomination attacking the theological positions of the other. Also, much space was given to Scriptural exegesis, and to religious movements such as foreign missions. They were hardly enough different from church papers of any other communion to warrant special description, except perhaps that there usually was in them a strong reflection of intellectual interests, less of the emotional appeal than is sometimes found in such publications.

Two church papers, one for each of the two denominations, had the character of permanent fixtures during much of the century of the Hollanders' life in America. The Holland-language organ of the Reformed Church, established in 1865, was called *De Hope,* as was the college whose first class graduated the next year. The church paper of the Christian Reformed Church, *De Wachter (The Sentinel),* was founded in 1868. The former suspended publication in 1933. The latter's life expectancy would seem to be conditioned by that of the language it employs. And as a language for Americans Dutch is of course doomed.

On the Iowa frontier it was not until 1855 that a newspaper appeared that was in part at least under the control of the Hollanders; it was an English-language paper with a department in it in Dutch. That year the Dutch leader Scholte and an American citizen of Pella, Edwin H. Grant, formed a business partnership for the publication of a weekly called *The Pella Gazette.* It served as a mouthpiece for Scholte in both languages, for the leader of the Iowa Hollanders had by this time learned to express himself well enough in the language of his adopted country to write in that tongue with considerable fluency if not quite with unselfconscious ease and grace. The flexibility of expression that he commanded in his native tongue could hardly be expected in an acquired language from anyone. But from the middle fifties on to the end of his life he was a frequent contributor, in English, to various weekly and monthly publications in Iowa. The versatility of the man was astonishing, and his instinct for expressing himself in a hundred different ways was protean. He had dreamed of establishing a Holland-language paper in Iowa, but the Pella area was not ready even for an American-language paper, and *The Pella Gazette* was forced out of business in 1857. Two years later, however, it responded to a resuscitation process, and in time it became one of the important weeklies of the area.

Finally, in 1861, ten years after the first Holland-language paper had been established in Michigan, a weekly exclusively in that language began publication in Pella. It was, however, not published by Scholte. The leader had for some years been an enthusiastic supporter of Lincoln, and *Pella's Weekblad* was Democratic in politics. Like the Holland-language weeklies in Michigan it printed news from Europe, especially from Holland, and it devoted space to telling about and commenting on American politics and state and local events. A monthly called *Pella's Maandblad* was published in conjunction with it to carry the religious news of the community, and comment on it. In time *Pella's Weekblad* became one of the largest and most successful Dutch-language newspapers in America, in a class with such Michigan publications as *De Grondwet* and *De Standaard*.

To offset its Democratic influence in politics, another group, in 1865, founded an English-language paper, *Pella Blade,* that served the purpose for which it was founded, for about twenty years. An attempt also was made in the Republican camp to establish a Dutch-language paper. Under the quaintly hybrid name of *De Pella Gazette* it began publication in 1867, but it died two years later. In 1866 Scholte established a religious monthly called *De Toekomst (The Future)* that he continued to publish and edit, until his death. It was highly influential in the more personal Iowa journalism of the time.

Dutch journalism in northwestern Iowa was more quickly active and successful than it was in the Pella area. Although the first sod of this settlement was not broken until 1869, and although the first locust visitation brought the community to the brink of disaster, so early as 1874 a weekly named *De Volksvriend (The People's Friend)* was issued. It had a hard time because of the locusts but served to maintain morale in those anxious years. Another influential Dutch-language weekly, *Sioux Center Nieuwsblad,* began publication in 1892; and in Orange City a semi-weekly was published for many years called *De Vrije Hollander (The Free Hollander)*. There were other papers, from time to time, printed in the language of the immigrants. All of them in time yielded to the inevitable trend of Americanization.

Sometimes an institution or movement that fails is more attention-arresting than those that succeed. As a kind of footnote to the record of Dutch journalism in America the story should be told of one such attempt, so late as the second and third decades of the twentieth century, that for sheer audacity and imaginative daring can have few parallels in American political and journalistic history.

It was no less a project than the formation of a national Christian political party and the establishment, in Chicago, of a Christian daily newspaper. The political party project never got so far as the convention-holding and resolutions-adopting stage; the newspaper was actually launched, and it succeeded in staying alive for a short time. Then the inexorable laws of economics wrote a period to its career. But the two projects, which were in essence and motivation one, represent a bit of almost forgotten history that stirs the imagination.

During the years just before the first World War some of the leaders of the Christian Reformed Church conceived the idea of translating their Calvinistic principles into political action. They had been doing this on a local scale in the city of Grand Rapids, Michigan, the home of Calvin College, through an organization bearing the Latin name of *"Fas et Jus,"* a kind of Calvinistic municipal voters' league that played an important part in local elections. Why not employ a similar technique on a national scale? A national political party on Calvinistic principles appeared to be the answer.

After a long period of discussion in the church press the movement arrived at the stage of platform building. A drafting committee was actually appointed, of which Professor Barend K. Kuiper of Calvin College was chairman. A contemporary interview perhaps reflects better than anything else what the initiators of the plan had in mind. It was in the spring of 1913 when Theodore Roosevelt's National Progressive party was still a going concern.

One might perhaps think [Professor Kuiper is quoted as saying] that it would be hardly necessary for us to organize a new party since one like the Progressive Party exists. But it would be perfectly impossible for us to co-operate with them. This new Progressive Party is thoroughly humanistic as to principle, not biblical, and when the principle is wrong, practices must necessarily be wrong also. . . . Man, and the authority and greatness of man, are placed on the foreground, while we wish to be obedient to God in the first place and desire to recognize his sovereignty in every sphere of life. We want the principles of the Bible worked out. . . Nor do I believe that we can cooperate with or join the Prohibition Party. I sincerely regret that a few years ago even the Fas et Jus, our Calvinistic political party in Grand Rapids, was led to battle for local option, and consequently for the Prohibition cause. Prohibition displays nothing more nor less than a self-willed religion. Prohibitionism has its root in unbelief. These people wish to be more religious and more holy than Jesus himself was. It's simply dishonoring God. It's what I call a Godless piety. No, Christendom is not ascetic in its nature. Far from it. We wish to enjoy every gift of God. Not in the things themselves, not in the world outside of us, but in the heart

of man sin is situated. There is where everything springs from. The whole
Prohibition movement is anti-biblical and therefore anti-Calvinistic.[1]

That gives an idea of what the architects of the new movement had
in mind. They would rebuild America's whole political structure in
terms of the neo-Calvinism that just then was revivifying their church
life. Although they represented one of the smaller denominations, they
hoped to attract to their political banners members of many other
church communions. They were practical enough to understand that
their new political party would not win state or national elections for
a long time to come; they seem to have expected that as a minority
party it would at least serve as an effective instrument for the dissemination of their political principles. But the year was 1913; within
a matter of months the first World War broke upon them as well as
upon the world in general. The national Christian political party was
never actually organized.

But the idea behind it, as well as the audacity that animated its pro-
jectors, had repercussions shortly after the close of the war that make
it a part of the story of Dutch journalism in America. In 1921 the
ambitious scheme was hatched of launching a national Christian daily
in Chicago. The paper made its appearance under the name of *The
Christian Standard*. The intention was to create a national publication.
Edited by a Christian Reformed minister, the Reverend J. Clover
Monsma, who had had some small experience on a Grand Rapids
paper, it started with more hope than cash. Nevertheless considerable
amounts of stock were subscribed by moneyed men of various churches
throughout the denomination, and a newspaper plant was equipped on
Ohio Street, in Chicago. After a career of about two months the paper
collapsed, and many who had taken a flier in newspaper financing were
wiser and sadder men.

While *The Christian Standard* was an English-language daily, the
spirit behind it was closely identified with Dutch ideology. The directors and publishers and editors were still fluent in the language of
their fathers, and, what is more important, in their thought processes
and points of view. Unfortunately, from a practical angle, they were
for the most part amateurish as newspaper men; their zeal for a phil-

[1] See author's feature article, "A Christian Political Party," in the *Detroit News
Tribune,* July 20, 1913.

osophy of life was much greater than their understanding of the ways of translating that philosophy into journalism. They were transcendentalists trying to run a newspaper, with the transcendentalists' usual lack of practical horse sense. Most unfortunate, from the point of view of their gambler's chance of success, was the fact that they did not understand the financing of a national daily newspaper. Their thinking was in thousands, when every practical newspaper man understands that anyone who plans to launch a national newspaper must train himself to think in millions. In any event, the scheme collapsed almost immediately, and the national Christian daily, established in Chicago by Hollanders, took its place beside the national Christian political party as a magnificent dream that has remained a dream.

This desire on the part of an aggressive church denomination to create a world of its own within the framework of the American social system was also responsible for the attitude of one branch of the Hollanders toward the organized labor movement. Not a few believed that it was their duty to promote unions built on Calvinistic principles. Their attitude of hostility toward conventional unionism has often been misunderstood and misrepresented. Just as they were not hostile to journalism as such but believed that they should develop a Calvinistic national journalism of their own, so they felt they should organize their own labor movement.

Consequently a Christian Labor Association came into being, and for some years it had considerable vogue in a limited local sense. It was almost inevitable that it should be bitterly attacked as a plot inspired by industrialists. It may be that employers used the movement for their own ends, but it does not seem likely that such considerations entered into the motivation of the Christian Labor Association. A group that had the magnificent audacity to project a national political party of its own, and to launch a national newspaper, would consider it possible and reasonable to organize its own labor on a national basis.

All three movements failed. Dutch labor remains somewhat difficult to organize in conventional ways; Hollanders are temperamentally individualists. But the so-called "Christian labor union" has not become national in scope, and it seems certain that it also will remain a dream that failed to come true.

In general, journalism on the Dutch frontier has followed the same lines pursued by the newspapers of other foreign-language groups. The volume of writing in the mother tongue during the early years was enormous, but it gradually yielded to the encroachments of English. The son of a Dutch immigrant publisher might continue the still profitable paper established by his father, while his brother formed a partnership with the son of an Irish Catholic immigrant for the publication of a parallel, if not rival, English-language journal. In course of time the papers in the alien tongue slowly but inevitably died, and today Dutch journalism in America is on the way to extinction. Many descendants of Hollanders conduct newspapers, but they are American papers indistinguishable from those edited by descendants of passengers on the *Mayflower*.

XXII

Serfs and Democrats

AT ABOUT THE time when Van Raalte, Scholte, and others were staging their revolt in the Netherlands, in the thirties and forties of the nineteenth century, the descendants of the New Netherland immigration were engaging in a life-and-death economic struggle in the Hudson River Valley. There was no slightest connection between the two events; the only thing they had in common was that they took place at the same time. The explosion in New York state has gone down in history as the Anti-Rent War. It is a part of the story of Americans from Holland.

The great manorial families were battling to retain the ancient privileges of their class; and legally, in a technical sense, they were on firm ground. Historians have shown a disposition to portray the farmers as a lawless rabble who engaged in insurrection; for the most part the history of this episode has come from the pens of people who were temperamentally hostile to the tenants, or else the "war" has been written down or ignored as unimportant. The other side of the story has recently been told, and it seems likely that future historians will be forced to reinterpret the "insurrection" of the Hudson Valley Farmers.[1]

The hosts arrayed against the tenants constituted an aristocracy of wealth and economic privilege. They were, quite impartially and indistinguishably, English and Dutch and hybrid. The nineteenth century descendants of Kiliaen Van Rensselaer were of them; so was James Fenimore Cooper, of pure British stock; so were the descendants of Alexander Hamilton, half British and half Dutch. So were the

---

[1] This chapter is based largely on the admirable book, *Tin Horns and Calico*, by Henry Christman, Henry Holt & Co., New York, 1945.

Livingstons, the Jays, the Van Cortlandts, and many others who ruled the state of New York, and some other states, regardless of who had been elected by the people.

Opposed to them were thousands of plain and simple farmers, many of them Hollanders. Whether they were technically right or wrong, they made an impact upon American history that set up reverberations far beyond their own valley or their own state. Their "war" made it certain once and for all that serfdom was incompatible with American democracy.

The men who fought and finally won that battle against the landed estates were the economically poor and the socially despised. But because many of them had Dutch blood in their veins, they also had tribal memories of economic and political freedom. They were the direct descendants of the Hollanders of the New Netherland occupation. But unfortunately for them, their Dutch forebears had lived on the wrong side of the frontier ox trail. Just as their great-grandparents had been the retainers and economic serfs of the great Hudson Valley lords like the Van Rensselaers, the Van Cortlandts, and others, so they were, in the thirties and forties of the nineteenth century, the bondmen of the scions of those same families.

In a republic that, out of its unruly West, had sent to Washington a champion of the people—Andrew Jackson—it was of course not possible to hold them openly as bondmen. The great manorial patroon families, so early as the days immediately following the Revolution, had been wise enough to work through democratic techniques. In the last quarter of the eighteenth century they had engaged Alexander Hamilton, a member by marriage of the Schuyler family, to fix things in such a way that the forgotten little men who had worked the vast estates of the Van Rensselaers and their kind would be kept in their place.

That common rabble had merely fought the battles of the Revolution. Many died for their country; when the war ended the rest were about as poor as they had been before. The Van Rensselaer patroon— and this was true for many of the Hudson Valley "lords"—fixed them up with contracts for clearing land, paying the taxes on it, paying rent to the "lords" in perpetuity, without the right ever to become the owners of the improved farms or to sell or dispose of them. The masters of the great estates could sit back, collect rents on land they had not paid for, enjoy immunity from taxation, and live happily ever after from generation to generation. The poor sons and daughters of equally poor Dutchmen were expected to wear out their lives in such a treadmill, and the unearned increment in the value of the farms by reason of their labor and enterprise would go to the masters. From the close of the Revolution until the thirties the forgotten little fellows remained forgotten; their masters were backed by the massed power of government, clergy, money, and society.

In the late thirties and early forties those average Hollanders began to organize for political mass action, and from then on for a generation they fought a political battle of far more than local significance. Although the revolt began to rumble under the surface during the Van Buren administration, it was in the forties that open insurrection broke out, and the "war" lasted on into the fifties. There was some bloodshed; there were acts of lawlessness. Certain leaders—"traitors" and "insurrectionists" were the terms applied to them by the landlords— were tried, condemned to death, later pardoned. Hot blood led to hot deeds; occasionally the "war" deteriorated into something very near to insurrection, and it is not clear that manslaughter did not become a part of the farmers' technique in their battle for freedom.

But only on a very small scale, if at all. In the main the Hudson Valley Dutchmen displayed Dutch common sense and tenacity throughout the long-protracted struggle. Their techniques were largely those of political action.

The details of the story, even after the lapse of a century, are as interesting as its broad outlines. It was finally in 1839 that the embittered and embattled farmers in the Hudson Valley southward from Albany broke into open violence—"insurrection" their enemies called it. Curiously, although very many of them were Hollanders, the farmers were not Hollander-led for the most part. Dr. Smith A. Boughton, descendant of a long line of French Huguenots, was the generalissimo of the movement; Thomas Devyr, born in Donegal, Ireland, served as the Patrick Henry of this war of the Hudson Valley farmers for independence from serfdom; William Brisbane, an intelligent, educated Scot, was another of the leaders and helped the cause of the farmers with his eloquence.

And there were others, men of education and culture who would have had much to gain by siding with the "lords and masters" of the valley and had everything to lose by championing the cause of the Dutch farmers. They shared in the blood and sweat of the battle, went to jail for the cause, and sacrificed money and goods in the conflict. They remain, for the most part, unsung heroes; most Americans today are unaware of their "war" and of their deeds, as they are unaware of the fact that in the forties of the nineteenth century scores of thousands of simple but staunch Dutch farmers fought a battle for freedom not only for themselves and their children but for America in general.

The death of Stephen Van Renssalaer, the last of the Dutch patroons, in January, 1839, touched off the "insurrection." He has gone down in the history of the valley as the "good patroon," and after a fashion he deserves the title. He had not tried to squeeze blood out of stones and had for years tacitly accepted the fact that in the America of the nineteenth century there was no place for serfdom. But neither had he or his fellow patroons done anything about the system that held hundreds of thousands of Americans as virtual bondmen to the land they tilled. They had created the wealth that such men as the "good patroon" had the legal right to appropriate to themselves. Stephen Van Rensselaer's "goodness" consisted largely in not insisting on the pound of flesh that his contract, the courts, the state government, to say nothing of the unofficial masters of the state, allowed him. He may have been afraid to press for rents from the tenants.

In any event, when he died the Hudson Valley farmers saddled with the feudal leaseholds owed him $400,000 in rents that had remained uncollected for years. The "good patroon's" very failure to exact, over a period of years, what was technically due him turned out to be a hardship for the farmers. Quite naturally, believing passionately that the system was unjust and that the rents were not an obligation, they accepted the long-continued failure to press for payment as an admission that feudalism in America was at an end. Suddenly they found themselves with a $400,000 debt. For the heirs of the "good patroon" were not as lenient as he had been; some of them may have felt that they were not as weak as he had been. They pressed for their money, and the law was on their side.

The Van Rensselaer name is prominent among the hosts arrayed against the farmers, and it has attracted more odium than have the names of most of the others. In 1839 the family still owned 1,152 square miles on both sides of the Hudson south of Albany. Legally the farmers who occupied and worked those vast holdings and who had turned them from wilderness into farms by their labor and sweat could be required to pay all the taxes, while the landlord had the right to withhold all wood, mineral, and water rights; and the leaseholds called for many galling tributes such as personal services and other duties more naturally associated with feudal serfdom than with American democracy six decades after the Declaration of Independence.

But although the Van Rensselaers attracted the lightning of the tenants' rage, they were not alone in the attempt to keep the feudal system alive in America. South of the Van Rensselaer holdings, in that part of the valley where the town of Hudson is located, lay Livingston Manor, with its 160,000 acres. West of the Hudson were other feudal principalities. Most of the great families were inter-related, and all of them together formed a close-knit aristocracy that was in complete control of the courts and the government. As a group they ruled over two million acres of American soil, for which they had not worked but that they "owned" in the sense that hereditary title deeds and feudal land contracts conferred the ownership on them. Those vast areas were tilled by some three hundred thousand tenants, very many of them Hollanders.

The farmers were not naturally a rebellious people; quite the contrary, they had put up with what most of them looked upon as an intolerable wrong, for decades. When the landlords pressed for back taxes, at the death of the "good patroon," many farmers asked for a revision of their leases, but the landlords refused. On July 4, 1839, the farmers held a mass meeting in the Helderberg hills that turned out to be a virtual declaration of war, as the landlords saw it; a new Declaration of Independence, as the farmers felt.

The war took the form of writs of ejectment that Stephen Van Rensselaer, son of the "good patroon," had the sheriff in Albany draw up. The farmers at first merely chased the writ servers out. But when the landlords organized a posse of seven hundred to "enforce the law," the farmers—Dutch, Irish, Yankee; they were not exclusively Dutch—surrounded the posse. Governor Seward sent a stronger army to subdue the farmers, who were by this time being called "insurrectionists," and the "war" was on in earnest.

But there were the usual lulls; neither side had much stomach for bloodshed. Moreover, the governor was inclined to try legislative relief. But his successor, Silas Wright, sponsored by Martin Van Buren in the latter's attempt to regain control of the Democratic party, was a landlord himself. The farmers saw themselves opposed not only by wealth but by government as well. And the battle of writ serving and opposition to the attempt of government to enforce the demands of feudalism rolled back and forth over the valley. The farmers had little else to sustain them than stout hearts and a determination to be free.

Under the leadership of Dr. Smith A. Boughton they adopted a curious strategy that has made the term "Tin-horn War" a variant of "Anti-Rent War." When the writ-servers appeared, the farmers disguised themselves in Indian paint and feathers—taking the hint from the "Boston Tea Party"—donned calico gowns for further disguise, and used tin horns to blare out the alarm down the valleys. By the time the officers arrived at the farms whose tenants were to be served with writs, said tenants had faded from the scene. It was a picturesque and, for a long time, an effective device. The farmers' leader, Boughton, came to be known as "Big Thunder," the "chief" of the "Calico Indians," and he became a thorn in the flesh of authority. His strategy was often brilliant; he had a flair for the dramatic that appealed to the popular imagination of the region, but to him the "war" was a holy cause for which he was ready to sacrifice wealth and life. In the end he was arrested and held in chains. Denied the most elementary human rights of an American citizen, he was tried and sentenced to life imprisonment.

For of course there had been some bloodshed. That was inevitable, given the explosive elements in the situation—officers serving writs; posses protecting the sheriffs with guns; farmers, also with guns, disguised to protect what they considered their rights; a few irresponsibles on both sides; "incidents"; a shot by—who shall say; an officer of the law falling victim to hot blood; hysteria; public outcries; state troops called out to enforce law and order.

The battles were dramatic, many of the incidents of the war lurid. But all things considered, the violence was not as great as might have been expected. One town was occupied by the militia in a scene that came nearest to the semblance of real war. The military officers arrested some scores of farmers and turned horses loose to trample their crops in reprisal for alleged atrocities.

But as the "war" dragged on through the years, from the late thirties to the early fifties, it was also fought in the courts, the legislatures, the newspapers, the pulpits as much as in the open field. Many took up the fight in other places than at the immediate scene of the conflict. In New York Horace Greeley's *Tribune* and James Gordon Bennett's *Herald* waged a journalistic "Tin-horn War," and ex-President Martin Van Buren became at least indirectly involved. Many other public men became involved in one form or another, even Daniel Webster, and also James Fenimore Cooper—who wrote Anti-Rent novels.

On the battle front itself violence presently gave way to legislative action; and the techniques of calico disguises and tin horns, to the less dramatic methods of the ballot box. The Anti-Rent War became a political issue that candidates for governor or for the Senate, or even for the presidency, took into consideration in conducting their campaigns; for the New York vote was important and the battling Dutch farmers in time won support from many unrelated sources. They had dramatized an issue that had far wider implications than they themselves understood at first—that a feudal system is incompatible with Americanism. They played an important part in the defeat of Governor Silas Wright, and when Wright's successor, John Young, pardoned the imprisoned leaders, the Anti-Renters were in a strong enough position to get ratification of a new state constitution, in 1846, that abolished feudal tenures and that represented a deathblow to the evil they had fought.

This, together with court decisions in the fifties, put an end to a system that had originated away back in the early days of New Netherland. The Dutch descendants of the folk of New Netherland, with the important help of thousands of people of other nationalities, had achieved a new Declaration of Independence in America, the effects of which were felt far beyond the Hudson River Valley. The most careful historian of the episode, Henry Christman, credits the movement with playing an important part in the birth of the Republican party; and in 1862 it led to the passage of the Homestead Act, a law that for half a century or more provided a new chance for the dispossessed and finally made any type of feudalism in America an impossible anachronism.

The Anti-Rent War was not, strictly speaking, a Dutch war. But the simple Dutch folk of the Hudson River Valley played an important rôle in it.

XXIII

Hollanders in American Politics

HOLLANDERS ARE NOT, like the Irish, born politicians, although a fairly large number of them have served as senators, congressmen, governors, or as appointive officers of national or state government. During for instance the first twenty years after the Revolution "sixty Dutch Americans served in the United States Congress."[1] Generally speaking, however, members of the Dutch race are hard to organize for political action, their native individualism militating against attempts to herd them into parties or blocs.[2] As a result they have developed comparatively few national leaders in the political field to whom the term "great" can legitimately be applied.

Dutch blood, however, has been traced in the veins of not a few important national figures who are seldom thought of as Dutch. Although such assertions are well founded, in most cases the Dutch blood has become so diluted that Hollanders themselves, eager to make out the best case possible for the political distinction of their race, would hesitate to claim them. Even the two Roosevelts, Dutch in name, were hardly or only rather faintly Dutch in blood after three hundred years of hybridization. They have, however, always been accepted as Hollanders both by descendants of that race and by the general American public. But it would be just as reasonable, for instance, to call Franklin D. Roosevelt a Swedish American as a Holland American, unless the maternal blood stream is held to be less potent than that of the male ancestor.

[1] Louis Adamic, "Americans from Holland," in *A Nation of Nations*, p. 101.
[2] Amry Vanden Bosch, *The Dutch Communities of Chicago*, p. 59.

But waive that for the sake of making out a case and accept the two Roosevelts as examples of Hollanders in American politics. Even then Dutch American blood turns out to be less political than that of many other racial strains in the American scene.

Martin Van Buren was truly Dutch in blood as well as in name. But although he reached the White House he does not loom large in the annals of Holland American chauvinism. Americans of Dutch blood probably seldom think of the sage of Old Kinderhook as one of them. And neither they nor many Americans of other racial strains know that the most ubiquitous American colloquialism of the present generation, "O.K.," very probably found its origin in the initials of that same Old Kinderhook, Van Buren's birthplace.[3] To Dutch Americans in general Martin Van Buren is not much more than a Dutch name.

This is all the more surprising because Van Buren cut quite a figure in the history of his own generation. As the political organizing power behind the Jackson administration he was, next to Jackson himself, chiefly responsible for the bloodless revolution that took place in American life during the decade of the thirties. His services to the Have-nots of that age and his abilities as a politician in the narrow partisan sense made him Jackson's inevitable heir. And during his single term in the White House he finished some of the reforms Jackson had begun, among them the final divorce between the government and the Bank. At a time when the word "democracy" was being metamorphosed from a term of reproach into one of political mysticism, he was the champion of "democracy." Strange therefore that his racial blood brothers in America's polyglot population have virtually forgotten that he ever lived. It might have been expected that they would cherish his memory as proof of the potency of their blood.[4]

The fact is that Van Buren has been relatively forgotten by America in general. He has been hopelessly dwarfed by the epic events and personalities of the Civil War period, as is of course true of all the presidents of the period except Jackson. Not by any means a nonentity in his own day, he gives the impression in history of having been

---

[3] Allen Walker Read, "The Evidence on 'O.K.'," *Saturday Review of Literature* (July 19, 1941).

[4] For a fuller portrait of Van Buren see, especially, *The Age of Jackson*, by Arthur M. Schlesinger, Jr. Also, *Martin Van Buren*, by Edward M. Shepard.

merely a shrewd politician; and it is hard to remember such a personality, even with the stimulus of racial pride. Roughly he is remembered as one of the group of presidents that followed Jackson and preceded Lincoln.

He is so remembered both by Americans in general and by his own racial group. Among the former the eclipse of the Van Buren reputation became associated with his record of post-presidential defeat, his failure to achieve a comeback, his inability to understand the new issues of a new age. The champion of the Jacksonian proletariate was not equipped politically or spiritually to join in the battle that reached its climax in the Civil War. When he died in 1862, at one of the darkest moments in the nation's history, Americans were too anxious to give the event much attention. For people of Dutch blood in his own Hudson Valley the magic of the Van Buren name had become dimmed in the Anti-Rent War.

It was not Hollanders or descendants of the New Netherland Dutch who dominated national politics either in colonial times or after the Revolution. Political power, for the most part, emanated from Virginia and New England, both the strongholds of British culture. Socially and commercially the wedge that had been driven between the two areas that were meant to "be forever England" continued to be dominated by a Knickerbocker culture; but in no other way does it become so clear as in national politics that Holland lost her chance to rule on the American continent when the States-General, in 1674, handed over to Charles II without a struggle what brave Dutch seamen had won by force of arms. Plymouth Rock and Jamestown ruled America during most of the eighteenth century in so far as England relinquished political power to colonials. And although Hollanders helped to fight the Revolution on both private-soldier and officer levels, the political policy making remained largely in the hands of men of British blood—the Washingtons, the Franklins, the Adamses, the Hancocks, the Jeffersons, the Henrys. Scions of Dutch families played an important part in financing the Revolution, but in the politics of the great upheaval they usually operated on secondary levels. Some of the great Dutch families were of course royalist, but so were some of the great English families; the score was fairly even between the two races, in that respect.

It is not unreasonable to assume that the descendants of the Hollanders of the New Netherland occupation lacked an instinctive aptitude for politics. In Virginia politics was the game of gentlemen, so much so that it was almost the only respectable profession besides law and the church. Throughout the South political oratory became a substitute for literature, and the manipulation of parties and factions was recognized as a worthy preoccupation of a well-bred man. In New England the long history of the political action in England that produced Cromwell was continued under frontier conditions. The members of a clan like the Adams family were born to politics.

The great Hudson Valley families were leaders in business but their genius did not run to politics as a profession; to them politics was usually a means to an end; business considerations might from time to time make it necessary to control governments, but politics was hardly regarded as an art. And on the higher levels, politics, like any art, is a jealous god; it does not brook dictation, and when it is not the object of worship for its own dear sake it is likely to deteriorate into a mongrel profession in which truly great statesmanship cannot breathe. In any event, whether that generalization is true or not, the great patroon families did not produce many statesmen. There were no Franklins or Jeffersons or Washingtons among them; not even many secondary figures like Patrick Henry or John Hancock. In national politics New Netherland Dutch influence was largely negative. It is fair to add that in numbers the Dutch were a very small minority.

Nor have the Hollanders of the nineteenth-century migration played an Irishman's rôle in national American politics. Of the two original leaders of the people, Scholte of Iowa was more the political animal than Van Raalte of Michigan. As for the third principal leader, Vander Meulen, he did not have the slightest aptitude for political action.

Scholte was political enough to be elected as delegate-at-large to the national Republican convention in 1860; he took pride in being recognized by Lincoln as his "Dutch friend," and he attended the inauguration in Washington. During the war and later, in newspaper articles, he engaged in political discussion in both Dutch and English and in that way exerted considerable influence on the political thinking of his people. As the leader in his community, and the best-educated man on the Iowa frontier, he was naturally looked up to for political advice, and it seems likely that his ideas in politics were more directly and more completely translated into votes than is usually the case. But it should be added that the number of people so influenced was never more than a few thousand; there is no evidence that he, or the Hollanders, strongly affected Iowa politics, and as for the nation, it could hardly have been aware of their vote.

On the Michigan frontier there was during the early years almost no consciousness of political affiliation with the nation. Such consciousness quite naturally is dependent on leadership; the attitude of the head man, or head men, is reflected in that of the people. If Van Raalte and his leader associates had been deeply interested in questions of government the people would have taken color from such interest. They were a simple folk, preoccupied with the hard business of cutting down the forests and growing enough food to stay alive. Moreover, epidemics hit them hard so that at times they were on the verge of despair. Death stalked through their ranks so that Van Raalte himself sometimes cried out in an agony of doubt. In the early years playing politics would have been incongruous for them, and later when ease of mind had come and they were no longer hungry they lacked training for such a rôle.

For Van Raalte and other Michigan leaders did not have the necessary training. Politically they give the impression of having been more unsophisticated than Scholte, in a purely political sense. Not that Van Raalte was unmindful of the claims of government on the people. He advised them immediately to develop the American citizen frame of mind, and through his influence they became naturalized as soon as the law permitted. But all temporal considerations remained secondary. Submission to the secular authority, whatever that authority might be, was a scriptural tenet, and Van Raalte conceived it to be his duty as the spiritual leader of the people to regularize their civic behavior. The motivation of such political action as there was, was not interest in politics, and his knowledge of national politics was limited. He was not the kind of man to be elected delegate-at-large to a national convention.

The one vital connection the people on the somewhat isolated Michi-

gan frontier had with national politics in the early days came through
the slavery issue, a moral question which could be discussed from the
pulpit; although even slavery had to be handled with discreet restraint
as it was also a secular problem. As for the other national political
issues of the day, during the first ten years or so the people hardly
knew they existed. Although they had become American citizens, they
needed time to develop in their hearts the feeling that this vast country
with Washington as its political center was *their* country, not the
fondly remembered Holland with its Amsterdam and Rotterdam.
Washington was too far away and the country was too big to be enclosed politically in their snug hearts. Local politics was another matter and they played their part in it to a limited extent, but the national
political system was probably hardly more than a blur.

Their lack of interest in questions of the secular government was
more than compensated for by their passionate devotion to ecclesiastical politics. That game was to them what a hot campaign always
has been and still is to the average American national. And it had this
advantage that it was continuous. In politics the big show comes only
once in four years, with by-elections to fill in the hiatus. The citizen is
reduced to seeking other interests to take up his full time. The Hollanders on the frontier, from the top-ranking leaders to the lowliest
man in the ranks, had in their religion a never-ending source material
for the same type of disputation in which most Americans engage during political campaigns. It served them as a catharsis of their emotions,
so that they did not feel the need of exercising their dialectical powers
on secular matters. Most of them were astonishingly well informed on
the minute distinctions between doctrines that would leave people with
other backgrounds confused and bewildered; and they argued the fine
points of scriptural authority and church discipline and doctrinal tradition with the same zest that others gave to issues of the protective tariff
and states' rights and, later, to free silver.

Ecclesiastical disputation was the Hollanders' perfect substitute for
the great American game, and their secular newspapers as well as their
religious press made a play to satisfy this absorbing interest. While
those papers took sides in the political campaigns and were party
organs, politics could not compete in interest with ecclesiastical questions. The editors understood, through the sixth sense that all true

journalists have, that questions of doctrine were much more real to their readers than secular political issues; and very sensibly they furnished what their subscribers wanted to read. The files of any of their papers are revealing on this score, and rather astonishing. It is questionable if they could be matched by the newspapers of any other alien element that has been built into the American structure.

That passionate devotion to ecclesiasticism on the part of the people on the Dutch frontier had another effect on their reaction to politics. In the early years the sermon was for them quite normally a substitute for the political speech. Their eloquence, and it was often very great, was channeled off into religious oratory. In that field they produced some speakers of first rank. In some other racial groups those men with silver tongues would have been the governors, the senators, perhaps the presidents of their day. The orators on the Dutch frontier felt they were playing for much higher stakes.

But as the nineteenth century drew to a close and the people on the Dutch frontier began to be indistinguishable from the standardized American type, this political aloofness changed. During the twentieth century citizens of Dutch descent have taken about the same interest in politics as have members of other racial groups. From time to time they have sent a second- or third-generation Hollander to Congress or a comparable national political body, and they have taken their full part in state and local politics. The period of political isolation came to an end for the Hollanders before the children of the original settlers had gone the way of all flesh. In fact, two members of the second generation achieved national standing in the American political scene —Gerrit John Diekema and Arthur Hendrick Vandenberg, both of Michigan.

Diekema was born in 1859, in what was then Van Raalte's little village of Holland. His parents had arrived there in 1848, one year after the founding of the settlement. He was graduated from the infant community's Hope College, on whose board of trustees he later served during most of his mature life. After a law course at the University of Michigan he plunged almost immediately into state politics, and served for a while as Speaker of the legislature.

At about the turn of the century he entered national politics when he was named a member of the Spanish-American War Claims Commission, and in 1907 he was appointed congressman from his district to fill a vacancy. After also serving an elected term, he was defeated in 1910 when he hitched his wagon to the Taft star, although his state was swinging to the "Hollander" Bull Moose candidate for president, Theodore Roosevelt. Later he made a bid for the Michigan gubernatorial nomination, but failed.

In spite of this record of ballot box failure, he was, during some forty years, a political power in Michigan, wielding an influence that went far beyond the racial group out of which he came. The Hollanders of America, in whatever state they might be living, recognized him as their political voice. In 1928 President Hoover appointed him Minister to the Netherlands, an office that he filled with distinction, due in part to the fact that he was genuinely bilingual and could use both Dutch and English with grace and linguistic discrimination. He died while on duty, in The Hague in 1930, and a warship was commissioned by the government to carry his body home.

His political power lay largely in the spoken word; nature had granted him a silver tongue, as it had blessed with eloquence not a few of his racial associates whose sounding board was the pulpit. In 1945 his oratorical techniques became the subject of a University of Michigan doctoral dissertation, when his methods and powers as an orator were subjected to an analysis more searching than is usually accorded the oratorical utterances of a public man. The fact that it was done at all is an indication of his standing in American political eloquence.[5] For him the speech was the norm of expression, so that even when he purported to be revealing himself in print or manuscript, what he wrote invariably had the look and tone of public speech. He had no personal literary style, aside from that of his oral expression, and he did not attempt any other form of communication. In private life he was a sucessful lawyer, particularly effective in jury pleading, and his business interests ranged from banking to serving on almost number-less boards of directors.

All this served as a background for the political activities that were his first love. He responded honestly and instinctively to the conservative interests in his political background, and when in 1910 he sup-

---

[5] Unpublished doctoral dissertation by Wm. Schrier in partial fulfilment of the requirements for the Ph.D. degree awarded June 23, 1945.

ported the reactionary Taft ticket he understood better than many that he was not on the winning side. It would, however, have been completely out of character for him to sacrifice his innately conservative spirit of party regularity to political expediency. He was not in sympathy with the forces that, in retrospect, have proved dominant in the politics of the first half of this century, but he was honestly expressing not only his own innate political conservatism but that of his race as well. Descendants of Hollanders have seldom been Utopians.

Senator Arthur Hendrick Vandenberg is also a second-generation Hollander. His father was born in the Netherlands; his mother, though born on American soil, was of unmixed Dutch descent. The future senator somewhat pointedly retained the Dutch form of his middle name when he began to dabble in Michigan politics during the first decade of the twentieth century. The Romantic Movement on the Dutch frontier was setting in, and in a city like Grand Rapids, with its scores of thousands of Dutch votes, that form of the name was a political asset. Not that he was at that time as yet making a bid directly for votes, but Vandenberg is an instinctively astute politician, and even in those relatively anonymous days he may have had a feeling of what was required for future political preferment.

The politics he played in those days were behind the scenes as a newspaper editor and the protégé of United States Senator William Alden Smith. He consistently and persistently resisted all the various pressures to draft him—and the influence of his Republican paper—for minor offices; his is one of the few cases on record of a man making the jump from private citizen to the United States senatorship. That habit formed in youth of refusing minor offices has stayed with him; it was completely in character for him, in 1940, to refuse to be considered as a candidate for the vice presidency.

Mr. Vandenberg is an effective speaker, but not an orator in the grand manner of the silver-tongued men of his race. But with him, too, speech is the norm of expression. For many years before he made himself heard on the floor of the Senate, his newspaper editorials were daily brief speeches. And very often even a routine interview takes on the same form. The style is instinctive and doubtless unconscious. The three books he has published: *Alexander Hamilton: the Greatest American, If Hamilton Were Here Today,* and *The Trail of a Tradi-*

tion, are in the same tone of oral eloquence. They give the impression of having been composed to be declaimed—which fact has made their style, aside from their substance, a too easy target for critics.

In substance the books are completely in character. The mere fact that young Editor Vandenberg considered Hamilton the greatest American—and he argued the point eloquently and sincerely—is a perfect forecast of the political complexion of Senator Vandenberg. For political and economic conservatism is the marrow of his bones. He has of course broadened his scope and changed his techniques to those of the atomic age. But at the heart of him he has remained the conservative Hollander who, like most men of his race, refuses to believe in a Utopia right around the corner. The conservatism of his hero Hamilton was no more innate than that of Hamilton's rhapsodist Vandenberg. Although he has become something of a world figure by reason of his connection with the San Francisco and Paris Conferences, he has no more faith in a world super-government than he had as a newspaper editor. Right or wrong, he is honestly a confirmed conservative, a reflection of the race that produced him and through the compulsion of the blood in his veins.

While the descendants of Hollanders have not assumed a commanding rôle in American politics, the parts they have taken have normally been played in character as honest interpretations of the life out of which they came.

XXIV

A Bilingual Culture

WHEN HOLLAND-LANGUAGE newspapers on the Dutch frontier had outlived their usefulness they simply died, without too much ado. When
the pioneers' children's children found themselves unable to understand
the tongue of their ancestors they quite sensibly refused to subscribe to
the newspapers printed in that language. And then the papers suspended publication.

It was not quite so simple a sequence in the churches on the Dutch
frontier. There the Hollanders' ecclesiastical transcendentalism came
into conflict with their common sense. Many Hollanders for a long
time continued to feel that Dutch was somehow a more *religious* language than English. The feeling sometimes found definite expression
as a fixed conviction, but for the most part it was an unexpressed
assumption. But not the less strong because it was held half-unconsciously.

Nor was it too unreasonable for simple, sincere people to feel that
way. The leaders like Van Raalte, Scholte, and Vander Meulen taught
themselves English as quickly as they could, and they counseled their
followers to do likewise. But to the average man religion was a form
of art, almost the sole method of artistic expression for him. To any
artist substance and expression are one; the style is the man, the language becomes part of the religion. Logically this feeling or assumption cannot be successfully maintained, but what religion was ever
primarily a matter of logic? The Dutch folk in America had a feeling
that the Twenty-third Psalm or the Lord's Prayer in English was not
so sacred, hence not so religious, as it was in the familiar phraseology

of their own tongue. It followed that religion in English was not so orthodox as in Dutch—again a feeling seldom put into words. Doubtless to the Americans of that day the Gettysburg Address pronounced in Dutch by Van Raalte or Scholte seemed less patriotic than it did in Lincoln's own language. Illogic in such things is the only logic a logical person should expect.

A considerable body of folklore grew up on the Dutch frontier about the nationality of God and His vicars. One of the best-known legends concerned an old farm woman who was convinced that God spoke the Dutch language. While that was recognized as a myth even by those who repeated the tale, it is not so certain that the same could be said of the asserted belief of some of the more unsophisticated that John Calvin, the revered founder of their theology, was a Hollander; they were at least likely to spell the name "Johannes Calvyn." *Pilgrim's Progress*, in Dutch translation under the title *Christenreise (Christian Journey)*, was popular among the Hollanders. There were those who took for granted that *Johannes* Bunyan was Dutch. And it seemed natural for some to spell Henry Hudson's first name "Hendrik," but in this last they did not differ from many Americans who to this day believe that the Hudson River was named for a Dutch sea captain.

It is of course impossible to determine how much of this represents frontier thinking; not infrequently folklore is fictionized to a degree to make a good story. But most men of whatever race can be depended upon to put their faith in the things they want to believe, no matter how fantastic; and the Dutch folk had a passionate affection for their own tongue and culture. To that extent even some of the more fantastic myths contain a truth that is truer than fact.

Inevitably in the course of human events the time came when English began to compete with, and then to threaten, Dutch as the language of religion, of business, of social intercourse. Almost from the beginning in Iowa, and not long after in Michigan, English departments began to appear in the Dutch newspapers, or else a Dutch section formed a part of an English paper. Public documents began to appear in both languages, in response to the fact that the community was bilingual. The language of business followed the same course taken by English five centuries earlier in England, when the "vulgar" jargon of the ignorant populace came into conflict with the respectable Latin of the educated. The time came in England when it was no longer convenient to sell mutton chops or onions in Latin, and a sense of folk humor militated against it. Hence English business life played an important rôle in the development of the English language.

And the Hollander on the Dutch frontier, even when he cherished the language of his fathers in religion, had enough good sense to try as best he could to do business with his American customers in their own tongue. There grew up in the business life of the Dutch frontier a kind of hybrid jargon that was neither English nor Dutch and that invariably offended the ear of the purist in either language. But the Dutch businessman cared little about that, so long as profits were satisfactory. Nor did he often understand that with all of his uncouthness of expression he was an important link in the chain of sequence from one language to another.

In social intercourse the story was somewhat similar, although often complicated by a shamed self-consciousness that did not trouble the soul of the business linguist. Confident and self-assertive enough among themselves and in their own tongue, the Dutch folk were likely to display a too great humility in the presence of Americans, and the very language of the latter seemed somehow sophisticated. The Hollander, of course, could not know how his American neighbor murdered his own tongue. He was given to a feeling of deference in the presence of spoken or written English, and he was perhaps more quick to adopt American vulgarisms and barbarisms than true speech, because he did not instinctively sense the difference. At any rate, he was likely to sing low in the presence of his American "social betters" until his tongue had learned to travel with some ease along the treacherous paths of the alien language.

But the story was quite different on his own ground, as a Hollander among Hollanders. In the war of languages in his churches he stood at Armageddon and he battled for the Lord. His opposition to the introduction of English was in the first place a religious matter. To him the logic of his opposition was very simple: Dutch was a more religious language than the tongue that was trying to displace it; in making his fight for the speech of his ancestors he was doing battle for his ancestors' religion. This logic was of course not expressed in words, unless it be now and then when someone half-unconsciously

let a cat out of a bag. Little evidence of it is to be found in the contemporary documents, but it was almost certainly in the background
of the thinking of many a Hollander who battled stubbornly for the
preservation of his ancestral tongue in the services of his ancestral
churches. The arguments he actually employed were based on reason,
but his main motivation was a mystic but unacknowledged sense of
the identification of his language with his religion.

In actual argument he was, for many years at least, on firm ground.
During the early days hardly any Hollanders understood English,
hence it would have been unreasonable to expect them to listen to
preaching or praying or singing in that tongue. No one expected that,
and it was not during the early years that trouble developed. The old
dogs of the immigrating generation could not be expected to learn
many new language tricks. Nor was the first American-born generation strongly insistent on replacing the Dutch church services with
English. But when their children reached maturity the battle was
joined. Many of them only half understood the sermons and prayers
they heard in their churches, and they knew that their children did not
understand them at all.

It was an irrepressible conflict. If all who joined in it had been completely logical, compromises would have come in the very nature of
things. But few men are ever quite logical when the emotions are
involved, as is the case in a religious issue. The older people felt with
a certain bitterness that the youngsters were frivolous and were depart-
ing from the ways of the fathers. The young "radicals"—actually they
were often painfully conservative—thought of Dutch as an old-fogey
language, uncouth and behind the times. They could not always see
that what suited them would not necessarily suit their elders. This
was the United States of America, and Americans should speak the
language of Americans. Sometimes, when they had the majority vote
in a given congregation, they would force the older members to come
all the way or get out. In other congregations, where the conservatives
were in the majority, that faction might stand like a stone wall against
even minor language changes.

The situation was complicated by the fact that the Dutch-language
faction was constantly getting new recruits, and hence new votes, from
the Netherlands. There was a continuing stream of immigration from

Holland from 1847 on to the time when the quota system was adopted by the United States government. After the first year or two the immigrants came as single families, not as congregations, but nearly all of this immigration converged on a few small areas like Holland, Michigan, Pella, Iowa, northwestern Iowa, Wisconsin, and Illinois. While the total number of Dutch immigrants was not large, as compared with those from Germany or even from the Scandinavian countries, they were not diffused throughout the United States, so that their impact on the communities in which they settled was relatively great. Quite naturally their vote in the language war was for the conservatives; it would have been unreasonable to expect anything else. But that did not prevent the young English-language advocates regarding them, and often sneering at them, as "green Dutchmen." This was authentically a war, and in war fairness is hardly to be expected.

As might have been foreseen, the break toward English came first in the cities. So early as 1861 a church was organized in the town of Holland in which only English was used. And the next year, in Pella, a similar church was organized. Increasingly, as time passed, other English-language communions appeared in those and other cities. Much more often a compromise was reached in city churches; forenoon and afternoon Holland-language services were held, as always, while a new evening service in English was added.

Since it was primarily the young people who were clamoring for English, this was a practical solution; those services, almost the sole social event of the week, served the purpose of bringing young people of the community together. Although the more conservative of the oldsters were inclined to cast a sour look on the innovation as one of the devil's booby-traps for their children, the younger people, biologically wiser than their fathers and mothers, used the innovation for purposes that were wholesomely sociological. In time the English church services in the evening of the Dutch Sabbath became a recognized feature of the techniques of religion on the Dutch frontier.

Moreover, they were the entering wedge for other English-language services. But oh, the battles that were fought between the generations on this issue! It was almost literally another Eighty Years' War, and it is impossible to estimate how many hearts were broken over it and how many tempers were worn thin in the course of the years.

Time was against the conservatives, but that did not prevent them from waging a losing battle to maintain the *status quo* in their own day. It is not clear that all of them understood that after them would inevitably come the deluge of English; such clarity of logic may not have been within the mental scope of all. But others, even though they understood it, still considered it their duty to fight valiantly in a lost cause and to postpone as long as possible the evil day when the less *religious* language would be employed as an expression of the very forms of religion. But they were forced back inch by inch, and slowly but certainly death eliminated them. By the time the Dutch frontier was a hundred years old the issue had been largely decided, although in many rural communities the language of Holland died hard.

The chief casualties in this protracted war of languages, although they did not always know it themselves, were the ministers. The spiritual leaders of the first decade or two, educated for the most part in the universities of Holland, were often men of great linguistic attainments—in their native tongue. Van Raalte, Scholte, Vander Meulen, and many others had a flexibility of Dutch style that made them truly great orators, and also writers of force if not of great distinction. They employed beautiful Dutch and passable English. But the ministers developed and trained on the bilingual Dutch frontier often used a language that was neither English nor Dutch.

In the days that are not yet wholly forgotten, many a pastor was required by his contract to deliver two sermons of a Sunday in Dutch and one in English, or perhaps one in Dutch and two in English. What those men of God did to the language of their fathers is difficult to estimate; what they did to the language of Shakespeare and Wordsworth was more than enough. The worst of it was that they did not realize what they were doing—men often of deep theological erudition. They were pronouncing English words, they were not speaking the English language, or the American language; to a reasonably sensitive ear their locutions were often ludicrous. They had been deprived in youth of a precious possession—a native language. They were forced by the exigencies of their jobs to learn two languages, each of them imperfectly; they were working with blunted tools.

The same thing was true of the earlier political speakers, as it was of many laboring under the tension of an occasional public address. Somewhat later the men in public life obtained their education in English in their associations in college and university, and particularly in rubbing up against all-English speech forms in courtrooms, legislative halls, and through social activities, and were likely to use English in a way that made it indistinguishable from the speech of non-Hollanders.

But the ministers spent their lives in a culture that was in its very nature imperfectly bilingual. They were not put to any objective tests in their speechways, and they did not even enjoy the benefit of ridicule; they were regarded with too much deference for that, and the people they addressed were often as lacking in the nuances of beautiful speech as they themselves were.

On the lower levels of education and culture the mingling of two tongues resulted in a great deal of bastardization that was neither flesh nor fish and that was not without its comic side. The comedy was inherent in the situation itself. Thus there happens to be extant some of the copy that an immigrant wrote for an English-language newspaper that had, incredibly, given him a job as correspondent in a neighboring community. This particular reporter was kept on because he had an unusually good news sense. The only historical and sociological value the excerpts here given have is that they are authentic copy exactly as they came to the city editor's desk. They have not been retouched; nor of course were they printed as written; all the Dutch reporter's copy had to be translated into American journalese before it could be served up to the readers.

The first sample is from the horse-and-buggy days, when the runaway was still legitimate subject matter for news stories: [1]

While going to Jamestown Henry Bos of Vriesland met a serious accident when the horse became frightened for a Gasoline Engine and run away with result that he was thrown out the buggy and fell upon a log who was laying there. Mr. Bos received two broken ribs and internal injuries.—Mr. Bos was just planning to go married next week.

Another runaway:

When Mr. G. Van Hoven was coming from Holland with his team of horses. Mr. Van Hoven was stopping at the Western Meat Market and there the horses were not hitched became his horses frightened and run-

[1] The samples of the immigrant-correspondent's English style are from the author's personal files.

away. They run through the Main Street (it was just the business hours) and run to Mr. Van Hoven's barn on East Main Street just before the cheese factory. Heavy damage was done at the wagon.

A traffic accident in those early days of the automobile:

Leonard Kieviet had a nice experience. While driving his Auto he met with a collission. The auto and a buggy were driving the same way and when by turning the corner from Maple Street and Main Street Mr. Kieviet drove into the buggy and did n't stop before he was in the cigar shop of Mr. Schulmeyer.

The Dutch correspondent's stories of accidents:

Walter K. Dyke who was found in a pool of blood of his own unconscious on the Interurban Track near this city on the night of January 30 is reported slowly improving. His brains who was weak are now stronger.

The youngest son of Mr. and Mrs. Simon Bos who was found unconscious several days ago in the stable there he was kicked by the horse with a scalp wound and a big gash on his forehead and internal injuries and who was given no hope for his recovering is by the prompt medical aid of Dr. J. Masselink that he is reported slowly improving.

While G. Gommers was laying in his hammock to rest he had the misfortune to fell out the Hammock and dislocated his shoulder.

While plowing in a field on Lincoln street Mr. G.J. Nykamp nearly lost his horse. An old cistern who was covered with soil was in the field after the horse and the horse fell in the cistern and after hard labor by the neighbors the horse was saved.

While working in one of the factories here Mr. B. Vander Weide had the misfortune that a bureau who was on a trunk fell upon him and cut a piece of his big toe off.

While working in his barn Mr. Henry Oetman who resides near Hamilton met a serious accident there he was doing to take some hay he had the misfortune to fell from the pile and broke three ribs.

In a fainting spell which Mrs. L. Bouwman of Drenthe had yesterday she had the misfortune to fell against the stove who was burning and cut a severely scalp wound and burned her face also.

While walking from one room to another and innocent that the cellar door was open who was between the rooms Mrs. H. Velzey had the misfortune to fell into the cellar and broke her left arm on two places.

Two samples of bizarre happenings:

It is strictly forbidden in Zeeland to stay on corners of the street on Sunday, but H. Gommers who was warned to move on was arrested for that charge and was brought to Justice Roosenraad court where he was fined to paid $4.20. First he was unwillingly to paid but after ward he paid up and paid the justice 420 pennies.

Thinking that Miss Jennie Meyer was married in silence the boys of Drenthe surprised her with a serenade in kettle music and with the Cow Bells and as a present they thrown two chickens into the house. They broke a fence and window and after finding that they made a mistake they went away. (Miss Meyer will be married next week Thursday.)

The history of the immigrant's struggle with the American language is still to be written. That struggle is almost identical with the process itself of his Americanization. In the very nature of things there are not many documents on which to base such a story, for the average immigrant expresses himself orally in the new language before he attempts to commit his thoughts to paper. Letters home usually do not serve—they are of course in the mother tongue. When documents that could be used find their way into the museums they are often show pieces that have been retouched, and usually they have a more or less self-conscious tone. It is not often that the kind of source material of which samples have been given here, survives.

Such things are interesting largely to one studying dialect patterns; the normal growth of the American language through unconscious importations and adaptations is quite another thing. It is not all a matter of bastardization. The Dutch immigrant writers, like those from other cultures, or their children or even grandchildren, have added flavors to our native American tongue which they did not know they were contributing, whose charm and vigor and freshness have served to revitalize our speech; the depth and variety and flavor of many languages, the Dutch included, are doing their part in building what can fairly be called the "American language."

Perhaps this is the place to speak of a third language of which there have been echoes on the Dutch frontier—neither Dutch nor English but Frisian.

Generally speaking, Americans from Holland refer to all nationals coming from within the boundaries of the Kingdom of the Netherlands as Hollanders. There are some who distinguish between Hollanders and Frisians. Politically Friesland is of course a province of the Netherlands, and throughout the three centuries that Hollanders have lived in America Frisians have usually been accepted simply as

Hollanders. Peter Stuyvesant, for instance, is so regarded by most people. In the story of Americans from Holland there could hardly be a place for any detailed analysis of the ethnic differences between Frisians and the people from other provinces of the Netherlands. But some descendants of Frisians, native or American-born, have been so earnest and enthusiastic in their endeavors to win recognition for their contention that Frisians are not Hollanders, that their labors deserve some attention.

The Frisians are supposed to have come into the Lowlands in the second century before Christ. Motley describes them as a people who were never conquered, not even by Julius Caesar, and they have maintained their ethnic identity for two millenniums. "They have existed as a distinct people, with a separate language and culture, for over twenty centuries." [2] But according to exponents of Frisianism themselves, "Friesland is politically a province of the Netherlands and wishes to remain so; nevertheless she is more than a province and different from others. . . . Friesland is not a nation in the political sense and does not want to become so; nevertheless she is a nation in the ethnic sense and wants to remain so in as strong and distinct a way as possible." [3]

The Frisians are ethnically closely related to the English, and there are many similarities between their language and English. They have a literature of their own and have cherished it century after century. In America, what may be called a neo-Frisian movement has developed among some of those whose ancestors came from Friesland. Not all who belong in this category have joined the movement; some simply regard themselves as of Dutch ancestry. Many of those who distinguish between Frisians and Hollanders do so with something of the same passionate enthusiasm with which a good many citizens of the Irish Free State distinguish between Gaelic and English.

The Frisian language has, however, never become a social "problem" in America, such as Dutch was at one time. It never became the bone of contention in the churches. The Frisian movement is largely one of ethnic patriotic sentiment. As such it has at least the interest of a footnote.

[2] Bulletin issued by the Frisian Information Bureau, Grand Rapids, Vol. I, No. 3 (March-April, 1944).
[3] Quoted in Bulletin of Frisian Information Bureau from Netherland Frisian newspaper *De Stim fan Fryslân*, Vol. III, No. 6 (August, 1946).

XXV

Dutch Domestic Mores

SUNDAY SUPPLEMENT FEATURES about the Dutch frontier in America often make much of the supposed "otherness" of the people who lived there. During recent years many of the communities themselves have been encouraging the growth of a reputation for a picturesque unique-ness—for advertising purposes. Actually the Dutch domestic mores that the original immigrants brought with them from Holland have long since, for the most part, been metamorphosed into the well-known American way of life, with only vestiges remaining of the ancient ways of the Dutch fathers. A description therefore of domestic life on the Dutch frontier belongs largely to history.

A custom that was virtually universal among the actual immigrants, and that remained so until beyond the end of the nineteenth century, called for the reading of a passage of Scripture after each and every regular meal—breakfast, dinner (eaten at noon), and supper. This ritual was a must in every respectable family, and it had the sanctity of an unwritten law. On the assumption that every word in the Bible had found its way there through divine inspiration, the head of a typical Dutch family played no favorites in the choice of passages to be read. After the first meal *en famille* of a newly married couple, the young husband would take down from the clock shelf the shiny new Bible—usually a big volume with double-column page of large, clear type—and begin with the first phrase of the Book of Genesis: "In the beginning . . ." By the time he had arrived at the last verse of Revelation, two or three little tots might be observing their father wide-eyed as he grimly pronounced each word. Never did he knowingly omit a single syllable, and he gave one word about as much emphasis as another. He was likely to devote as much of his eloquence to the reading of a list of the names of forgotten Hebrew kings as to the Twenty-third Psalm or the Sermon on the Mount. Omitting a chapter or a paragraph was unthinkable; selecting a passage for its beauty as literature was equally unthinkable.

This grim determination to avoid doing violence to textual continuity was the source of no little shamed embarrassment to adolescent Dutch maidens who might be introducing their special boy friends to the family. Already nervous about the impression her family might be making on the young man, the daughter of the house whose timing had been unlucky would blush to the roots of her hair when her father, through the innocent compulsion of mere sequence, read a passage in which the facts of life were stated with the frankness of primitive honesty. To have selected another passage would have seemed faintly sacrilegious to him.

The ritual had an inevitable tendency to become routine. Some flexibility there was, so that in haying time, when rain was threatening, the passage read might be briefer than on a winter day with time no consideration. But usually no thought was given to adapting the Scripture reading to seasons or occasions. If Christmas overtook the family while the bookmark was in the middle of Leviticus—well then, Leviticus it was that the father read to the assembled family.

Thus—the story is too pat to be other than mythical—an anecdote gained wide currency about the father of a Dutch household who was in the habit of reading a column from his big Dutch Bible after each meal—a column, not a chapter. The page was printed in double-column, and so he plowed through a page and a half on each of the 365 days of the year. When he had arrived at the bottom of the column he had fulfilled his full and complete obligation and nothing further could reasonably be expected of him. But it was disconcerting to hear him stop in the middle of a sentence—some versions of the anecdote even asserted in the middle of a word. But stop he would, or so the story had it; taking off his glasses he would place the bookmark at the top or bottom of the page in accordance with a private code of his own to prevent accidental re-reading of a column, and replace the Bible on the shelf beside the clock.

While such an anecdote contained a little of the truth that is truer than fact, the ritual of Scripture reading was not the mere lifeless routine that some have said it was. Often the unlettered frontier Hollanders were endowed with considerable native eloquence, and although their lips were hardly touched with the divine fire of the poet, something of the music of the book imperceptibly found its way into their voices, and not infrequently the ritual became a moving exercise.

At the very least, over the years it served to familiarize the generations as they came and passed with a culture that could hardly help enriching their lives; and it was almost the only deliberately cherished culture to which many of them were regularly exposed. Without their realizing it consciously, the great stories and poems and essays and chronicles became part of them, of the mental furniture of their lives. One drawback was that, up until about the opening of the twentieth century, the Bible reading was almost exclusively in Dutch; often Hollanders of the third generation had some difficulty in translating the culture thus acquired into what in their maturity must of necessity be their own language. But even in spite of this difficulty their cultural gain from the routine was considerable.

Saying grace at meals hardly calls for special mention, because of the custom's fairly wide acceptance in many racial groups. Except perhaps that Hollanders made it a ritual both before and after meals. The prayer before meat was genuinely "asking a blessing," and the one that followed the Scripture reading was just as consistently and logically a prayer of thanksgiving. Some households also followed the custom of holding "family prayers" in the evening just before going to bed, but that too is familiar to other racial groups, including Victorian English families, and hence does not call for special description. Nor was this custom universally followed by Hollanders on the Dutch frontier in America; perhaps it was rather the exception than the rule.

A Dutch custom subject to almost no exception was that of copious coffee drinking. Babies began to consume this beverage almost as soon as they had been weaned, and octogenarians continued to delight in it when death was just around the corner for them. The Dutch housewife usually had a pot of coffee brewing on the back of the kitchen range, and anyone who stopped in for gossip or a chance errand was forced by the laws of Dutch frontier etiquette to drink a cup—or two or three, together with "coffee cookies" or some other confection. Regularly, on the Dutch frontier farm, the men came in from the field for coffee in mid-forenoon and again in mid-afternoon—for coffee and bread and butter generously topped with home-smoked dried beef or ham, or sometmes with cheese. Dutch farmers worked hard and they needed the snack between meals.

In some cities of what was once the Dutch frontier, vestiges of that custom linger on even though the reason for it has disappeared. In such places business and professional men betake themselves in droves to the local restaurants in mid-forenoon, and again in mid-afternoon, for a cup of coffee and perhaps a doughtnut. They don't need the snack; most of them would be better off without it. But it is an occasion for a half hour's respite from the cares of business, for juicy man-gossip, for recounting the latest stories—with or without off-color accompaniments. Doubtless some of them do not realize that they are merely carrying on one of the tribal mores of their fathers. Restaurant owners reap a considerable harvest from the trade that is half a social ritual and that is itself a vestige of an older Dutch way of life.

When the Dutch frontier was still genuinely a frontier, coffee at meals—invariably more than one cup—was as much taken for granted as Scripture reading. And on all likely and even unlikely occasions between meals. And, usually, at night just before bedtime; no Hollander on the frontier ever feared insomnia from the consumption of strong coffee—his system had become inured to it from before he had learned to talk. Tea, too, was a recognized frontier beverage, but more among women gathered for afternoon gossip than among men. Farmers working too far afield to come home for the between-meals snack carried a jug of coffee and a lunch to be enjoyed at the end of a corn row, while the horses had their heads in the feedbags. Coffee was the universal Dutch drink. A frontier "poem" describing the disillusionments of many of the emigrants in the hard early days puts high on the list the fact that instead of "Java koffie" the settlers were forced to drink a brew made of burnt rye. That was hardship indeed!

As for stronger drinks, the folk on the Dutch frontier were not addicted to them. Occasionally a group of young fellows might add zest to a local jollification with a keg of beer, but whiskey drinking was

HOLLAND, MICHIGAN, IN 1875

Four years after the big fire that destroyed most of the town.

Netherlands Museum, Holland, Michigan

ST. JOHN'S CHURCH AT LITTLE CHUTE,
WISCONSIN
Erected by Catholic immigrants from Holland.

Netherlands Museum, Holland, Michigan

extremely rare; what is more significant in terms of Dutch mores, it was not respectable. Now and then a Dutch veterinarian or even a doctor might develop a reputation for tippling from his medicine case, but there was a social stigma attached to such a habit. Many families kept a little whiskey or brandy on hand against colds or for medical emergencies, but it was normally used only for the purposes intended.

Except perhaps on New Year's Day, when even children who knocked on neighborhood doors for first of the year good wishes were likely to be rewarded with a tablespoonful of brandy and raisins that went under the name of *boeren-jongens* (literally *farmer-boys*). They might gag on the unaccustomed drink but would be consoled by the cookies or cake that went with it.

That was about all the tippling there was. The cities had their quota of saloons, but Dutch ministers preached against them when the occasion offered, and such places were not considered respectable at any time on the Dutch frontier.

Dutch food was not markedly different from the diet on any frontier; of necessity the Hollanders ate what the land produced, and their eating habits underwent some changes from the ones the people had been addicted to in the Netherlands. But they brought some dietary habits with them from Holland, and such foods to this day are known as "Dutch dishes"—indulged in for the most part only as a kind of romantic adventure in eating.

Thus there was the elusive dish known as *hutspot*, a combination of potatoes and some vegetable, like cabbage or kale, boiled together and crushed. The dish was elusive because every culinary expert had her own ideas on how to make it, and the most important ingredient appears to have been a mystic ritual. *Hutspot* is now and again attempted on the Dutch frontier to this day, on some super-special occasion; but old-timers shake their heads sadly—modern cooks, they are convinced, have lost the know-how.

Less mysterious was the dish known as *balkenbry*, a loaf made out of pork liver and lean pork cooked together; it came to the table sliced and fried. Then there was the concoction known as *botermelk pap*, a dish made, ordinarily, of barley and buttermilk boiled together as a soup, and served sweetened with brown sugar or syrup. The dish was, however, not treated as a soup course but came to the Dutch farm table in a huge steaming cauldron, to be ladled out generously to hungry Dutch children. Also, there was the vegetable dish known as *snij-boontjes*—sliced flat-beans subjected to a mild fermentation in a stone jar; the process of manufacture was somewhat like the one used in making sauerkraut—which is of course a German dish, not Dutch. Perhaps the best known of Dutch foods was *beschuit,* which has made its way to the American table as rusk. So popular was it in the early days that not a few bakeries were devoted exclusively to its manufacture, and some frontier bakers became locally famous for their art.[1]

Perhaps the greatest work of culinary art in frontier diet was Dutch pea soup. But it was not a soup in the American sense; it was a hearty meal in itself, not a first course. It took its name from the whole dried peas used—never the powdered or split variety; pea soup from a modern tin can is only a very distant relative of the real thing, hardly a fifth cousin. The peas were set to soak the evening before the great and solemn day that the Dutch housewife had set aside for the creation of her work of art. The first step in the creative process was usually that of peeling and slicing a huge crockful of onions; no mere flavoring of the dish with onions—their tissue had to be in every spoonful and they were simmered with the soup in its slow three hours of cooking, from the very start. Rice was added to the brew, also at the beginning, in amounts that varied with individual taste. Seasoning too depended somewhat on the cook's knowledge of what her constituency demanded; and there might be minor ingredients dictated by family tradition. But true Dutch pea soup always contained little cubes of potato, added a short time before the work of art was taken off the fire, so they would keep their shape in the finished product.

Most important of all, and put into the kettle in the beginning along with the peas and onions and rice, was the meat that would later be served as a separate course. If the Dutch pea soup was made in the best tradition large and meaty pig hocks were used that had been scraped until even an imaginary speck would have disappeared; cleanliness has of course always been a Dutch tribal trait. The incredible

---

[1] For a discussion of Dutch foods and Dutch language adaptations see an article by Peter Veltman, "Dutch Survivals in Holland, Michigan," in *American Speech,* February, 1940.

tenderness and sweetness of this meat, after its three hours of simmer-ing, made the phrase "work of art" more than a figure of speech.

Dutch pea soup was not for delicate appetites; but robust eaters found in it valid reason for ecstasy. The generation on the Dutch frontier that knows it not has missed one of the minor pleasures of life.

But aside from a few such dishes, Dutch diet was not markedly different from that of the rest of the population.

If the folk on the Dutch frontier did not do much hard drinking, they more than compensated for their abstinence by hard smoking. An adult man who did not smoke was rare; the chances were that he had formed the habit at twelve or thirteen and had never so much as pretended to "swear off." If he lived to be ninety, or even a hundred, he might slough off many another habit of indulgence of his youth, seldom his enjoyment of tobacco.

In the cities, where they were readily obtainable, the Hollander often went in for cigars; on the rural frontier he was likely to smoke a corncob pipe, sometimes cut with a jackknife from one of his own cobs, sometimes purchased in the village grocery store, for they were incredibly cheap—perhaps, at times, two for a nickel. Or he might smoke a clay pipe, also obtained in the grocery store and equally cheap in price. Briar pipes did not make their appearance on the rural Dutch frontier until quite late in the century of the Hollanders' life in America.

But the Hollander kept his corncob or clay pipe warm most of his working day; it was his solace during long hours of toil in isolation. He might admonish his growing boys on the evils of smoking—for boys doing so, perhaps, between puffs from his corncob. Occasionally he would even promise them a gold watch if they refrained from smok-ing until they were twenty-one. The boys did not usually earn their watches—but they got them anyway!

And as likely as not by the time they came of age they had also learned their father's habit of chewing tobacco. Two brands of chewing tobacco popular on the Dutch frontier were known as "Rob Roy" and "Peerless," shredded tobacco that could be either smoked or chewed. Another kind that was popular came in the form of a solid cake known as "plug." About a half-inch thick, it could be carried conveniently in a hip pocket. It was made of leaf tobacco cemented together into its mold by a kind of sugar extract, and its bitter-sweetish taste was greatly relished by some. A chew was cut off with a pocket knife, or sometimes torn off by strong teeth.

Social life on the Dutch frontier would perhaps not have appeared very exciting to people in other communities. Not to people whose literature contains many descriptions of life in the early days on the Anglo-American frontiers. The American rural population in the era of oxen, and later in the horse-and-buggy days, had a fairly crowded social program, if the story writers can be believed. While it was different from the life of today, it was not necessarily less crowded or enjoyable. *The Hoosier Schoolmaster,* as a single example, paints a fairly typical picture of that life—frontier people gathering for spell-downs, for husking bees, for harvest moon entertainments, taking advantage of all sorts of excuses for social jollification.

On the Dutch frontier participation in spell-downs was likely to be confined to adolescents on Friday afternoon in school; they were not used as social events to mask love-making and eating and drinking. Husking bees, beloved of Hollywood in the portrayal of rural America, were virtually unknown; the practical Dutch farmers did their corn husking during hours of daylight, when conditions were right for it.

There was in fact comparatively little communal labor on the Dutch frontier; in the cities and villages there was no occasion for it, and in the rural areas Dutch individualism militated against it. Now and then there was a barn raising that a farmer could not manage in the family, and when that happened it was turned into a social event for eating and drinking, with sometimes even a keg or two of beer half-surreptitiously tapped in a cowshed. But a barn raising might not occur once in five years in a community. Threshing recurred each fall and it was of necessity communal. The threshing outfit traveled from farm to farm, and all the land owners and their grown sons manned the job cooperatively on all the farms. The women meanwhile toiled and moiled and worried to outdo one another in providing generous feasts, and children and dogs gathered to share in the leavings. Threshing thus grew into a social event of a kind.

Sharing movie honors with the husking bee, the barn dance has these many years been a Hollywood symbol of rural social life in America. On the Dutch frontier it was wholly unknown as a community social activity engaged in openly, for the very simple reason that all dancing was "sin." Dancing, card playing, attending plays, boozing, indulging in fornication—such were the sins most frequently fulminated against from the pulpit, and the Dutch preacher seldom minced words or indulged in euphemisms out of regard for the sensibilities of his mixed audience.

Dances were of course held by the entertainment-starved young people. They were called "square dances," the participants going through various intricate gyrations in response to semi-primitive "calls." Calling for dances was, an art that shared honors with "fiddling" for them. The "fiddle" itself was regarded on the Dutch frontier as an instrument of "sin" because of its association with dances; it was not quite respectable to own a violin.

In the cities the young people gradually came to adopt the dancing conventions of the general population. But even a century after the establishment of the Dutch frontier, dancing there was still half-unconsciously associated with "sin." In one prosperous and progressive city dominated by people of Dutch descent dancing was barred from the public schools within recent years by a formal vote of the people in a regular election. And in the various colleges, whose scholarship and general academic standing have won the respect of educators, dancing is hardly even an issue; for students to dance under school auspices is simply unthinkable. Of course, young people, many of them, dance. Perhaps they get more pleasure out of it than others because, in spite of sophistication, they continue to savor in dancing the taste of a faintly delightful wickedness. Dancing also continues to be the theme of occasional fulminations from the pulpit.

Cards likewise were under the ban during the century of life on the Dutch frontier. "Devil cards" they were called, and the pulpit was likely to thunder against them along with its denunciations of boozing; there was a natural association in the Dutch frontier mind between a deck of cards and a saloon, and a typical respectable Dutch father or mother would not have dreamed of touching the things except perhaps to toss them into the fire.

As a result "Pedro" cards, as they were always called, were likely to have a fascination for youngsters of about the third generation that was out of all proportion to their entertainment value. By the end of the nineteenth century very many boys—girls were likely to be more respectable—were learning some of the simpler card games like "Pedro," "High, Low, Jack," "Five Hundred," and others; bridge did not come in until considerably later. But all such games with "devil cards" had to be played under cover. A friendly family game would have been unthinkable up until recent decades. Games played with other kinds of cards were entirely respectable; "Pedro" (bridge) cards alone were "wicked."

Aside from cards, most of the games that have always been popular with an isolated frontier people, such as checkers and dominoes, were respectable if not particularly popular. They could always be played with parental approval and would not have to be hidden even from the minister.

The theatre was of course definitely a "sinful" institution during the early decades on the Dutch frontier. This association of moral turpitude with drama was the inheritance of centuries of hostility toward the theatre in Holland, a hostility that began before a similar opposition developed in Puritan England of Cromwell's time, and that continued long after eighteenth century London had swung back to its Covent Gardens and Drury Lanes. There is probably something racial in Dutch hostility to theatricals; Hollanders don't normally express themselves in terms of drama.

While on the Dutch frontier in America, during the closing decade of the nineteenth century, an occasional "Opera House" offered entertainment in the cities, such places were seldom conspicuously successful. By the time the movies appeared, in the present century, the Dutch frontier had virtually ceased to be a real frontier; with the exception of an occasional community that holds out against them, the cities today support about as many picture palaces as are found in average American communities.

Less definitely racial perhaps was the no less determined hostility toward novel reading. But in fairness it should be added that throughout the first half of the nineteenth century the general American public also regarded novel reading with at least official disfavor. So late as the forties and fifties the fantastically and absurdly romantic lady fiction writers, whom Hawthorne called a "d—d mob of scribbling women," often pretended that their novels were not really novels but "true rela-

tions," with only names disguised. Or sometimes the novel was justified by its moral purpose, such as *The Wide, Wide World* and
Ben-hur. But throughout much of the nineteenth century novel reading was considered at least frivolous even if not definitely wicked, by
the general American public.

On the Dutch frontier it was normally considered wicked, especially
if the novel was what was known as a "love story." Boys and girls
devoured as many of such books as they could lay their hands on, and
usually they were the more meretricious kinds. The young readers
might hide them guiltily when their elders appeared upon the scene,
and they might keep the books in safe places along with dog-eared
packs of "devil cards" and other such contraband, but they usually
managed to acquire them somehow and to keep them circulating
through underground channels.

And while the more respectable and more "serious" older people
considered it their duty to fulminate against the practice of novel
reading, they managed to read some novels themselves, under the impression, or at least the official assumption, that they were reading not
novels but something else. *Uncle Tom's Cabin* was as popular on the
Dutch frontier as it was in the rest of the nation. Long after slavery
had been abolished, and while in its English editions and in the
theatrical versions Mrs. Stowe's story was slowly turning from propaganda into caricature, the book continued to be an excellent seller on
the Dutch frontier, in its Dutch translation under the title of *Neger-
hut* (literally *Negro-hut*). It was not thought of as a novel. Didn't
the author assure her readers that it had all *really happened*? Nor was
Ten Nights in a Bar-room considered really a novel. Nor *The Wide,
Wide World*. Nor Dutch translations of some of the sentimental
concoctions that Hawthorne so bitterly damned. (Hawthorne himself
was unknown.) Moreover the popular Dutch secular newspapers
usually kept a serial going that had enough of the unction of piety to
be eagerly read by story-hungry people in their isolated communities
who were officially opposed to novel reading. And almost any story
about the Eighty Years' War was not really a novel; it was accepted
rather as a kind of history.

There were many such books in circulation on the Dutch frontier.
Dutch children who heard them read out loud around the evening

lamp imperceptibly developed the feeling that the Eighty Years' War had been a fairly recent event, roughly contemporaneous with the American Civil War they learned about in school. Also, they acquired from those Dutch novels a bitter and passionate hatred for Catholics, that sometimes later in life flowered into such unshakable convictions as the belief that all Catholic churches in America had secret arsenals in their basements that would at the proper time be used to kill off Christians. Novels of this type were often lurid love stories as well as religious propaganda, but that was all right—the lovers were always unctuously pious. It is hardly necessary to add that as literature those books were without exception tripe. The boys and girls on the Dutch frontiers fed on such husks and starved for the nourishment they might have obtained from truly great fiction.

But on the whole, social life was not grim and bleak, in defiance of the impression given by such a recital of the various taboos that were in force during much of the Hollanders' century of life in America. During the early decades life was inclined to be rather too real and too earnest, but those were the years of struggle when the battle against the wilderness or prairie was a form of entertainment in itself. Later there was considerable mitigation of the racial austerities; and even before that came about, the folk had their own good times in their own undramatic ways. It is somewhat difficult for the citizens of today to understand what the entertainment consisted in, but all in all there was far less dourness on the Dutch frontier than the official documents would lead one to believe.

Perhaps the whole story cannot be told in terms of exposition or description. It may be that the re-creative imagination of the novelist is needed to paint the picture truly and to paint it whole. The growth-of-the-soil life at Sellanraa would have seemed drab and dull and austere to the outsider, but the people on that frontier had good times in very simple ways that they found thrillingly exciting. Life was inclined to be somewhat more sober than on other frontiers, but there was room also for joy and playfulness, and for the social amenities that are designed to turn living into an art.

XXVI

Lost Generation

JUDGING BY SUCH books as O. E. Rölvaag's *Peder Victorious*, as well as by some of the short stories of such writers as Ruth Suckow and Anzia Yezierska, there is often a "lost generation" among the descendants of immigrants. Not the children of the newcomers, at least not usually so; more often the grandchildren. Or it may be the children in one family and the grandchildren in another, and they may lose their way at different times. It is not so simple as the case of the generation Gertrude Stein counted lost, who had all been battered by life at the same moment. At least on the Dutch frontier the wanderers in the wastelands were scattered through several decades; which is the reason their lost condition has usually been overlooked.

Even those writers among them who have turned their own race into fiction have usually no more than hinted at the truth, perhaps because they were not objective enough to see the whole picture. Writers for some other alien groups have been more successful in this respect. There are numerous portrayals, for instance, of the lost condition of the second or third generation of Russian children in America. If their fictional biographers are to be believed, such children invariably reacted dramatically, often even hysterically, to the obstacles thrown in their path by the older generation. Confronted by similar social crises, Dutch young people were likely to take it quietly, too mortally afraid of scenes to be dramatic about it.

But not too insensitive to suffer, to develop the unhappy feeling of being condemned to live between two worlds, one dead and the other powerless to be born. And intelligent enough to understand that even if they did keep their mouths shut, they would still win the condemnation of such writers and speakers as took cognizance of this irrepressible battle between the generations. The parents have almost always been portrayed as rough diamonds, sound and noble at the heart of them, even though socially they might fall short; the children have usually been condemned as shoddy sons and daughters of essentially noble sires. "O Pioneers!" "O tempora! O mores!"

At least that is the line most of the writers about the Hollanders have taken. Those writers, in the very nature of things, have usually been recruited from the ranks of those who were no longer lost—perhaps the third, perhaps the fourth generation. They could comfortably be sentimentally romantic about the crude forefathers of the hamlet; they had roots of their own in their own soil, and to them the very crudenesses of their ancestors were picturesquely interesting. To the generation bearing the brunt of the transition to a difficult Americanism, trying desperately to hold its own in the sex and business competition with more fortunately born natives, the battle with their own parents often meant something very close to tragedy.

For the parents, the actual pioneers—and sometimes their immediate sons and daughters as well—continued to live spiritually in Holland after they had arrived in America; they merely made a living in this country, they did not authentically live here. Some of their children—more often their grandchildren could not live or breathe in the European land of their fathers; sometimes they thought of it with bitterness and hatred. But they found breathing somewhat difficult here too; they were conscious of a baffling sense of "otherness." They did not "belong," in the wholly unconscious way in which the young natives did that they were thrown with. If their natures were positive, the fact filled them with rage; if timid, with fear; if gentle and thoughtful, with a sense of frustration.

If they had an instinct for expression they sometimes tried to compensate for their sense of lack by turning on the generation that brought them here and that complacently, often self-righteously, continued to dwell elsewhere. They turned in savage hatred, or in sorrow, or in bewildered reproach, depending on temperament. Often what they wrote had little more than a catharsis value. But no matter how feeble the product might be, it served as a release, and those who could resort to expression were the lucky ones.

It was not primarily they who made up the "lost generation," but their inarticulate fellows who were forced to live in an atmosphere of an alien culture at home and were expected to be "American" on the street, in the schoolyard, on the athletic field, in the sex and job competition. Deprived of the compensation of expression, they often arrived at semi-frustration. Without realizing it themselves, they frequently became no better than half-Americans; they had to wait for their own children to go all the way. They represented the hyphen that used to be regarded as necessary in describing alien cultures; they lived partly homeless between two worlds, neither alien flesh nor quite American fowl.

They, not their fathers, are the "forgotten men" of the Dutch mass migration. It is quite the fashion, and properly so, to celebrate the courage and the endurance of the immigrant generation. They left the settled life of home and friends, braved the terrors of the Atlantic, and settled in the wilderness. Tearing up one's roots is no small thing. The terrors of the Atlantic were not imaginary; the accounts alone of the funerals at sea on those six or eight weeks' journeys in the crowded steerage of sailing ships wrench the heart of the reader even a century later. And the wilderness, the mosquito-infested swamps, or locust-menacing prairies were not havens of rest and comfort. The men and women who stood up to such things are deserving of all the paeans of praise that are offered up to them. "O Pioneers!" is not mere romanticism.

But many facts are conveniently forgotten by the rhapsodists to keep their poems of praise keyed to the tune of heroic drama—such, for instance, as the fact that weaklings were not unknown among the pioneers, and that there was narrow-mindedness, and sometimes stubborn insensitiveness. The specific gravity of genuine heroism was not as high as legend, romanticized by racial pride, would have posterity believe. It never is, whatever the race. And after the romanticism has been corrected and compensated for by sober realism, there is reason enough left for panegyric.

But there is also something to be said for those who came later, for the "lost generation." The pioneers had something to sustain them.

Their American-born sons and daughters bore the brunt of many of the physical hardships, but what they had to sustain them was at best secondhand. The pioneers had grown up in Holland, with its centuries-old culture. For them the greatest evil was exile; they suffered from loneliness and homesickness. But—and this was important—they had a spiritual home to be sick for. Some of their children had no home at all in the true sense. The older people had brought their lares and penates with them from Holland; their children or grandchildren had no household gods—it takes a true god as long to grow in a new soil as it does a fir tree. The children had to face the rigors of near-frontier life with the support only of the gods their elders had grown in an alien civilization. Cut off from the culture that had produced those gods, and also cut off, sometimes even more completely, from an American culture through which they might have grown their own deities, they often gave the impression of being somewhat degenerate sons of heroic sires.

The pioneers on the Dutch frontier did not lack books; many of them had brought some from Holland. But that was small comfort to the younger people when their own language had become, or was in the process of becoming, English. Nor did the foreign-language newspapers like *De Grondwet, De Standaard, De Hollandsche Amerikaan* fill the cultural vacuum. Perhaps as a great concession to the new generation, a family might take in a paper in which a few columns in English were found, but written by men who did their thinking in Dutch.

The language used in the family was normally Dutch, or rather one of the provincial dialects of the Netherlands—all of which have an uncouth sound to sensitive ears. Only a very small minority of the people on the Dutch frontier spoke a language that did not make the educated Hollander wince. The Dutch American child was likely to develop the mistaken feeling that the language of his fathers was inherently crude. The members of one provincial group were quick to ridicule the dialectal peculiarities in the speech of another group. The grandchildren of immigrants from Groningen might mingle in the school yard with pupils whose ancestors hailed from Gelderland or Drenthe. Gelderland jeered at survivals of Groningen pronunciation, and Groningen jeered back with still more seering ridicule at the alleged uncouthness of the ancestral speech of Gelderland. There was no way for such children to learn that one was about as grotesque as the other, that the speech of both had about the same relationship to classic Dutch that the dialect of Hardy's Wessex peasants has to the language of Wordsworth. Nor was there much opportunity for them to learn that Dutch is one of the most beautiful of Europe's languages. Some smattering they got of the real thing from the pulpit, but that weekly lesson in linguistics could not begin to compete with the drag on them of Dutch dialect the rest of the time. Quite understandably a member of the "lost generation" might become ashamed of the speech of his fathers, something that should have been reason for pride.

Nor was the substance of the talk he heard at home usually adapted to the needs of the young American of the "lost generation." The history of Holland was the native history of the pioneer generation, the national heroes of the Netherlands were that generation's heroes. But they were not the history or the heroes of a larger number of growing boys and girls than the older people suspected. Those European demigods remained as unreal to a Dutch boy as his own national heroes—Washington, Franklin, Jefferson, Hamilton—were shadowy to the pioneer elders. Lincoln was well known to both generations: the pioneers had voted for him, or against him, and slavery had been their first real political issue in this country; and the younger generation had of course met him in a history book in school. But for the most part the two groups had two different sets of national gods. Because of this not a few of the imperfectly rooted young Americans developed the feeling that they were somewhat less than native to *their own* country. It was from such that the "lost generation" was constantly being recruited.

Usually they had but small opportunity to make compensating corrections through reading. Even in the days of the third generation, public libraries, except in the larger towns, were unknown. If, as occasionally happened, a sketchy township library was maintained, it was almost certain to be inaccessible to most of the eager ones by reason of distance and a lack of understanding on the part of the guardians of the volumes that books are meant to be read. For the most part, until about the close of the nineteenth century, libraries were non-existent, at least on the rural and village frontier.

Not that some of the young Americans of those communities, who were likely to be hungry for American books almost in proportion to the degree to which they sensed their "lost" condition, did not often manage to read English classics. Now and again they were the beneficiaries of fortunate accident. A broken set of Dickens or a stray volume of Cooper or even a mammoth one-volume Shakespeare might seep by a process of a kind of cultural osmosis into a community. Perhaps no one would be quite clear where they came from; to book-starved boys and girls they might seem like an oasis of cool water springs in a desert.

But there was always the hazard that it would prove a Tantalus find. Parental suspicion of the uncomprehended was often so great that the legends are legion of eager boys being forced to read Shakespeare himself in secrecy behind the barn, the way other boys learned to smoke there. Shakespeare's works were plays, and to many Hollanders of the pioneer generation all plays were lures of the devil. Many members of the "lost generation" merely went without books; the foreign-language volumes of their fathers meant nothing to them, the books of their own America were considered unnecessary if not positively harmful.

They were thus compelled to go without many of the tools of their own culture; they were unable to convert those of their European fathers into tools that would serve their own needs. And they lived one life at home, another in the schoolroom. It is hardly surprising that some of them became confused and lost their way. For they had to travel their own road to the world—usually more or less alone. The majority of their contemporaries simply, and for them sensibly, followed the path of least resistance.

Not that all this was clear to the unhappy members of the "lost generation" on the Dutch frontier. For the most part they understood their own trouble only as acute discomfort, and were incapable of making even a loose diagnosis. To be lost is one thing; he who understands that he is lost has already half found his true way.

The result often was a kind of racial inferiority complex. It is too easy to suggest that the sons and daughters of immigrants, or their grandchildren, were under a kind of personal obligation to rise above such feelings; the feelings often went too deep for such facile solutions. Many were ashamed of the very thing that should have filled them with the greatest pride, their blood. It carried for them connotations of a kind of taint, so that the phrase, "the Dutch of it," was made up of racial self-reproach when it was used by members of that race, as it often was. That was obviously an unwholesome feeling, but a feeling that very many acquired at one stage in their racial history in America.

Holland itself was thought of as a land of uncouth peasants, primarily perhaps because there was of necessity a good deal of uncouthness among a race of pioneers, and it was therefore that type that any member of the "lost generation" would be conscious of. Often too ignorant to correct his mistake by reading, and unable by reason of finances and a passionate distaste to correct it by visiting the land of his fathers, he carried through life the feeling that Holland was the one land in the world that was without glamour. Often he was that unhappy person, a man without an ancestral country.

Was that through his own fault, and because he had grown what Louis Couperus has called a "small soul"? In part yes, but his losing his way must have been due to something more than an individual lack; there have been too many instances of it on the Dutch frontier in the course of the race's history to make such an explanation tenable.

Now and again a member of the "lost generation" would attempt to find himself by losing his racial identity in the general American population, going as far away from the home scene as possible. Occasionally this involved disguising his name, perhaps as much to reassure himself as deliberately to deceive others. The members of the "lost generation" were likely to regard a "Van" or a "De" in their names as a special slap at them by fate, and there are many other marks of Dutchness in the racial names, some of which the average American might not recognize as racial; but that fact did not make the suffering any the less for one who was saddled with such a name. A name ending in the syllable "ga," for instance, has been known to make its possessor cringe in self-conscious discomfort; or a name ending in *"weg,"* which is simply Dutch for "way."

Not infrequently Dutch pioneer parents had bestowed their own given names on their children, or more often those of their parents. In Holland those ancestral names had been normal and natural; in the American scene they often had a grotesque look and sound, and to none more so than to the unfortunate ones who bore them. How would Americans pronounce a name like Sjoerd, or one like Foppe? It is not remarkable that a boy bearing such a name should be self-conscious about it when he enrolled in an American university or college or became a member of any other American group. Even later, when the Romantic Movement on the Dutch frontier had set in, and men in public life like Senator Vandenberg took pride in the possession of a name like Hendrick, those who bore the more grotesquely unfamiliar names remained self-conscious about them. Very sensibly some members of the "lost generation" simply changed their Dutch names into American equivalents. But others, and they were the unlucky ones, had qualms of a kind of racial conscience about changing a name bestowed by revered parents. Also, a young man who spent his life in the home surroundings where he had been born, often found it impossible to gain acceptance for a change he might make.

Some members of the "lost generation" had a similar feeling about the place names on the Dutch frontier. Van Raalte and his associates had valiantly tried to mitigate their sense of *heimweh* by giving to their crude settlements in the woods the dear names from home—Holland and Zeeland and Drenthe and Vriesland and Overisel and Harderwijk and Graafschap. In Iowa Scholte had given the Biblical name of Pella to his first settlement, but he and others also commemorated Holland's place names in their frontier towns—Amsterdam and Holland and Maurice and Middelburg and Nassau. The time came when not a few of those who were desperately trying to free themselves of that sense of "otherness" developed a feeling almost of hatred for the names that made up their home addresses. Sometimes the more aggressive ones even tried to persuade their neighbors to join them in Americanizing those Dutch place names. Their children and grandchildren would not thank them if they had succeeded; they are the generation of the Romantic Movement, and their home place names have taken on a sentimental glamour.

Many of those forms of self-consciousness experienced by members of the "lost generation" were relatively harmless. Often they merely meant acute discomfort; but sometimes they had unfortunate consequences. Racial pride, an emotion that in the main is wholesome and vitalizing, often became a species of racial shame. And the rather extreme parochialism into which the Holland Americans had been born and under which they had been brought up, became for them a curse that for some poisoned life.

This parochialism was perhaps no narrower than that of some other racial groups, but to the sensitive member of the "lost generation" it seemed unique, and he often rebelled against it with a passion out of all proportion to its importance. When he had been told from the cradle up that his people were the chosen people; that the institutions of all other communities should be judged—and largely condemned— in terms of the Dutch norm; that Dutch home life was the best, Dutch churches were the only possible churches, the Dutch way of life was the most desirable—when he had learned to accept all that as a matter of course, he not infrequently lost his bearings and swung about to an extreme of revolt that was as ridiculous as his father's parochialism had been.

His greatest hazard in his personal battle for wholesomeness and social sanity, while he was traveling as best he could along his road to the outer world, consisted in the fact that he had to travel alone. He was usually not conscious of thousands of others like him plagued by the same fears, hindered by the same tribal disabilities. The Dutch "lost generation" was not a group with a group consciousness; it was spread over half a century or more in time, and it counted its members on several levels of culture, education, and social development. One youngster might belong to it while his twin brother did not even understand his trouble. Or a father might feel himself a member of the "lost generation" while his son might fit perfectly into the background of the Dutch frontier. Seldom did one of them have the support of a group or even of a small coterie. Usually he did not find himself in a spiritual sense until he had blundered into some "outside" setting in which he belonged. When that happened the tribal associates of his youth were likely to count him "lost," but if he could succeed in developing the consciousness of having truly found himself, he knew that he was "saved."

But no amount of analysis can ever give an adequate conception of the "lost generation" on the Dutch frontier. It is a subject for a future great novelist.

XXVII

Later History of the Dutch Hyphen

BY THE END of the nineteenth century most of the members of the "lost generation" had found themselves. Their fathers and mothers who had represented the hyphen on the Dutch frontier had passed out of the picture, eliminated by death or transformed into unhyphenated Americans by inclination or necessity. The labor pains in the birth of Americans from Holland had been long and cruel; in terms of individuals the casualties had been many; for some the process had spelled tragedy, a tragedy that was no less hard to bear because it could not be dramatized. But all that had largely come to a happy end when the twentieth century dawned. For individuals the pains might persist, for one reason because immigration from Holland was continuing; for the Dutch frontier as a community the hyphen had been erased. Even individuals were seldom losing their way; for the most part they had their roots imbedded by that time in their own American soil.

As of today, at the close of their century of life on this continent, Americans from Holland do not feel that they are alien in any sense. Even those rare members of the community who may continue to speak Dutch intermittently for reasons of convenience or religion, or as a bond between themselves and newcomers from Holland, seldom feel the presence of a hyphen in their background. Most of the very newspapers that, in the now fading past, perpetuated the Dutch language because it served a useful purpose on the frontier, were even then "American to the last word and every word American," to apply to them the motto of an English-language publicist at the time of the first World War. And many individuals who fought to retain the

274

tongue of their fathers in the worship of what they conceived of as their fathers' God, were not less sincerely devoted, because of that fact, to the institutions and ideals of the land of their adoption. A few were alien in spirit, and often such people were noisy out of all proportion to their numbers. There can be no statistics on such a point, but it seems likely that hyphenates were in the minority long before the close of the nineteenth century.

At the time of the mass migration some few of the more provincial-minded pioneers had dreamed of a kind of Dutch Utopia or City of Refuge in the forests and on the prairies. They were the isolationists of the movement, who wished to establish a replica of their home provinces in America; they had dreamed of retaining their own customs, perhaps even the dialects of their home communities, and above all their own religion. Their language and institutions were to remain Dutch permanently; Dutch culture was to rule not only their own lives but the lives of their children and grandchildren; they were to live separated from the life of America in a kind of spiritual and cultural, if not economic, ivory tower. They were to keep themselves unspotted from the American world. A few, a very few, had even acted on this plan. They had refused to learn English, and years later they confessed sadly that "we made a mistake"—they couldn't converse with their own grandchildren whom they adored; they themselves were unable to speak or understand English, and to the children their talk was gibberish.[1]

But their number had been negligible. In any considerable social group there are bound to be a few eccentrics. Such pioneers are remembered today on the Dutch frontier with a tolerant smile, if remembered at all; most Americans of Dutch blood are unaware that there ever were such people among their ancestors.

But some non-Dutch Americans labor under the suspicion that such a spirit still exists, that it is not generally recognized merely because it is deliberately concealed. There is a disposition on the part of some so-called "native Americans"—by which term is meant Americans of British stock—to deprecate pride of race in non-English Americans as manifested in folk festivals, in ethnic institutions, in various attempts to keep alive the story of their European origin. The Americans from

[1] Aleida J. Pieters, *A Dutch Settlement in Michigan*, p. 130.

Holland are now and again admonished by such well-meaning patriots to forget their Dutch origin as quickly as possible, certainly to refrain from taking pains to recall it. Even such dramatically picturesque activities as the Tulip Festivals in Holland, Michigan, and Pella, Iowa, are sometimes regarded with suspicion; they are occasionally thought of as keeping alive Old World points of view that are not organically a part of the American scene. And as for recalling the fact that there was a William the Silent in their racial background, that is usually regarded as irrelevant if not an encouragement to the spirit of alienism.

But many of the more thoughtful Americans from Holland, at the close of the first century of life in America, have an instinctive conviction today that their racial memory of a William the Silent is an important element in their Americanism. While such a thought may seldom become articulate in the masses of people, it is not an unreasonable assumption that it is present in them also. Men capable of giving expression to the idea often employ it on the Dutch frontier in defense of their Americanism. Seldom or never do they suggest that their would-be mentors should not revere a Shakespeare in their British ancestral background, or a Cromwell, or a Milton. Normally it seems natural to Americans from Holland that Anglo-Saxon nationals should be better Americans because of the fact of such figures in their ancestral history. They would not dream of advising Americans of British stock to forget *their* Old World origin. A tree, wherever it grows, does not repudiate its roots if it wants to stay alive. For Hollanders to deny their genesis would be a kind of cultural suicide.

Such a conviction is not incompatible with the growth of an organic Americanism. During the early decades it did retard the process of Americanization. But that was inevitable. Men do not make their national gods; they are born to their gods and inherit them. There could be no such thing as erasing their tribal heredity from the slates of their minds.

That same thing was true of colonial Englishmen in the early days of our history. Franklin and Washington, as young men, and most of the nationals of that time, were Englishmen at heart until they had had time to grow into Americans; for them the process was accelerated by violent revolution. Americans from Holland were subject to all sorts of cross currents that swept over their souls and retarded what later appeared to be inevitable. That, for instance, they fought bitterly for their native language has often been cited as a proof of alienism. Basically it was one of their birth pangs.

And Americans of British stock are inclined to forget that their own ancestors fought just as bitterly against the encroachments of what H. L. Mencken has called the "American language." In so far as the language of this country differed from that of the British they regarded it as barbarous and sneered at it as "Americanese." That opposition is continuing even today. Many Anglo-Americans see nothing incongruous or unpatriotic in preferring English speech to American. In a choice between the two, they are inclined to be apologetic in regard to the speech of their own country when it differs from the language of England—as if American speech were a kind of bastardization. They would consider as wholly unfair the implication that they are poor Americans for saying "again" with a long *a*, or "either" and "neither" with a long *i*, or for referring to a movie as a "cinema." And it would of course be unfair, but not more so than to suggest that Americans from Holland are less than truly "native" because their ancestors clung as long as possible, at least in the exercise of their religion, to the speech to which they or their fathers had been born.

The people on the Dutch frontier are sometimes told that it is their duty to adapt themselves to the political and cultural patterns they find here. In the main, as of today at least, they subscribe to that injunction with enthusiasm, but they are not convinced that their forefathers migrated to a finished civilization. They are inclined to feel that the very essence of Americanism is progressive change, that it is not of the true nature of Americanism to freeze social or political institutions. To do that would result in a dead world, and their fathers' reason for migration was to escape from that type of life. To fix the American pattern in terms of the social and political structure of any country— England or any other—seems peculiarly un-American to them. They insist, quite unconsciously for the most part, on modifying the cultural and political pattern in terms of their own cultural and political inheritance, and to remodel such institutions as have grown up in America to serve them best in the exercise of their Americanism. They have little desire to make themselves over into "native stock" Americans, and see no reason for denying their blood, believing that their blood gives them their opportunity to add something to the term "American" that men of no other race can give, not even the nationals of purest English stock.

For they are good enough Americans to feel that the opportunity is theirs to pump rich new blood through the pulses of American institutions. America, the vast majority unconsciously believe, is more truly America because its life blood has been enriched by them and by other continental European groups. That blood is not better than the plasma that came to present-day America from the Pilgrims or from the Virginia Cavaliers, but it is different, and the strength of America, they are convinced, lies not in homogeneity but in differentness.

That otherness has played a part, they believe, in America's cultural Declaration of Independence that Emerson called for in his revolutionary Phi Beta Kappa address in 1837. From occupying the position of a satellite, in literature and language, their country, America, has finally taken its place as an independent member of the United Nations of the spirit. They take a sober pride in believing that they have helped a little in transforming their native land from a parochial community tied to Anglo-Saxonism by the apron strings of language, into a country whose culture is fed not by a single English spring but by many springs in many lands.

Individuals do of course feel, and sometimes they say so passionately, that an elixir of special richness courses through the veins of Hollanders. But that is inevitable, and very human. The same thing is true of stray members in almost any other racial group. It seldom means that the group as a whole has a sense of superiority; rather, usually, that individuals who feel themselves racially inferior, loudly assert their superiority because of that very fact. On the whole the folk on the Dutch frontier are inclined to be reasonably free from racial self-consciousness. They pride themselves on the great men and institutions of their ancestral country, and on the ways of life of their fathers, not to draw an invidious comparison between Dutch ways and those of the English, but because it is natural and wholesome to keep one's roots in remembrance. Sometimes such manifestations of ethnic pride give an impression of tribal boasting. It is hardly to be wondered at that individuals of Anglo-Saxon stock should so interpret this spirit when, as minority members of such a community, they are subjected to the cumulative impact of many individual boasts.

In any event, the men of "native stock" on the Dutch frontier sometimes break out in long-suppressed resentment against neighbors and friends, business associates or clients or customers, who have boasted too often of their racial achievements. The resentment is not less real for being expressed under the cloak of banter or persiflage.

Thus one community with a very Dutch name cherishes a tradition of how one Anglo-Saxon worm turned. A prominent attorney of "native stock" created a sensation by indulging in public address, not on the familiar local theme of the achievements of Hollanders but on that of non-Dutch contributions to the local economy. His own ancestors had come from New England. His lot, as well as that of his father, was cast in a community that was predominantly Dutch. Nationally a member of the dominant race, locally on the Dutch frontier he was a unit in the minority group; subconsciously that position of racial inferiority irked him. All his life he had been forced to hear the Dutch and their contributions extolled. But the Dutch had not built the whole town, in spite of its Dutch name, Dutch traditions, and Dutch flavor. All the major industries—he laid stress on the "all" —had been organized by non-Hollanders. The city had never had a school superintendent of Dutch descent, he pointed out triumphantly. (It has not had one to this day.) The very exploitation of Dutch tradition that had brought something like national fame to the community had been suggested by one who could not claim a drop of Dutch blood.

His oratorical riposte was completely fair, and the community in general so regarded it; every word he spoke was true. The people were mildly surprised at his heat, because it did not occur to them at the moment to attribute it to his sense of a community minority status. The fact is often forgotten that thousands of "native stock" Americans are living as minority members in communities founded and dominated by socalled "aliens"—Hollanders or Germans or Scandinavians or Italians. The term "minority group" is invariably applied by writers of Anglo-Saxon stock to people whose ancestors did *not* come from the British Isles. But people of English stock, like this attorney, are quite likely to be members of a "minority group" with reference to the local majority. When this happens they are not immune from a community inferiority complex. And it is natural that they should engage in a compensating assertion of superiority.

That may be the reason why they sometimes stress unduly the alleged continued existence of the hyphen on the Dutch frontier. They may derive a sense of superiority from the assumption that their numerically dominant neighbors and friends are after all lacking in American quality. And the more aggressive ones among them are not always backward in advice to their neighbors to erase the hyphen that is supposed to be separating them from Simon-pure Americanism.

Actually, in a community sense, the hyphen no longer exists on the Dutch frontier. The folk for the most part are quite simply Americans, and nothing else. They would not dream of resenting the fact that, if they are Dutch from both sides of the family, they cannot join the local chapter of the Sons of the Revolution, or that their wives, if similarly of Western Dutch ancestry, are not eligible for membership in the D.A.R. Those are simply facts. Their ancestors happened to arrive some decades too late. But they themselves do not feel less American because of this fact than do authentic "Sons" or "Daughters." The very fact that their sense of Americanism has become unconscious —often more unconscious than that of the Anglo-Saxons among them —is an indication of its reality.

Normally the hyphen between the two words "Holland Americans" is being placed there today by people whose chief concern seems to be to erase it. They think of themselves as *Americans* in a deeper ethnic sense than are "Holland-Americans"—for no better reason than that their ancestors arrived here decades, perhaps centuries, earlier. It is they also who engage in "Americanization" activities. Such projects are well meant and honest enough, even if they are sometimes stupid. The assumption is that citizens of Dutch blood have to be "born again" into Americanism, that the work of regeneration is incomplete. The necessity existed for an older generation, and it exists today for stray individuals, but the mass of the folk are Americans to the heart of them, whatever Dutch dialect their fathers spoke. They do not feel that they are hyphenates.

Rather with a certain unconscious pride they feel that they are contributing an essential element to the dramatic mixture that is American blood. Similarly, the Bohemians of Nebraska, as Willa Cather has demonstrated in her fiction, furnished another essential element. So did O. E. Rölvaag's Scandinavians in Minnesota and the Dakotas. So did many other racial strains whose blood has gone to the making of the American. People on the Dutch frontier are inclined to believe with a certain racial stubbornness that anemia would long ago have sapped America's strength if it had not been for such enrichments.

Not biologically only, although that is important. Also culturally and in terms of the political and social blood stream of the nation. That may be the main reason why Holland Americans so often engage in racial self-panegyric. It seems natural to them to glory in their special racial strengths, as it is natural for Scandinavians to rejoice in theirs, and for Bohemians in theirs. The oak tree delights in its own sap, and the fir tree does likewise, and the maple and the redwood and the hemlock; each extols its special virtue to the world in the riot of its own leaves and in the texture of its own fibre. As a race Americans from Holland do not exult unduly because of their blood. But they feel that their pride in it is legitimate; they are better Americans because of it.

The folk on the Dutch frontier think of their race as one of the pieces in the intricately beautiful mosaic that is America. The rock from which they were cut was imported, not native; but so was that from which all the other pieces were carved, including the Anglo-Saxon, excluding only the Indian. Americans from Holland do not regard the pattern as complete; they are not disposed to deny to the cosmic artist the right to add new pieces in the future. But neither do they think of themselves as an alien intrusion because they were placed in the design later than some others.

To return to the more familiar figure of speech, they are stubbornly refusing to erase the hyphen because they are convinced there is no longer a hyphen to erase.

XXVIII

The Romantic Movement on the Dutch Frontier

IN RETROSPECT IT is not difficult to recognize the fact that a Romantic Movement has set in on the Dutch frontier. But it is not possible to fix a date for the change, any more than a man can recall the exact point in time when he put off adolescence and assumed maturity; he merely gets the feeling some day that he is a man, no longer a boy. In rare circumstances of crisis, as in Joseph Conrad's story, this "shadow line" may be crossed in a single night that is identifiable; normally there is no recognizable wall between epochs in life or in history that can be scaled again through an act of memory.

At any rate, it is impossible to fix the date of the beginning of the Romantic Movement on the Dutch frontier. There were probably many dates for many different people. It seems likely that for some the time is still in the future when they will look at the life of the Dutch race in America through the haze of romance, when a Dutch spinning wheel will take on a glow of antique beauty, and an old Dutch book in a private library will be given a place of special honor.

About all that can be asserted with any confidence is that during many decades Dutch American response to life was in terms of prose; today large numbers of people, many of whom hardly retain even a smattering of the language of their ancestors, think of the history of their race in America in terms of poetry. It may not be possible to fix the date of the change, but it is certain that at some point a change came over the Hollanders in this country. If there were any members left of the "lost generation" they had probably made their individual adjustments with life; their children were the ones who waxed senti-

282

mental over all things Dutch. They had arrived at the beginning of
the period of collecting Dutch antiques. Their wives drove through
the countryside and peered into abandoned chicken coops for forgotten
pioneer spinning wheels tossed into cobwebby corners generations ago
when their owners were only too glad to get them out of sight. The
men themselves might even, somewhat shamefacedly perhaps, negoti-
ate with a farmer customer for a long-abandoned pair of wooden
shoes to be placed picturesquely on the floor of the den. Their newly
race-conscious sons began to discover that the wooden, steel-runnered
skates, which were still to be found in the community, were greatly
superior to the American brands. And Dutch brass hanging lamps,
with pictured shades and crystal pendants, began to make their appearance in summer cottages—with however electric bulbs replacing oil
wicks.

The next step was to perpetuate in symbols the tradition of race.
Furniture factories began to erect enormous neon-lighted signboards
in the form of wooden shoes. Merchants brightened up their letter-
heads with little vignettes of windmills. A bakery might call its brand
"Dutch Boy," and a confectionery shop might put a candy on the
market under the name of "Holland Maid." A restaurant called itself
"The Tulip," and a transportation concern painted a picture of that
flower on its cabs. The owner of a speedboat might even give his craft
the incongruous name of "The Wooden Shoe," just to be in line with
the current romanticism; and a gas station might be built as a copy of
a Dutch windmill—with stationary flails!

There are four main symbols through which the tradition of Dutch
race is perpetuated in America today—the windmill, the wooden shoe,
the dyke, and the tulip. There are some others favored by individuals,
but these four are universally recognized as authentically Dutch in the
sections where descendants of the Hollanders live, although one or two
—notably the wooden shoe—is as characteristic of other European
strains as it is of the Hollanders.

The windmill has become a common municipal showpiece. Park
commissioners outline it in flowers facing the city fountain. A park
has even been known to be created for the express purpose of accommodating an imitation windmill as an attraction for tourists. Such a
bit of created scenery is certain to be one of the most photographed

scenes along the line of travel. City councils erect wooden shoe sign-boards over trunk lines into town to tell speeding tourists they are entering a Dutch community. Novelty manufacturers cannily pay a salary to the last wooden-shoe maker of the community, and place him in a show window to ply his trade before the eyes of fascinated tour-ists. The traveler parks his car in front of the hotel and is greeted by the words over the door: *"Welkom, Vreemdelingen"* (Welcome, Strangers"); when he leaves next morning he can't miss the sign over the exit: *"Vaarwel, Vrienden"* ("Farewell, Friends").

The dyke has given the symbolists of the Romantic Movement the greatest trouble, in spite of the fact that it is one of the most universally recognized marks of the Dutch tradition. No American is so illiterate that he does not know the myth of the Dutch boy holding his finger all day in a hole in the dyke, taking his legendary place beside the other little prig who loitered too long on the burning deck. But it is difficult to turn a dyke into a symbol; a dyke does not photograph readily, it would look odd on a letterhead. And it would seem silly to erect a replica of it on dry land, without any water to hold back. It might have its uses as a levee to hold back a river given to overflowing its banks, but that would be too practical for use as symbolism; and besides, unruly rivers are not often accommodating enough to do their overflowing near trunk lines where their act can be seen of tourists. But even the dyke is likely to have its symbolic day on the Dutch frontier when advertising genius solves the technical problems involved in its adequate and convenient display.

It is the tulip that has become the outstanding symbol of Dutch tradition—in Michigan, in Iowa, and in some other sections that de-scendants of Hollanders call home. This flower, in America as in Holland centuries ago, represents an odd mixture of poetry and busi-ness that assures its permanence as a symbol. In the Netherlands, some hundreds of years ago, when the tulip had been imported from Turkey, its bulbs were sometimes concerned in stock market crashes, as the medium of exchange in Dutch trader gambling orgies. To the growers, in the area between The Hague and Haarlem, the tulip has for cen-turies meant wealth, one of the important articles of Dutch export. In America, growers in many sections have long been reaping a golden harvest by cultivating the bulbs, and the poetry of the flower has extracted the dollars from the pockets of hordes of tourists. Millions of tulips flaming along the curbs, in private yards and public parks, become the poetry in color and living flowers of the Romantic Movement of the Dutch migration.

In 1929 a high school biology teacher, Miss Lida Rogers, suggested to the chamber of commerce of the little city of Holland, Michigan, that as a Dutch community the town might make use of the tulip as a living symbol of racial origin by annually holding a tulip festival Not of Dutch descent herself, she was objective enough to see the flower's community-advertising value. From 1929, when the festival was first held in the Michigan city, until 1942, when it was interrupted by the war, the city of Holland sometimes entertained between eight and nine hundred thousand guests during its annual "week"—its normal population is about sixteen thousand. A single day's attendance might rise to 225,000. During that period the people of the community accumulated plantings within the city limits of more than a million tulips, of some seventy-five varieties. They laid out a twelve-mile "Tulip Lane" that led to farms which annually produced more than two million bulbs, of some four hundred varieties.

Those farms, in fact, began their bulb culture some years before the first Festival was held. Now and again motorists would observe pigmy figures far out in the swamp lands grubbing away at something and would wonder what they were about. Bulbs? Tulip bulbs? People smiled. That kind of thing was all right in a backyard flower garden, but in an open field! What in the world did those growers expect to do with so many bulbs?

And, it should be admitted, they were not the main source of the original community plantings; the bulbs for the early festivals were imported from the Netherlands, paid for by money municipally appropriated. Such was the modest beginning of one of America's most successful folk festivals.

The fame of it penetrated to every section of America and to some foreign countries as well. But it did not pay in the usual narrow sense, and the community's businessmen knew that it would not. That is, the immediate business it brought to the town during the "week" was not only negligible, many were convinced that the Festival hurt business for the time being.

But the people thought of their "week" in terms of long-range values. They were willing to pay in inconvenience and loss of immediate business, for the all-over benefit; to the community the "week" was a kind of annual advertising appropriation.

What was the Tulip Festival like during the dozen years from 1929 to 1942? A composite picture in the form of a word-sketch may give a fairly satisfactory idea. . . .

There are a hundred thousand or more people milling about in search of entertainment. Their cars, bearing license plates from as far away as Missouri and Minnesota and Pennsylvania, make the outlying districts look like vast parking lots. The two intersecting main streets have been closed to traffic to serve as an avenue of march for visiting bands and pageants and city officials and school children and fraternal orders: they are like a European High Street in carnival time.

On the opening day every inch of space from store front to curb is occupied by visitors (some natives, wise in the ways of their "week," prefer the quiet of their own homes). To symbolize traditional Dutch cleanliness a battalion of women with brooms scrubs the pavement to musical accompaniment, the water supplied by a bucket brigade of men—all dressed theatrically in somewhat Hollywoodish versions of Dutch costumes, including wooden shoes. But those who take part, and the native spectators, understand perfectly that such clothes have not been worn in most of the provinces of the Netherlands for a century, except in Dutch folk pageants; the clothes are costumes, the buckets and brooms are props, the scrubbing of the pavement is a symbol.

And then the processions: City officials lead the way in costumes out of Rembrandt's "Night Watch." The fire department displays its bright red motorized equipment. School children in parade battalions, happy over a day off, are proud or giggly or bashful, depending on individual temperament. Commercial concerns enter floats in which various Dutch motifs of windmills and wooden shoes and baggy pants provide symbolism and color and tinsel romance. And spaced between the brigades march thirty bands from many communities in Michigan, Ohio, Indiana, Illinois.

And then follow seemingly spontaneous but artfully rehearsed folk dances on the pavement, the dancers often joined together with garlanded strings of flowers—dances in wooden shoes, in pumps, in baggy pants of the famed island of Marken. (And the folk dancers are not ignorant of the fact that their costumes are imitations of imitations— that the Marken folk also wear costumes for business reasons, to attract the tourists.) Loud speakers at convenient intervals blare out the numbers of the program or give information about coming events— punctuated by announcements of a child lost, or a car improperly parked, or a doctor urgently wanted on the long-distance phone.

Perhaps the most romantic feature of the Festival, romantic that is to visitors, is the twelve-mile tour along Tulip Lane, carefully marked by temporary road signs but more unmistakably, at least within the city limits, by tulips in bloom. Along both curbs of the street, mile after mile, the awed visitors see the marching lines of tulips until the eyes become dizzy with shimmering color. Bumper to bumper the cars crawl along Tulip Lane, miles of cars, thousands of drivers, all a part of the Big Parade of tulip worshipers. Past the city parks, where skilled flower specialists have worked out tulip-bed patterns with intricate designs—a wooden shoe, a windmill, the Dutch lion rampant. Then on to the city limits, across the bridge, and to the "loop" that runs past the tulip farms where the bulbs are grown. On a busy festival afternoon the cars crawl foot by foot, with many stops; the drivers cuss, because they are seldom allowed by the ubiquitous road cops to get out of line. Most of them take a rest from crawling when they arrive at the tulip farms, deploying on to the spacious pasture parking lots. But when they have glutted themselves on the colors of acres of tulips and take to the highway once more, the story is the same—crawling bumper to bumper, mile after mile, almost foot after foot. But a half million people annually seem to think that the sight is worth it, and who can say that they are wrong?

Even in the difficult business of feeding the visitors the community has succeeded in introducing something of the Dutch symbolism that is the motif of the entire play. The woman's club has paid off the mortgage on its spacious clubhouse by serving "Dutch dishes." The waitresses wear "Dutch costumes" as a matter of course (the quotes are used advisedly), and the cooks are sometimes advertised as being skilled in concocting the ancestral dishes of the Netherlands. The tourists eat up the propaganda as readily as the food, but there are amused rumors among the natives that the "Dutch cooks" have been imported from metropolitan hotels and are visiting the town for the first time. In any event, the flavor of the bill of fare is Dutch. And the hungry tourists do not appear to care. They are interested in something to eat, and they are charmed by the quaintness of a food that, they are happily convinced, is a faithful copy of dishes set before Queen Wilhelmina and Princess Juliana. But of course, it is good honest food, as are the other "Dutch dishes" in the restaurants and hotels.

Lodging is difficult. The strain is eased somewhat by the fact that scores of thousands come for only one day and leave on the long trek home before nightfall. The space in the city's community-built hotel is reserved weeks, sometimes even months, in advance. By a stroke of fortune a Great Lakes transportation company has for years used Holland Harbor as winter quarters for its two palatial excursion steamers, and those vessels can be turned into floating hotels—their season does not open until July. More thousands travel for hotel accommodations to towns within a radius of fifty miles; and the tourists camps and resort hotels are also pressed into service.

In Pella the folk festival is similar, with regional variations dictated sometimes by geography, sometimes by the imaginative ingenuity of the people of the community. When the fame of the Michigan festival was spreading throughout the Middle West and even to more distant states, the people of Pella began cannily to think of their long-neglected racial asset. So they sent a committee to Michigan to attend a festival and to ask questions about ways and means.

The first Pella Tulip Festival was held in 1935, and since then the fame of the Dutch folk show there has traveled to many states. Very many of the features of the festival have, from the start, necessarily been identical with those of the Michigan show—street scrubbing, wooden shoe dances, tulip lanes, windmills in parks, bands marching, choruses singing Dutch anthems, girls in native costumes going through colorful drills, bell boys and waitresses in hotels dressed in Dutch clothes, children proudly lining up in parades, and city council members falling in behind the mayor in costumes designed by specialists at local museums.

But the Pella Festival has developed a few features of its own. One of them is a town crier, a copy of the official who used to call the time

A TYPICAL LCG SHELTER ERECTED BY MICHIGAN DUTCH PIONEERS

The lower part, which dates back to the first years, gives an idea of how a people virtually without tools solved their building problems.

Netherlands Museum, Holland, Michigan

R. KONING.

FIRST SETTLEMENT ZEALAND TP. OTTAWA CO.
MICH.

MRS. R. KONING.

RESIDENCE OF R. KONING, Overisel, Tp. Allegan Co., Mich.

PIONEER FARM AND VILLAGE

of night or day in the Holland of a century ago. He is dressed in buckled knee breeches and flowing cape, and goes from street to street ringing his bell and crying the events of the program. Another Pella feature is the selection of an official "Queen," chosen by popular vote to represent Wilhelmina of the Netherlands.

But in the main these Dutch folk festivals during their first decade have followed a pattern that has by this time become fairly well standardized. They are the reflection of the innate romanticism concealed beneath the shell of Dutch practicality, and they give evidence of a continuing pride of race.

When Holland was invaded by the Nazis in 1940, the pageantry was suspended for the duration, to be resumed on a limited basis in 1946.

When the festivals made their appeal once more to the touring thousands, after the war, there was a deeper note of Dutch racial consciousness in the festivities. At least some who observed them before and after have testified to the difference. Before 1940 the people of Dutch descent, or at least the preponderant majority of them, had almost forgotten their tribal origin and heritage; their very sentimentalism about racial institutions and customs was often no more than skin deep, expressing a very human need for a background of some kind. Most of them had never seen the Netherlands and never expected to see it; born here, they thought of Holland as a *foreign* country. The tulip festivals of necessity focused their attention on the land that their pageantry portrayed, but most of them could not quite make their ethnological connection with the people of the Netherlands seem real; that connection was almost as stagey as the festival itself.

Then came the invasion, and many who had never given a thought to the land of their fathers discovered that they had a consciousness of *"land en volk."* In attacking a "foreign" country on the edge of the North Sea Hitler had somehow mysteriously attacked *them*. Their Americanism was as real and as strong as ever, but they began to develop a curious feeling that a rape had been committed on their own race-chastity when people of their ancestral blood were deprived by the invader of life, liberty, and the pursuit of happiness. The Americans of Dutch descent were shocked by the invasion into a consciousness of their Dutch blood.

That consciousness is revealing itself in the tulip festivals of the post-war era, as well as in many other manifestations of life on the Dutch frontier. The pageantry is somewhat less theatrical and more truly dramatic, less "romanticistic" and as a result more genuinely romantic. The festivals, like the people themselves, have had their roots imbedded not merely symbolically but to a greater degree organically in the soil of Dutch culture.

But it would be a mistake to assume that Dutch flower culture is confined to the sections in Michigan and Iowa that have dramatized it. Those areas, in fact, do not take first place in this Holland American enterprise. The geography of the American continent is studded with little dramas of this type of business.

Thus there is Jan de Graaff, the king of the daffodil growers in this country. Arriving here from Holland in the early thirties, he located in Oregon at the foot of Mount Hood. His ancestors had grown flowers in the Netherlands since 1611, and the skills he had inherited quickly spelled success for him in this country. On land that had been abandoned by less imaginative farmers, he began operations on credit, breeding hybrids. In this enterprise he developed seven hundred acres, eventually growing six million daffodils in 1,500 varieties. Adopting the most modern methods in mechanized flower culture, he displayed an imagination in business that had in it a touch of genius. What would Wordsworth have said about a field of six million daffodils? [1]

Diagonally across the continent, in North Carolina, another flower king, Hendrik van Dorp, became the largest individual tulip planter in America. At the full flood of his operations he shipped the flowers to the markets in New York, Philadelphia, Baltimore, and Chicago by the hundreds-of-thousands dozens, and sold his bulbs in millions. Finding that the bulbs and blooms mature early in that area, van Dorp hit on the idea of using the same land for a profitable crop of corn and beans for the same market. Hollanders first took over the rich black swamp lands of Beaufort County, North Carolina, in 1925. But dissention developed and many moved away. Van Dorp and a few fellow Hollanders stayed on, and others soon moved in. When van Dorp began his tulip culture in North Carolina many said it couldn't be done. He did it and became the "tulip king" of America. [2]

[1] Henry A. Wallace, "Report from Oregon," *The New Republic,* June 3, 1947.
[2] Bill Sharp, Department of Conservation, Raleigh, N.C., *New York World-Telegram,* April 27, 1940.

XXIX

A Dutch Who's Who—Highly Selective

In the nature of things there are only two ways of compiling a Who's Who among Holland Americans. One is to catalogue them. Any newspaper man knows that the average person is interested in his own name, even if it appears in a mere list, but he also knows that nobody else cares to read it there. In a record intended to be read, a catalogue would seem to be a waste of space.

The other way is to select a few representative names and let them reflect that wider group of Americans from Holland whose achievements would entitle them to recognition if space permitted. The thumbnail sketches that follow represent an attempt to suggest that during their life in America citizens of Dutch descent, as well as naturalized Hollanders, have won distinction in many fields—education, theology, literature, science, music, art, the theatre, invention, business, social work, military life, journalism, life insurance and prison management. The mere enumeration of the fields in which Holland Americans have made names for themselves threatens to degenerate into a catalogue and hence to become dull; and in a story dullness is the unpardonable sin.

In a selective treatment, such as this aspires to be, the principle of selection deserves explanation. Of first consideration has been the general recognition value of any name selected. Cecil B. DeMille, in an absolute sense, may not be more important than, or so important as, many other Americans of Dutch blood who might be chosen, but his name wins instant recognition from the general American reader. And the name of Lee De Forest is identified more readily than many another name that would have an equal right to be included in an un-selective list of prominent men of Dutch blood. An attempt has also been made to achieve variety, to suggest that distinction has been won by Holland Americans in many fields.

Edward Bok may conveniently serve as a representative of the Holland Americans who won the equivalent of an Eagle Award in journalism. For nearly half a century he was recognized as one of the most distinguished figures in the slick paper magazine world; some have credited him with being the father of that type of journalism. Chosen, while still in his twenties, by Cyrus H. K. Curtis, Philadelphia publisher, as editor of *The Ladies' Home Journal,* which at that time was almost gasping for survival, he built it up into one of the best-paying magazine properties in the world. When Bok retired in 1919, the *Journal* had a circulation of more than two million and carried in excess of a million dollars' worth of advertising.

This record of success was due largely to the sure sense this Holland American had of what would interest the American woman. He was forever introducing circulation building projects: campaigns against patent medicines, for a higher grade of pictures in the American home, for the elimination of public drinking cups, for woman suffrage. Bok was bursting with such ideas, and he appears to have believed in them himself. That fact may have helped to turn them into circulation—there was hardly a dud among them all—and circulation turned into money. Before he died Edward Bok had accumulated enough millions to offer $100,000 American Peace Awards and numerous other prizes that ran into many thousands, among them a $10,000 annual Philadelphia Award for community service. And he established the famous "Singing Tower" wild life sanctuary at Lake Wales, Florida.

Of course, he had married money, in the person of the daughter of Cyrus H. K. Curtis, but he was in his own right the best possible example of "rags to riches" Americanism that won the worship of his generation. Born in Holland, he was brought to America at the age of six. He went through all the romantic stages of a Horatio Alger character—window washer, messenger boy, newsboy, cub reporter. A half-century after his arrival here, in 1920, this American from Holland told his own story in *The Americanization of Edward Bok* that won the Pulitzer Prize and sold a quarter of a million copies.

The biography of Edward Bok was a greater "success story" than was ever published in the fiction columns of the *Journal*'s co-property, *The Saturday Evening Post*.

Hendrik Willem Van Loon is almost the inevitable selection not from the field of literature with an upper case *L,* although he wrote many very fine books; but rather as a sample of those Holland Americans whose ideas were seminal in American life. There have been not a few of that type among Americans from Holland. Not all have expressed themselves in books, as did Van Loon. Nor were books Van Loon's sole method of expression, or perhaps even the most important method. Although he illustrated his own books, and the pictures were often even more exciting than the text, it seems likely that his best drawings were never published. He often carried about with him some dozen or so fountain pens filled with different colored inks, and a pack of drawing cards, and he improvised pictures with protean prodigality.

An inveterate lecturer, he talked to scores of thousands of American women, and no one who ever heard him can forget the delightful irreverence he displayed as he gaily skated over the slick surface of American woman's-club romanticism. His audiences loved it all, including the mild profanity that sometimes broke through the lecturer's platform manner.

And he spawned ideas in many other ways. Big and burly and bluff, he was a human dynamo, the intimate of Presidents and the personal friend of Queen and Crown Princess; but also of the humble Midwestern farm mother for whose personal stationery he designed a letterhead that was a work of art.

His books sold in hundreds of thousands—*The Story of Mankind, R.V.R., The Arts,* and a score of others. It is doubtful if they will ever find a place in the canon of America's beautiful letters, but they are infinitely zestful, as was their author. It was like Van Loon to call his last book, an experiment in autobiography, *Report to Saint Peter;* the title carries a Puckish Van Loon smile on its face, and he himself would have enjoyed the incongruity between the ideas of Puck and the Gargantuan Van Loon. The book remained a fragment; its author died in 1944.

Van Wyck Brooks will serve as the representative of Holland Americans who won recognition in belles-lettres. While Edward Bok and Hendrik Van Loon were both born in Holland, Van Wyck Brooks can trace among his ancestors Holland Americans of pre-Revolutionary days.

His career as a writer began early. Graduating from Harvard in 1908, he published his first book, *The Wine of the Puritans,* in 1909. Five other volumes followed during the next several years, but it was not until 1920 that he won national attention with *The Ordeal of Mark Twain,* an attempt to prove that the great American humorist was a frustrated satirist, a theory that drew the fire of writers of the Bernard De Voto school. He wrote many other volumes, some of them of high literary distinction. But he is best known for the book that formed the first volume in what he has described as a "literary history of America," *The Flowering of New England;* it won the Pulitzer Prize for history in 1937. Later volumes in this "literary history" are *New England: Indian Summer* and *The World of Washington Irving.*

The best of the work of Van Wyck Brooks has already found a place in the canon of American literature. Possessed of a graceful, urbane style, and of a critical judgment that is marked by warmth and intellectual maturity, he has been one of the more reliable literary voices of America.

In quite a different field, a direct descendant of the New Netherland Hollanders has won distinction that is national in scope—or rather, international. Lee De Forest, widely credited with being the "father of radio," traces his Dutch blood to the New Netherland days before Peter Stuyvesant arrived in New Amsterdam as governor-general. In 1637 a Jesse De Forest left his home in Leyden and cast his lot with the American pioneers. He was the distinguished radio inventor's ancestor in a direct line.

Lee De Forest has patented over three hundred inventions in wireless telegraphy, radio telephone, wire telephone, sound-on-film talking pictures, high speed facsimile and picture transmission and television.

In 1916 he organized the first radio news broadcast. If anyone can be called the "father of radio," the title can be applied to this descendant of a New Netherland Hollander.

The American Dutch ancestor of Cecil B. DeMille, of motion picture fame, arrived in New Netherland twenty-one years after the arrival of Jesse De Forest, but early enough to be classified as a citizen at the time of the Dutch surrender in 1664. He was one Anthony deMil—as the name was spelled at that time. With his wife and two children he arrived in New Amsterdam in 1658. Several descendants of this New Netherland Hollander occupied positions of distinction. Cecil B. DeMille's father, Henry Churchill DeMille, was a dramatist of some note, producing many plays in collaboration with David Belasco.

Cecil B. DeMille has been a power in motion pictures since 1913. He is president of the Cecil B. DeMille Productions, Inc., and from 1928 to 1930 he served as president of the Motion Picture Producers Association. Among the productions that have made his name famous are: *Ten Commandments, The King of Kings, The Sign of the Cross, The Squaw Man, Male and Female,* and *The Volga Boatman.*

During the Golden Age in the seventeenth century, Dutch industrialists were among the best businessmen in the world. The tradition of acumen in trade was maintained during the three hundred years that followed. In the eighteenth century Dutch-descended businessmen played an important part in American life, taking among others the rôle of helping to finance the Revolution. In the nineteenth century there was Cornelius Vanderbilt, and there were many others.

In the twentieth there have been enough important Dutch American businessmen to make the choice of a representative figure unusually difficult. Several might be chosen from both the first and second migrations whose names have a familiar ring to the American public. That of Walter P. Chrysler is selected for the picturesque, if somewhat irrelevant, reason that he was a descendant of the first male child born in New Amsterdam—one Tuenis Van Dolsen. Chrysler was at least as much of a Holland American industrialist as the Roosevelts were Dutch American statesmen.

Chrysler's career is another case of "rags to riches." At seventeen he was working as a locomotive wiper at five cents an hour. Nineteen years later, in 1911, he became manager of the American Locomotive Company of Pittsburgh. He studied motor car construction on the side, and General Motors offered him a job as works manager for Buick cars. A little later he became executive vice president of General Motors. In 1924 he established the Chrysler Corporation, which within four years was recognized as one of the "big three" in the automobile industry, manufacturing, besides the Chrysler, the Plymouth, the Dodge, and the DeSoto. This Holland American wrote his name so large in the motor car industry that it has international recognition value. He died in 1940.

In the field of music Gladys Swarthout is a Holland American of national distinction, if the term "Holland" may be said to retain its meaning for three centuries. The earliest American members of the family settled in New Amsterdam in 1653. The spelling of the name at that time was Swarwouldt, which later was shortened to Swarwout, and still later changed to the present form. Twenty-nine members of the family fought in the Revolutionary War.

Gladys Swarthout had her debut in 1924, and for three seasons she sang with the Ravinia Opera Company. Discovered by the Metropolitan, she sang the part of La Cieca in *La Gioconda*. Her chief rôles have been in *Mignon, Carmen, Norma, Forza del Destino, Tales of Hoffman,* and *Peter Ibbetson.* Her voice moreover has become familiar to millions via radio on various programs, and she has won popularity on the concert stage.

Pulpit eloquence has always been a marked characteristic of Holland Americans. Among the original leaders of the nineteenth century migration there were not a few minor Dutch Savonarolas. And among the descendants of the pioneers the silver tongue was fairly common; there were several orators whose fame became national at least in their own church communion, and sometimes in the larger Calvinistic body, the Presbyterian Church.

One such pulpit orator of far more than local or sectional fame was Dr. John M. Vander Meulen. The choice falls on him rather than on some others who might be chosen because his endowment of dramatic eloquence was very great, but also because he was a grandson of the co-leader with Van Raalte on the Michigan frontier, the Reverend Cornelius Vander Meulen.

Like his pioneer forebear, he had not only the gift of eloquence but also the perhaps even more precious grace of humor—even in the pulpit, where humor has always been rare among Hollanders. His sense of pulpit drama was also highly developed, but tempered and controlled by an intellectualism that was characteristically Dutch and that saved it from sensationalism. In his best days he had a considerable following among younger clergymen in two denominations who almost recognizably adopted his pulpit techniques, often without understanding the sobering truth that the style is the man and cannot be adopted from without, but must be generated from within.

Born in Milwaukee in 1870, Dr. Vander Meulen grew up in Michigan. He filled several pulpits in that state; also in New York City, Louisville, Kentucky, and Chicago. For a time he served as a humble missionary among the Indians of Oklahoma, in sharp contrast to his occupancy of wealthy metropolitan pulpits in two denominations, the Reformed and the Presbyterian. His restless energy drove him into many other activities, among them that of college professor and president of a Presbyterian theological seminary. But always, his real power lay in the spoken word. He died in 1936.

In the field of history, biography, and criticism the name of Carl Van Doren has won national recognition. His is by no means the only Holland American name in this field, but he is perhaps as representative as any of the others who might be listed in such a highly selective Who's Who among Hollanders as this of necessity is. The Van Dorens made their first American appearance in the person of Pieter Van Doorn, who settled on Long Island some time before 1657, the year he was first mentioned in a New Amsterdam record.

Carl Van Doren himself was born in Hope, Illinois, and he was educated at the University of Illinois. He became associated with Columbia University as faculty member, and won distinction as literary editor of the *Nation* and of the *Century Magazine*. He held several other positions, among them that of editor of the Literary Guild.

But his chief claim to national recognition lies in the publication of a long list of books in the fields of criticism, biography, and history. In criticism such books as *The American Novel, Contemporary American Novelists,* and *The Roving Critic* have won wide acclaim. In biography his life of Benjamin Franklin is perhaps the best study yet published of that many-sided Revolutionary figure; it won the Pulitzer Prize for biography in 1939. In the field of history Van Doren's *Secret History of the American Revolution* is his best-known work.

This Holland American man of letters, who has now and again expressed pride in the Dutch part of his ancestry but is American to the heart of him, is one of many continuing indications of the seminal vitality of the people who came to these shores from Holland three centuries ago.

Along with the name of Carl Van Doren, that of his brother, Mark Van Doren, may be conveniently mentioned—not merely because Mark Van Doren is the brother of a distinguished man, but because he has won national recognition in his own right as an educator and a poet.

The American academic profession is almost literally swarming with Holland Americans. There are few universities that do not contain several of them on their faculties, and there is also a large sprinkling of them in very many of the colleges in most of the states. One authority estimated in 1942 that "one hundred Dutch-born professors—nearly all American citizens—are teaching in American colleges and universities."[1] And for every educator actually born in Holland there are several second- and third-generation Hollanders on American college faculties.

Dr. Clarence A. Dykstra may be taken as a representative figure. Both college professor and executive, as well as an active figure in municipal government management, he has attracted far more than sectional attention; his reputation is national. Not strictly a product of the Van Raalte-Scholte migration, he yet belongs, in origin, to the Middle West. His forebears first settled in New York state, later moving to Michigan, and Dr. Dykstra's father graduated from Van Raalte's Hope College. He himself grew up on the Iowa Dutch frontier and graduated from the University of Iowa in 1903.

He occupied chairs in the University of Chicago, the University of

---

[1] Vlekke and Beets, *Hollanders Who Helped Build America,* p. 3.

Kansas, and the University of California, and held other teaching positions. Moreover, he held important managerial positions in Cleveland, Chicago, Los Angeles, and served as city manager of Cincinnati. From that post he went to the University of Wisconsin as president, and then he became provost of the University of California. Also, he served as adviser to numerous governmental agencies. No less than ten educational institutions have conferred honorary degrees on him: Ohio Wesleyan, Otterbein, Knox College, University of Cincinnati, Hope College, Hobart College, Northwestern University, Harvard, Johns Hopkins, and Rutgers.

In some ways Dykstra is an exception rather than the rule as a representative of Holland Americans in education. The educators of Dutch descent are more likely to be pure scholars than of the executive administrative type. A sample of the scholar group may be briefly mentioned in the person of Martin Luther D'Ooge, for many years a truly distinguished professor of ancient languages at the University of Michigan. Professor D'Ooge was a scholar of high attainments in his field, recognized in a national sense by classical scholars. He was a product of the western Dutch frontier, a native of Grand Rapids. He died in 1915.

Hollanders are found in so many fields that it would be impossible, in a selective Who's Who, to list representatives of them all, even of those who have won national distinction. Astronomy is a somewhat unusual interest, and hence it seems appropriate to select a representative from that field. He is Jan Schilt, professor of astronomy at Columbia University.

Born and brought up in the Netherlands, Dr. Schilt came to the United States in 1925 as a Fellow of the International Education Board to work at the Mount Wilson Observatory. The next year he went to the Yale Observatory, and in 1931 was appointed head of the department and associate professor of astronomy at Columbia. He is also director of the Rutherford Observatory.

Dr. Schilt has done original work in astronomy that has attracted the attention of the scientific world. Among other achievements, he has established the fact that individual stars of the Pleiades cluster are following slightly divergent movements. This conclusion contradicts previous observations and is a discovery that has had important results in the study of astronomy. And he has made other observations that represent original work in that field. His invention of the Schilt photometer is another of his achievements. Among his professional publications are: *On a Thermo-electric Method of Measuring Photographic Magnitudes* (1924); *Remarks on Various Statistical Properties of Galactic Cepheid Having Periods Longer than One Day* (1926); *The Short-period Variable Star RV Canum Venaticorum* (1927).

But noted Americans from Holland are not all persons who have won distinction of so solemn a nature as may be suggested by the list chosen as samples. The record of honors of a lighter nature may be of interest; perhaps it may even be important. As, for instance:

That a Holland American, John Vander Meer, is the no-hit, no-run pitcher of the Cincinnati Reds; that John Roukema has won wide fame as a skater; that David Christiaan Henry was a leading American expert in dam building; that Garrett Heyns was appointed director of Corrections of the biggest penitentiary in the world, the Southern Michigan Prison; that Daniel De Leon wrote pamphlets so early as 1905 which, in the opinion of Lenin, "contained the germ of the Soviet governmental system"; that Theodore P. Dykstra, a noted potato expert, won fame adapting American potatoes to Chinese soil; that Cornelius Bol invented the "midget sun," the Bol lamp, important in the movie industry, which "enables one to read a newspaper at a distance of a mile."

There are other instances of somewhat unconventional achievements by Americans from Holland:

John Amans, an American born in Amsterdam, married a Polish woman, began his professional career in Helsinki, Finland, and became flute soloist of the New York Philharmonic Orchestra.

Harry Cornelius Beumer won a prize of $100 for an essay written in English on "Dutch Influence on the Establishment of the United States," on the occasion of the Olympic Games in 1928, one year before he came to America to live.

Herman E. De Vries, born in Friesland, offered his services free, in 1930, to a New England manufacturer, under a royalty agreement, and became one of the country's highest paid furniture designers.

John Van Druten, born of a Dutch father and English mother, combined the career of a highly successful playwright with that of lecturer in English Law and English Legal History.

Hendrik de Leeuw, traveler and writer, rubbed shoulders with peoples of all kinds and hunted tiger, boar, and wild bulls. The high civilization of the Javanese and Balinese fascinated him and he became known as the "man who made the world Bali-conscious."

Henri Frankfort, a native of Amsterdam, became one of the world's outstanding archaeologists. Excavations were directed by him in Khorsabad, Tell Asmar, Khafaje, Ishcholi, and Tell Agrab.

Charles Lester Marlatt, entomologist, directed the effort that resulted in the Plant Quarantine Act of 1912. Against strong opposition he provided America protection against imported insect pests and plant diseases.

Three Iowa brothers, each bearing the name of Pella's founder, won three types of distinction. Gerard Scholte Nollen became president of the Bankers Life Company, Des Moines; Henry Scholte Nollen rose to the presidency of the Equitable Life Insurance Company of Iowa; John Scholte Nollen became president of Grinnell College.

Louis Raemaekers, born in the province of Limburg, after his escape to America in 1940 became a cartoonist for the newspaper *PM*. During the first World War his anti-German cartoons caused the German government to put a price on his head.

John Theodore Scheepers, born in Arnhem, "revolutionized the bulb industry in America." His tulips won him "several hundred Gold Medals."

Leon Monroe Schoonmaker became one of the leading authorities on fencing in this country. He was a member of four American Olympic fencing teams: Antwerp, 1920; Paris, 1924; Los Angeles, 1932; Berlin, 1936.

William Brantley Van Ingen, mural painter, has to his credit panels in the Congressional Library in Washington, the United States Mint in Philadelphia, and the United States Administration Building in the Panama Canal Zone.

Alfred van Ameyden van Duym, born in The Hague, became an important figure in the noble guild of book sellers in this country. As a sideline he forged a link between Holland and America by translating Dutch books for the American market, among them *The House of Tavelinck, The Platter,* and *The Field is the World.*

A complete catalogue, even if such a thing were a possibility, would be tedious and unprofitable. Enough instances have been cited to show that variety marks the distinctions that have come to Holland Americans.

In a selective Who's Who there can in the nature of things be no inevitable end. The decision on where to leave off must of necessity be arbitrary. If enough samples have been cited to show that Holland Americans have been active in many fields of activity and that they have won distinction in those fields, little more can be asked for. And it has seemed desirable to select figures that could legitimately be placed against a national, not a local, background, without their being dwarfed or lost.

XXX

Centennial Year

THE DUTCH FRONTIER in America came within sight of the Pacific at about the turn of the century. It had taken Dutch culture nearly three hundred years to march across the nation. When the final group settlements were made in such places as Lynden and Oak Harbor, Washington, and in some sections in California, the New Netherland beginnings of the long journey were so far away and long ago that it is doubtful whether the actual settlers felt any identity with those countrymen of theirs who had begun the march. But as the bearers of a culture, standing at last on their mystic Peak of Darien and staring on the Pacific toward which they had begun to reach out their unconscious tentacles three centuries ago, the Hollanders could look back on the long journey that had come to an end. Individuals might remain unconscious of the epic quality of the march, but as a race the people of Dutch blood in America understood its true significance. They knew that the fur traders of New Netherland and the bulb growers of Lynden, Washington, were linked together over the breadth of a continent and across three centuries.

But they knew it with their blood rather than with their thinking minds. In their actual consciousness of the past, individuals were more likely to look back only a century, to the time when their immediate ancestors had begun to make America their home. They fixed upon 1947 as their centennial year, a time to look back along the road their culture had traveled, to try to get into perspective many things that had been out of focus while they had actually been experiencing them.

The first fact they understood now in the perspective of their racial history was that the Dutch occupation of New Netherland had not come to a close when the English had taken over the government. A culture is far tougher than a political system. The Hollanders of that first migration lived on in the bone and sinew of millions who followed them, many of whom had lost the very memory of their racial origin; they achieved a kind of biological immortality by passing into something rich and strange—Americans. And their way of life was perpetuated in American institutions that served a new age and were serviced by a new race of men. Their very language had reappeared to a degree in the speech called "American" as distinguished from "English," enriching it and helping to contribute to it some of the tang that distinguishes it as a national language; and their literature had broken out from time to time under new forms in the national letters of a people that did not even exist at the time of the New Netherland occupation.

What had seemed like a political tragedy long, long ago when a culture had appeared to arrive at frustration, in the perspective of three centuries was not so much reason for sorrow as for wonder at the strangeness of history, which seldom makes the turnings that any given generation expects of it. The very men and women who, three centuries ago, would have given their lives for the maintenance of the *status quo,* could they only have stood at the end of the long road might have felt not merely reconciled but triumphant that things had turned out against their wishes. For an America dominated by any single race would have been a poor thing; that composite of cultures that has become the real America is richer, more exciting, more alive. And while it might have been racially satisfying to give a language to this continent of destiny, those of Dutch blood who feel most deeply their identity with the culture of their fathers love best that language that is Emerson's and Mark Twain's and Mencken's and would not have it any other. At the end of the long road across the continent and the centuries it is possible to see that it was best to become not Hollanders or Englishmen but Americans, to understand that hybridization of cultures makes for health and life and rejuvenation.

All that, the bearers of a culture could see after its three hundred years' march across the continent. And they could see other things in better perspective in the nearer distance of a century of time. They could understand at last that what had once seemed like religious fanaticism had in reality been destiny's means of steeling the hearts of thousands of simple people to stay with the march of their national culture along its second stage. Pushed out as they had been like fledglings from the home nest, their flutterings would have ended in disaster and despair if they had not been sustained by a fanatical faith in the rightness of their philosophy.

The very tendency to divisiveness that strongly characterized them was not without its uses. To Van Raalte and other leaders their people's centrifugal spirit seemed disastrous, but those leaders were too near to the history of their own day, and to the personal traits of the people, to see the picture wholly in focus. A spirit of unity is comfortable for the leaders of any people, and it is always held up as the greatest good. But destiny reveals itself in many forms, and the individualism that divided the people on the Dutch frontier is beginning to appear as being far more precious than any surface unity that might have been achieved. For an American culture that almost worships uniformity Dutch individualism serves as a wholesome corrective. Standardization has become an American evil, and any force that counteracts it is wholesome. Looking back over a hundred years, the bearers and inheritors of Dutch culture in the West thought they saw in the very fanaticism of the individualism of their ancestors something that they, and America, needed.

And there were other tribal traits that they could see in better perspective when they set aside a centennial year for the business of looking back. Their ancestors' want of progressiveness, for instance, an alleged charateristic of which many had been secretly ashamed who themselves had it in their blood. The Hollander, during that century, had normally tried to appear less than he was, to have less money than his bankbook revealed, to know less than his mental attainments gave him a right to claim. He had an inbred horror of putting on "front," and he carried this fear to such extremes that he often failed to put his best foot foremost. He took an inner delight in the possession of powers and attainments that people did not suspect he had, and when by accident they were revealed to men they lost some of their charm for him. When he was charged with being unprogressive he did not resent the charge; he knew that Utopia did not exist, and that most new things are old ones with new names. As a race he was not given to romantic flights of the imagination; he remembered with satisfaction that people who travel familiar ways seldom break their necks. But he was charged with being too conservative, and to many of those whose blood itself was Dutch this undoubted tribal trait had often seemed an unmixed evil.

But as the heirs of Dutch culture looked back during the centennial year their sense of perspective suffered modification. They understood that their race could be depended upon, and that in general the Dutch folk on the frontier had been "solid." Business failures there had been, as elsewhere, but in the main an instinctive refusal to believe in the romanticism of getting rich quickly or of getting something for nothing, had kept their manufacturing plants among the most prosperous, their banks among the soundest. It had been a tribal trait to land on one's feet, and financial panics were alien to Dutch character. In the hard times of the early 1890's, and again during the panic of 1907, and later still during the depression of the thirties, the savings deposits in many of the banks on the Dutch frontier had actually increased—when much of the rest of the nation had been drawing out savings to buy bread and beefsteak.

The Hollanders had often been charged with being "tight." In perspective, what had had the look of parsimony turned out to be something not far removed from common sense. Where now were many of the glorious "causes" to which they had stubbornly refused to contribute? Those movements had gone with the wind, but carefully conserved Dutch funds had not gone with them. And in perspective it appeared that there had been no narrow parsimony in support of the time-tried institutions of churches, schools, or for investment in personal or family comfort. What had to many descendants of Hollanders themselves looked like parsimony, from the end of the road appeared to be a sensible determination to get one hundred per cent of service or goods out of a dollar invested.

And Hollanders and descendants of Hollanders, during centennial year, gave themselves leisure to see that some things and persons had loomed too large through the distortions of proximity. They learned to understand that ecclesiastically the folk on the Dutch frontier, during their century of life there, had not been the "chosen people" they had fancied themselves and that their parochial eulogists always assured them they were. Theirs was about the mixture of good and bad, of strength and weakness, that characterizes the philosophy and the way of life of other nationals. A retrospective view helped them to gain perspective on their tribal history and achievements, and to acquire that objectivity that is always necessary to a true appreciation of things as they are. Although they looked back with legitimate pride on the past of their race in this country, the centennial year served as a kind of shadow line between what they and their fathers had been as Hollanders and what they themselves now were as Americans.

The time had come to place their race not against a temporary drop-curtain of parochial history but against the background of America and its history. Seen in that perspective their culture filled them with a quiet pride of race, but at the same time with a sober sense of racial achievement. They read with satisfaction a large tome that an enterprising publisher issued as a Dutch *Who's Who* in contemporary America, but they had advanced too far beyond the parochial attitude to take it with portentous seriousness. They honored those of their race who had been, or now were, men "mighty in words and deeds," but they remembered with a racial sense of proper proportion in all things that such a word as "mighty" is relative, and that the time had come to measure their own "great" men by the yardstick not of the Dutch frontier but by the measure of the nation.

The Dutch frontier in America, like that of other Old World groups, is passing and is about to fade out. There is much in the story that is heroic and there is much in it that is crude. Inevitably so, because it is of the stuff of which life is made; and just as nature in the raw is seldom mild, so life not yet reduced to art seldom has finish. There frequently is a disposition to ignore the crudities and to indulge exclusively in heroics. But the crudities, too, are a part of the story, and a necessary part. Even Walt Whitman did not omit them from "Pioneers! O Pioneers!" Thomas Hardy's phrase, "the raw material of a divinity," applies to the history of the Dutch frontier in America; there is in that story the raw stuff, if not of a divinity, at least of a human dignity that is worthy of celebration in art. Unfortunately, the artist is not yet in evidence. When he appears he will have ready to hand the materials with which he must work. Not until he shapes them into forms of enduring beauty and truth will the epoch that has come to an end on the Dutch frontier in America attain that inner unity that alone can give the illusion of its continuing life.

BIBLIOGRAPHY

Abbott, John S. C. *Peter Stuyvesant, the Last Dutch Governor of New Amsterdam* ("American Pioneers and Patriots" Series). New York: Dodd, Mead & Co., 1873.

Adamic, Louis. "The Hollanders: They Made Their Pella," *From Many Lands*. New York: Harper & Brothers, 1940, pp. 165-181.

———. "Americans from Holland," *A Nation of Nations*, New York: Harper & Brothers, 1945. Pp. 94-121.

Barnouw, Adrian J. "The Seventeenth Century: the Golden Age," *The Netherlands,* edited by Bartholomew Landheer. Berkeley and Los Angeles: University of California Press, 1943. Pp. 39-59.

Beets, Henry. "Dutch Journalism in Michigan," *Michigan History Magazine* (Lansing), Vol. 6, pp. 435-41.

Blok, Petrus Johannes. *History of the People of the Netherlands,* translated by Oscar A. Bierstadt and Ruth Putnam, 5 vols. New York and London: G. P. Putnam's Sons, 1907.

Bowers, Claude G. *The Young Jefferson 1743-1789.* Boston: Houghton Mifflin Co., 1945.

Brooks, Van Wyck. *The World of Washington Irving.* New York: E. P. Dutton & Co., 1944.

Brown, Herbert Ross. *The Sentimental Novel in America 1789-1860.* Durham, N. C.: Duke University Press, 1940.

Brown, Willard Dayton. *History of the Reformed Church in America.* New York: Board of Publications and Bible School Work, 1928.

Christman, Henry. *Tin Horns and Calico.* New York: Henry Holt & Co., 1945.

Classis Holland: Minutes 1848-1858, translated by a Joint Committee of the Christian Reformed Church and the Reformed Church in America. Grand Rapids: The Grand Rapids Printing Co., 1943.

College English (Chicago). Organ of the National Council of Teachers of English.

Common Ground (New York). Quarterly published by the Common Council for American Unity.

Daane, P., Sr. "History of the First Settlement at Sheboygan, Wisconsin," *De Hope,* July 21, 1897.

De Crèvecoeur, St. Jean. *Letters from an American Farmer.* New York: Fox, Duffield & Co., 1904.

De Grondwet. Weekly newspaper published in Holland, Michigan, 1860-1939.

De Hope (Holland, Mich.). Weekly organ of the Reformed Church in America, 1865-1933.

De Jong, Rev. C. D., "The School in Parsonage and Upper Room," in *Theological School and Calvin College,* 1876-1926. Semi-Centennial Volume. Grand Rapids, 1926.

De Leeuw, Hendrik. *Crossroads of the Zuider Zee.* Philadelphia and New York: J. B. Lippincott Co., 1938.

Detroit News Tribune, "A Christian Political Party," by Arnold Mulder, July 20, 1913.

De Vries, Tiemen. *Influence of Holland on America.* Address at the University of Chicago, Oct. 15, 1911. Grand Rapids: Eerdmans, Sevensma Co., 1912.

De Wachter (Grand Rapids). Weekly organ of the Christian Reformed Church, established 1866.

Diekema, G. J. "Holland Emigration to Michigan: Its Causes and Effects," *Michigan History Magazine* (Lansing), Oct., 1917.

D'Ooge, Martin L. "The Dutch Pioneers of Michigan," *Michigan Pioneer and Historical Collection* (Lansing), Vol. 38 (1912), pp. 204-12.

Dosker, Henry E. *Levensschets van Rev. A. C. Van Raalte, D.D.* Nijkerk, The Netherlands, 1893.

Fuller, George N. "Early German and Dutch Settlers," *Michigan: A Centennial History of the State and Its People.* Chicago: The Lewis Publishing Co., 1939. Vol. I, pp. 294-301.

Goodwin, Maud Wilder. *The Dutch and English on the Hudson* ("The Chronicles of America" Series, Vol. 7). New Haven: Yale University Press.

Grattan, Thomas Colley. *History of the Netherlands.* New York: Harper & Bros., 1855.

Greshoff, J. *Harvest of the Lowlands.* Anthology of Dutch prose since 1880. Introductory chapter on the history of Dutch literature by J. Greshoff. New York: Querido, 1945.

Griflis, William Elliott. *The Story of New Netherland.* Boston & New York: Houghton Mifflin Co., 1909.

——. "The Dutch Influence in New England," *Harper's Magazine,* LXXXVIII (1894), pp. 213-21.

Hoekstra, Peter. *Thirty-seven Years of Holland-American Relations* 1803-1840. Grand Rapids: Eerdmans, Sevensma Co., 1917.

Holland City News. Weekly newspaper in Holland, Michigan, established 1872.

Holland Evening Sentinel. Daily newspaper in Holland, Michigan, established 1896.

Hollandsche Kookery Boek. Holland, Mich.: Steketee-Van Huis Printing House, 1936.

Honigsheim, Paul. "Religion and Assimilation of the Dutch in Michigan," *Michigan History Magazine* (Lansing), Winter Number, 1942.

Irving, Washington. *Knickerbocker's History of New York,* 2 vols. New York & London: G. P. Putnam's Sons, 1893.

Karpinski, L. C. *Bibliography of the Printed Maps of Michigan* 1804-1880. Lansing, 1931.

Kellogg, Louise Phelps. "The Story of Wisconsin," *Wisconsin Magazine of History* (Madison), Vol. 3, pp. 314-26.

Keppel, Anna Kremer. *The Immigration and Early History of the People of Zeeland, Ottawa County, Michigan, in 1847.* Zeeland, Mich.: Zeeland Record Press [1925?].

Knickerbocker Weekly. New York: the Netherland Publishing Corporation.

Kregel, J. H. "History of the Reformed Church of Alto, Wisconsin." Seventy-fifth Anniversary Souvenir Pamphlet. Alto, Wisc., June, 1930.

Landheer, Bartholomew. *The Netherlands.* Berkeley and Los Angeles: University of California Press, 1943.

Lucas, Henry S. "The Beginnings of Dutch Immigration to Western Michigan," *Michigan History Magazine* (Lansing), Vol. 6 (1922), pp. 642-74.

Mencken, H. L. *The American Language.* New York: Alfred A. Knopf Co., 1936.

——. *The American Language: Supplement One.* New York: Alfred A. Knopf Co., 1945.

Michigan, Michigan Writers' Project. New York: Oxford University Press, 1941.

Michigan History Magazine (Lansing), Vol. 6, pp. 642-74 and pp. 435-41.

Motley, John Lothrop. *The Rise of the Dutch Republic.* New York: Harper & Bros., 1856.

Nieland, Dirk. *Yankee Dutch*. Grand Rapids: W. B. Eerdmans Pub. Co., 1919.
——. *'N Fonnie Bisnis*. Grand Rapids: W. B. Eerdmans Pub. Co., 1929.

Parrington, V. L. *Main Currents in American Thought*, 3 vols, in 1. New York: Harcourt, Brace & Co., 1939.
Pieters, Aleida J. *A Dutch Settlement in Michigan*. Grand Rapids: The Reformed Church Press, 1923.

Quaife, Milo F. *Lake Michigan*. Indianapolis: Bobbs-Merrill Co., 1944. Pp. 39-59.

Raderus, Sipko F. "The Dutch Settlements in Sheboygan County," *Wisconsin Magazine of History*, Vol. I (1918), pp. 256-65.
Read, Allen Walker. "The Evidence on 'O.K.'," *Saturday Review of Literature*, July 19, 1941.

Schlesinger, Arthur M. *The Age of Jackson*. Boston: Little, Brown & Co., 1945.
Scholte, H. P. *Eene Stem uit Pella*. Pamphlet printed March, 1848, at Amsterdam by Hoogkamer & Co., translation by Jacob Vander Zee, in *Iowa Journal of History and Politics*, October, 1911.
Scholte, Leonora. *A Stranger in a Strange Land*. Reprinted from April, 1939 number of the *Iowa Journal of History and Politics*, Iowa City, State Historical Society of Iowa.
Sheboygan Nieuwsbode, Aug. 14, 1855. Property of Grand Rapids, Mich., Public Library.
Shepard, Edward M. *Martin Van Buren*. Boston: Houghton Mifflin Co., 1897.

Vanden Bosch, Amry. *The Dutch Communities of Chicago*. The Knickerbocker Society of Chicago, 1927.
Vander Meulen, Jacob. *Hollanders: The Development of Their Objectives in Europe and America*. Sponsored by the First Reformed Church of Zeeland, Mich., 1946.
Vander Zee, Jacob. *The Hollanders of Iowa*. Iowa City: State Historical Society of Iowa, 1912.
Van Eyck, William O. *Landmarks of the Reformed Fathers*. Grand Rapids: The Reformed Press, 1922.
——. "The Story of the Propeller Phoenix," *Wisconsin Magazine of History*, Vol. VII (March, 1924), pp. 281-300.
Van Hinte, J. *Nederlanders in Amerika*, 2 vols. Groningen, The Netherlands, 1928.

Van Loon, Hendrik Willem. *The Fall of the Dutch Republic.* Boston: Houghton Mifflin Co., 1913.

Van Rensselaer, Mrs. Schuyler. *History of the City of New York in the Seventeenth Century,* 2 vols. New York: The Macmillan Co., 1909.

Van Schelven, G. "Early Settlement of Holland," *Michigan Historical Collections* (Lansing), Vol. 26 (1926), pp. 569-79.

——. "Michigan and the Holland Immigration of 1847," *Michigan History Magazine* (Lansing), October, 1917.

Veltman, Peter. "Dutch Survivals in Holland, Michigan," *American Speech* (Feb., 1940), Columbia University Press, New York, pp. 80-83.

Verwyst, Chrysostom Adrian, "Reminiscences of a Pioneer Missionary," *Publications of the State Historical Society of Wisconsin.* Proceedings for 1916. Madison, 1917. Pp. 148-85.

Vlekke, B. H. M. and Beets, Henry. *Hollanders Who Helped Build America.* New York, 1942.

Wabeke, Bertus Harry. *Dutch Emigration to North America 1624-1860.* New York: The Netherlands Information Bureau, 1944.

Walker, P. C. Gordon. "The Sixteenth and Seventeenth Centuries," *A Modern History of Europe 1046-1918,* edited by J. Hampden Jackson. New York and London: Harper & Bros., 1935.

Wecter, Dixon. *The Saga of American Society.* New York: Charles Scribner's Sons, 1937.

Wedgewood, C. V. *William the Silent, Prince of Orange.* New Haven: Yale University Press, 1944.

Wilson, Ruth Elaine. "Little Holland of the Prairies," *Successful Farming,* May, 1937.

Wisconsin, Wisconsin Writers' Project. New York: Duell, Sloan & Pierce, 1941.

Wormser, J. A. *Een Schat in Aarden Vaten: Het Leven van Albertus Christiaan Van Raalte.* Nijverdal: E. J. Bosch, Jbzn., 1915.

Yearbook of the Christian Reformed Church, 1946. Grand Rapids: Christian Reformed Church Publishing House, 1946.

INDEX

315